"AND IT CAME TO PASS . . . THAT BEHOLD THERE APPEARED A CHARIOT OF FIRE, AND HORSES OF FIRE. . ."

—The Bible

From the hanging gardens of Queen Semiramis at Babylon, to the Temple of Mysteries of Tibet, comes evidence that the theory of civilization from the stars is not only possible but highly probable—so much so that we must look at ourselves and the universe around us in a totally fresh way.

GODS AND SPACEMEN IN THE ANCIENT EAST is a book for those who are not afraid of new ideas. *It is for those who wish to experience the greatest widening of our horizons that this century of scientific marvels and revelations has yet offered the mind of man.*

Gods and Spacemen in the Ancient East

by

W. Raymond Drake

A SIGNET BOOK
NEW AMERICAN LIBRARY
TIMES MIRROR

Acknowledgments
The warmest gratitude is due to Miss Edith Nicolaisen, of 'Parthenon', Halsingborg 6, Sweden, that inspired and selfless Leader for the New Age, for her encouragement and advice.

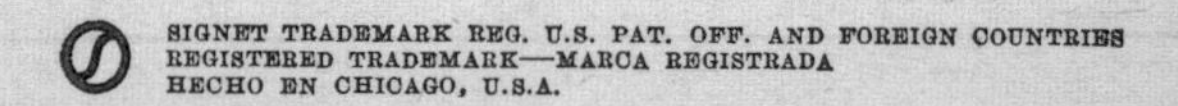

SIGNET, SIGNET CLASSICS, SIGNETTE, MENTOR AND PLUME BOOKS
are published by The New American Library, Inc.,
1301 Avenue of the Americas, New York, New York 10019.

FIRST PRINTING, DECEMBER, 1973

1 2 3 4 5 6 7 8 9

PRINTED IN THE UNITED STATES OF AMERICA

To my wife, Marjorie

CONTENTS

CHAPTER ONE

The Inhabited Universe

In those glorious days when our Earth was young and Nature shone in newness, Celestials winged down from the stars to teach the arts of civilisation to unsophisticated Man creating that Golden Age sung by all the poets of Antiquity. For centuries the whole world basked in a brilliant culture, humanity prospered under the benign rule of the Space Kings, who mastered a psychic science attuned to the cosmic forces of the universe and the powers within the human soul; they worshipped the Sun, the divine Androgyne, symbolising the Creator; they taught of life after death, reincarnation, ascending through existences in different dimensions to Union with God. Earth's development was fostered by the Solar Planets in a higher octave of evolution; they fringed the Galactic Federation whose myriad worlds flowered in dazzling splendour; on treasured occasions Beings of transcendent wisdom would descend to Earth and impart their arcane secrets and technology to chosen Initiates.

Man evolves through suffering. As light requires the dark to realise illumination, so divine Law decrees that good should be tempered by evil. God is Absolute, eternal Truth beyond all vicissitudes of mortal men, but mystics suspect that God though perfect, needs deeper perfection, so is dreaming into existence an endless sequence of universes, each conditioned by the character of its predecessor that He might learn vicariously from the experience of all creatures, humans, spirits, on all planets in all the planes of His Creation. Man needs God; most wondrous of all, God needs Man, else He would not have created him. Life is not Illusion nor is the Universe some Cosmic Joke played by the Deity; from the lowliest insect to the loftiest archangel, from a grain of dust to a galaxy, all have meaning; each Man's brief life, his joys and sorrows, contribute their purpose to the divine Plan. This concept of existence may be questioned but seems as close as human fallibility can approach the infinite Truth. Can Man, who does not know himself, know his Creator?

Such esoteric speculations are not without relevance to the study of Spacemen, our fellow-souls throughout the living universe. Man stands on the threshold of a new age, of cosmic affinity with the stars. Man must now forget his selfish geocentric philosophy; he must expand to cosmic consciousness and realise his oneness with all Creation. To re-orientate his thoughts comprehending all sentient Beings in all dimensions of the universe Man must humble himself and begin at the Beginning. In the Beginning was God.

All religions teach of the Angels of Light warring against the Powers of Darkness for possession of Man's soul. This conflict between Good and Evil on the spiritual plane may be symbolic of that real War in Heaven described by Apollodorus,[1] Hesiod[2] and Ovid,[3] exemplified by the Tower of Babel in Genesis and by legends all over the world.

Throughout the universe few men are saints, many are sinners, most have virtues balanced by vices; in all stages of evolution none is wholly good or wholly bad.

Maleficent invaders from Jupiter or its moons usurped the Saturnians of the Golden Age and enforced a tyranny provoking Earth's Giants to revolt. World-wide legends agree that war was waged in Earth and Sky with fantastic nuclear weapons, aerial-craft and laser death-rays, shrivelling cities and blasting the mountains with titanic bolts of electricity in destruction still visible today. Later as in divine retribution a comet ravaged our Earth, the wondrous civilisation was destroyed, the climate grew cold, distortion of spatial tensions interrupted communications between the planets, most men perished, the few survivors plunged to barbarism. After centuries of isolation the old sciences and technologies were largely forgotten, though fragments of the ancient wisdom were preserved down the generations by Initiates in all countries including witch-doctors today. Garbled race-memories and folk-lore imagined the Spacemen to be Gods with superhuman powers glorying in aerial battles or descending to Earth for more amorous exploits.[4]

Human consciousness divined that Man was not alone in the universe, somewhere in the Heavens above existed Beings of great beneficence who might help mankind. Certain sensitives claimed influence with the Gods, compounded a theology and communication through prayer, from their ritual and morals developed religion.

Such novel interpretation of the past bewilders experts and laymen alike; both for different reasons dismiss it as dubious science-fiction hardly worth consideration. Extraterrestrial domination of our Earth millennia ago presupposes planets inhabited by Beings far more advanced than ourselves mastering a science transcending our own today. The astronomers and biologists who suggest life elsewhere, are careful to stress that none of our neighbouring worlds can be inhabited,[5] planets are not certain around the near stars, and if Supermen do exist in other galaxies travel across thousands of light-years seems unlikely. Archaeologists smile about digging up skeletons not spaceships, forgetting that in a few hundred years all our own aircraft would dissolve to dust; historians say the Classics never mention Spacemen, surely Plato[6] and Livy[7] would have known? Perhaps they did, if you read them properly? Mythologists seldom consider legends as basically true, they hypothesize more primitive meaning or suggest religious symbolism. Schliemann believed the 'Iliad' and discovered Troy; Sir Arthur Evans fascinated by Theseus killing the Minotaur unearthed Knossus and the Minoan civilisation of Crete, yet scholars still regard the old Gods as personifications of natural forces, anthropomorphisms of human moods, surely an effort of the intellect beyond most of us today. Probably the greatest obstacle to accepting the advent of Spacemen lies in dogmatic religion. Theologians believe God's sole concern is Man on Earth, if Man exists elsewhere must Christ be crucified millions of times on all the worlds in the universe? Immersed in their own subjects, the most brilliant specialists become intolerant of new concepts confounding their pet philosophies.

The man-in-the-street prides himself on his commonsense, a commodity most uncommon; usually he lives in a trance bemused by the pleasures and pains of daily existence and brain-washed by the pressure of propaganda from Press and Television. Ordinary people languish a generation behind the latest discoveries, their main concern is to conform with the social conventions of their community; they believe only what they see and know only what they want to know. The group-consciousness evolves slowly, mass-education promises enlightenment but the bloody history of our twentieth century makes the average person suspicious of new ideas and disillusioned with the traditions of the past on which our civilisation is based, his mind muddled by theologians preaching threadbare doctrines and the scientists threatening his life with bigger bombs, he feels the world would be better without them. The ordinary man reasons with a basic logic undistorted by the questions troubling theology and science; when he gazes at the glorious heavens he senses the wonder of the universe and knows that God did not create those shining stars just for men to look at. Like his ancestors in Antiquity he feels all creation throbs with life and believes whatever astronomers might say that in those starry depths of space live Beings wise and passionate, weak and sinful, human like himself.

The concept of Spacemen landing on Earth throughout history would, if proved, revolutionise our views of the past, inspire our present and promise a glorious future; mankind would wake as from a dream to cosmic reality. At last Man would discover his real self and soar in regeneration to his Brothers in the stars; humanity would spiral to a higher plane closer to God.[8 9]

Before we can comprehend the co-existence of Spacemen, we must first understand ourselves and evaluate our Earth's position in the Universe; we must open our eyes, unstop our ears, attune our very souls to the cosmic wonder of Creation; we must expand beyond space and time to embrace eternity.

The real universe is what God thinks[10] not what Man imagines. Man's finite mind synthesises information cognised by his five senses extended by science into a pattern which he terms the Cosmos; as his awareness intensifies so does his conception expand in grandeur. Were Man's vision sensitive to lower frequencies of radiation he would marvel at those dark stars now detected by the radio-astronomers and be blind to those glorious constellations spangling the heavens; to an earth-worm the universe must appear as a one-dimensional darkness; some wondrous advanced Being on Sirius may cognise an infinity of vibrations to experience a transcendent Creation beyond our imagination.

Much of what exists we do not see, much of what we see does not exist. Astronomers cannot see the void into which the galaxies allegedly recede,[11] the physicists cannot see inside the atom; the light we see from countless stars was emitted millions of years ago, many may have long since exploded; now—and what is Now?—our senses are stimulated by radiations from them, our brain computes a pattern based on its memory-bank and frames a reality. Esoterically all we ever see is ourselves, a secret most profound.

The exoteric science of the cosmologists collates observable phenomena in the heavens and escalating backwards through time, propounds plausible theories to explain the origin of the universe; the esoteric wisdom of the occultists begins with God and thinking forwards divines how the universe has evolved until the present day. Our materialist philosophy bedazzled by the practical benefits of science, which have transformed the world, tends to scorn the occultists, who operate in the realms of Spirit, but in the infinite wonder of Creation both science and occultism constitute different view-points of the manifestation of God in Whom we live and move, and both have equal validity. Super-Intelligences in other galaxies may cognise the universe and its origins in terms beyond our comprehension; their conception and our own are relative to Reality, only God the Creator knows Truth.

Occultism is the science of Divine Unfoldment.[12] The occultist regards Deity as the All, no manifestation can exist outside of God. From His Own Spirit the Absolute begins each Cosmic Day by involving Mind through myriads of forms to the grossest vibrations of matter; when Involution is complete, Evolution begins; through countless ages matter evolves to finer and more complex forms gradually attenuating to pure Spirit returning to God, Who then broods over the Experience during a Cosmic

Night when nothing exists. Some Hindus believed the Day of Brahm lasts fifteen million, million years and is followed by a Night of equal duration when the Absolute withdraws Its manifestation entirely into Itself and dwells in Infinity. At the end of this period the Absolute invokes a new Universe, a refinement of its predecessor; Day then Night in endless succession beyond the comprehension of Man.[13]

The fundamental Rhythm, activity and inactivity manifests from Universes to Atoms including Man himself, and is the basis of all Secret Doctrines. The highest Hindu teachings however insist that this principle does not apply to the Absolute Himself Who is constantly creating and holding in His Mind millions of universes in different stages of evolution; Night in one series may be Mid-Day in another. Rhythmic Change, Rise and Fall, profoundly influenced the philosophies of the Ancients; Heraclitus taught that the Universe manifested itself in cycles; the Stoics believed the world moved in an endless cycle through the same stages; the followers of Pythagoras claimed each universe exactly repeated all the others over and over again in Eternal Recurrence preached by De Siger in the Middle Ages and Ouspensky[14] today. The Yogis teach cyclic evolution in infinite progression.

Oriental writings, the sublime Upanishads, stress that our whole universe throbs with the One Life, divined by the Chinese philosophers, illumined Meister Eckhard, mystics of all religions, Spinoza, Kant and our modern physicists. Atoms have consciousness, all matter is alive; some sensitives assert the planets themselves are glorious Beings; we infest and influence our living Earth like microbes. Occultists believe that co-spatial within our own universe exist universes of varying frequencies of matter, astral planes inhabited by the so-called dead and souls awaiting rebirth, also different dimensions peopled by devas, nature-spirits, faeries, elementals, races of Beings in a different stream of evolution from Man himself.

Cyclic progression includes Man too. The human soul evolves by metempsychosis, reincarnating life after life ascending to perfection in God. This wonderful doctrine was taught by the Egyptian Priests, the Eleusinian Mysteries of Greece, Pythagoras, Plato, Virgil, the Druids, Hindu sages, Tibetan Yogis, Persian Magi, the Jewish Kabbala and the early Gnostic Christian Fathers. Many great souls like Francis Bacon, Paracelsus, Giordano Bruno, Schopenhauer, Goethe, Gandhi and almost all the East today, believed in reincarnation governed by Karma, the Law of Cause and Effect. Man suffers for his own sins. The Earth is a training-school to which the soul returns to learn its lessons, then is reborn on a more highly developed planet, ascending through a chain of worlds assimilating experience.[15]

Occultists, Yogis and psychics like Swedenborg believed in countless inhabited worlds in various stages of evolution; many planets were apparently allied into associations, grouped into Galactic Federations and possibly ever greater organisations. To our sardonic minds this conception smacks of science-fiction with its inter-planetary wars and galactic rivalries, yet behind the phantasy lies Cosmic Truth. Occult traditions hint at Adepts and Masters dwelling on Earth, who in secrecy and silence direct the evolution of our planet; they are said to maintain telepathic or astral communication with Avatars on neighbouring worlds, all are subordinate to Celestials on the Sun, who probably obey some great Intelligence controlling the Galaxy, Himself obedient to yet Higher Entity ascending through a Hierarchy approaching the infinite, ineffable Absolute. There is reason to believe that some of these Super-Beings have appeared on Earth by incarnation, astral manifestation or landing from spaceships; here they have taught Man cosmic truths, the arts and crafts of civilisation, and prompted human evolution in accordance with the divine plan.[16]

Conventional thought conditioned by the Judaic-Christian conception of the Intervention of God in human history as the supreme revelation of the Creator, and the materialistic philosophy of our twentieth century, ridicules the sublime cosmic design of the occultists as lunacies, yet as astronomers peer into galactic space and as physicists probe inside atomic nuclei they are startled to find their new illumination approaching the old transcendent Secret Wisdom, Hermetic philosophies of the occult Initiates.

All the great religions of the world express the yearning of men and women throughout the centuries to learn the

Truth of terrestrial existence; their questing souls soared beyond material surroundings and hungered for illumination, for at-one-ment in that hushed, sweet Mystery transcending the universe. Man marvelled at the myriad stars studding the sky, the miracles of nature in all her moods, the procession of humanity from the remote past across the peaks and depths of history on to the veiled uplands of the future, the pageantry of noble deeds, the drama of mortal passion, all the infinite wonder of life itself. Logic, reason, philosophy, science, triumphs of the human intellect, enable Man to fashion tools to modify his environment and to devise persuasive systems of thought-patterns explaining the apparent universe, yet as his awareness sharpens so Man's ignorance intensifies until the truly wise know nothing.

Wisdom brings humility; in this tortured twentieth century which began in a golden age and now stumbles to suicide, men see no purpose to their lives and like the cynical pagans of the past eat, drink and make merry for tomorrow they die. The schizophrenic masochism, the mad rush to mass destruction, so manifest in national crime and international conflict are evidence of humanity racked with inner tensions and fear of the future, frightening ignorance of the infinitely expanding universe; science has reduced Earthman from Lord of Creation to a meaningless ant; God from being a benevolent Father has receded to an inexpressible, unimaginable Mind conjuring a universe of countless worlds in endless dimensions where Earth is less than dust.

In their hearts, never in history, were men so religious; cruelties to man and beasts condoned by prim society a century ago are now condemned like the orgies of Nero's Rome. Capitalists and Communists wage open war for domination of the world yet behind the blatant materialism quickens the urge to benefit all mankind; though methods differ, in cosmic analysis the social betterment of Man must surely earn the blessing of God. Men are human, life is struggle against ignorance. No longer can people accept the dusty dogmas of the past without question, mankind has followed so many false Messiahs, today Men search for Truth but find no answer. Men wonder why five rival religions in two thousand years should culminate in spiritual sterility, and bedazzled by the illusions of modern enlightenment they smash the old images of God only to find their souls plunged into a nothingness from which there seems no escape. Today humanity awaits a Message; men gaze at the silent, shining stars and listen. Earth sighs with weariness. Salvation must come from Space.

It is wrong to criticise religion, to censure officious priests, to pity their deluded dupes and to scoff the tortuous dogmas which stifle men's souls. Religion must suit Man's evolution. The stone idol of the primitive savage represents to him some occult force he cannot comprehend; indeed witch-doctors appear to possess remnants of an ancient wisdom transcending our own sophistication. The conception of a personalised God or Saviour like Osiris, Orpheus, Krishna, Buddha or Christ, gave the deepest spiritual solace to countless millions, whose limited intelligence could not conceive of the formless, infinite Absolute, the teachings of the holy books and the lives of saintly men and women inspired multitudes in their pilgrimage from darkness to light; men are in different stages of evolution; the guidance from wondrous Teachers down the generations surely proves the presence of Higher Powers and demonstrates the beneficence of God.

The existence of Supermen in the skies was accepted by the peoples of Antiquity all over the world; in reaction to paganism the Christian Church dethroned the old Gods and closed men's minds to the living universe. For two thousand years Christians have been conditioned to believe that Earth was the centre of Creation and Man the sole concern of God. Although modern astronomers now teach that the old conceptions are false and that our Earth is an inferior planet of a dwarf sun near the edge of the Milky Way, only one of countless galaxies, this awareness has hardly permeated the contemporary consciousness, for most people's knowledge of astronomy seems actually little better than the ignorance of the early Christian Fathers; some scholars like St Augustine and the Venerable Bede, familiar with the writings of the Greeks, were aware of the planets, the sphericity of the Earth and phenomena of the heavens, but their views on scientific matters were suppressed by the Church. For two thousand years science was asleep. Even today, scientists, who should surely know better, seem reluctant to relinquish their pre-conceived contention that life exists only on our Earth, though admittedly a growing number realising the irrationality of this belief now teach that life must exist throughout the universe but not on the other planets in our solar system. *Information telemetered from our artificial satellites is said to prove scientifically that life cannot possibly exist here on our own Earth; photographs from rockets show our world as barren as the Moon with an atmosphere of unbreathable hydrogen.*[17] Since we believe those same instruments when we deny life on Mars, scientifically speaking we should not exist.

Scientists do not take themselves seriously, nor do the people they try to impress; so swift is the avalanche of new knowledge that everyone knows that what a scientist swears to be truth today he will scoff tomorrow. The fundamental disbelief in spacemen today may be due to the geocentric thought-pattern imposed by religion.

Many sincere Christians reject life on other planets arguing that Christ must then be crucified on every star in the sky, although Pope Pius XII declared that men on other worlds may live in a State of Grace without redemption by the Son of God, a theological subtlety beyond most laymen. The Protestant Church of Germany declared that God would create Man throughout the universe to praise His Wonders but most people find this claim difficult to equate with Christianity.

Modern scholarship makes the Mystery of Christ more profound. We ask ourselves whether God the Creator of countless worlds in many dimensions possibly paralleled by a universe of anti-matter would incarnate a unique Being on our tiny Earth for a purpose which is still not clear. The Virgin Birth and the Resurrection were not confined to Christianity but were common to most of the religions of Antiquity; some theologians speculate that the Crucifixion of Christ represented the murder of Tammuz, the Babylonian fertility God or the Dying King of many ancient cults. The Dead Sea Scrolls surprise us by not mentioning Christ or Christianity, their Essene teachings suggest that some of the Christian doctrine originated a century earlier.[18] Nothing is gleaned of Christ from contemporary sources, surprising in an age of classic writers; almost all we know of Him is from Gospels written by imaginatives decades later. Some scholars while accepting the reality of the Man Jesus believe that He was a pious Jew, patriotic Leader of a Resistance movement against the Romans for which He was crucified; others allege that Christ survived the Cross and lived in Rome, then died in India. Cogent arguments suggest that the historical Jesus was really Apollonius of Tyana, that great spiritual Teacher, who nineteen hundred years ago wandered throughout the known world, worked miracles, healed the sick and raised the dead, to whom Emperors built temples and worshipped as a God.[19]

Voltaire said, 'If God did not exist, Man would invent Him.'[20] Perhaps Christianity is a Myth necessary to the evolution and inspiration of Man during this lost Piscean Age? A denial of Christ is not a denial of God; our conception of God transcends His humanisation on Earth in a glorious expansion embracing all the sentient Beings on all the worlds in all the realms of all the universes.[21] The gentle Image of Christ conceals a Mystery beyond our understanding, mankind on the threshold of Space spirals to a new octave of evolution; man's questing soul soars beyond the dogmatic creeds of yesterday to the cosmic religion of tomorrow.

CHAPTER TWO

The Search for Extra-Terrestrials

Science parallels religion in refuting Spacemen, while many scientists theorise inhabited planets light-years away, most hesitate to admit Beings elsewhere in our solar system, and ridicule Extra-terrestrials landing on Earth. Like the Church, official science arrogates to itself presumptions that cannot be proved: the fundamental belief of the scientist is that the nature of the universe and its evolution can be discovered by Man following that scientific method which has transformed our modern world. Science assumes a space-time universe composed of mass and energy governed by immutable laws; this conception would be challenged by miracle-working Saints, who view Creation as a manifestation of God, or Adepts performing magic, who regard the universe as a great Mind. Our occultists evoke psychic phenomena, and there possibly exist Supermen in the stars who manipulate forces beyond our cognisance. Science with all its wonderful instruments perceives only a narrow slit of the real universe, only God can know His whole Creation.

Today theoretical science plunges into depths as esoteric as religion, expanding into an ever greater area of ignorance; whereas religion closes on inner truth transcending question. The once proud claim of science to know reality dissolves into a dream.[22] The solid atom disappears into a hundred particles, vibrations of energy approaching pure thought. Science cannot know the real world; the physicists cannot see the electron, the astronomer views stars not as they exist now but as millions of years ago. Einstein's Theory of Relativity is not wholly proved, Heisenberg's Principle of Uncertainty seems to introduce into physics the religious problems of fate versus free-will; there is a growing reaction against Darwin's Theory of

Evolution; instead of gradual development through countless ages sudden mutations appear to have occurred through cataclysms or changes in cosmic rays. Some thinkers suggest that Man is not indigenous to our Earth but ages ago arrived here from another planet.[23]

Scientific reasoning is based on deductive or inductive logic following the axiomatic methodology of the Greeks. Recently Goedel has proved to mathematicians with masterly revelation that deductive logic must be incomplete since questions can be legitimately asked without apparent answers, inductive logic seeking to generalise a theory from known facts can never be wholly true since it cannot completely include the future or evidence beyond its experience. Logic is unreliable. Many fundamental discoveries are made by practical inventors unencumbered by scientific training. Simon Newcomb proved conclusively that heavier-than-air machines could not fly.[24] While he was brilliantly theorising William and Orville Wright built their aeroplane, the *Kitty Hawk*, and flew it. Many great inventions are born by chance, pure luck or sudden intuition, defying logic, inspired by occult sources or from Man's subconscious mind. Man cannot know himself, how can he know the Universe?

Scientists consider their experiments take place in an isolated system whose evolution dominated by the Principle of Carnot tends to thermodynamic equilibrium in the ultimate state of entropy; Giorgio Piccardi, Professor of Geophysics at Florence, in a brilliant series of experiments has proved that the methodology of research based on initial conditions is false.[25] Chemical tests performed with strict precision day after day, year after year, have shown that the results vary surprisingly according to solar phenomena and extra-terrestrial force-fields; the Earth gyrates around the Sun which moves through space towards the constellation of Sagittarius.[26] The Earth thus moves in a spiral trajectory crossing lines of force created by the Milky Way, whose galactic field in motion is influenced by all the moving matter and energy in the universe. Each human being is a concretion of electrical energy. A man might influence a star, which influences him. This is not occultism, astrology or mysticism; every experiment, every human passion, is performed against the background of the entire universe. All Creation is in constant change; our Earth and all upon it are influenced by cosmic forces, whose total intensities we cannot measure but whose variations alter preconceived results, both in the world of matter and in our minds, too.

Science like religion has given much to mankind; its mastery and manipulation of the physical world have revolutionised men's lives for good or ill; the scientific method remains a glory of the human intellect. It must be recognised that in the consideration of Extra-terrestrials in the present and in the past we are dealing with phenomena beyond the experience of geocentric science and religion; the valuations by both these disciplines may offer enlightenment but illumination can come only from Space. While orthodox science mesmerised by its spectroscopes denies intelligent Beings on other solar planets, scientists realise that since all the stars seem apparently composed of the same ninety-two basic elements as our own Earth, life-forms are likely to exist throughout the universe. Some astronomers believe that planets are by-products in the creation of stars from accretions of atoms born from cosmic energy. The slow angular speed of our Sun is said to be due to its family of planets, since in our own galaxy there must be millions of suns like our own and of approximately the same age most of them probably having planets.[27] Biologists declare that life appears anywhere conditions favour its development and they regard life itself as an electro-chemical rather than a spiritual phenomenon. The primeval atmosphere of Earth consisted of ammonia, nitrogen and hydrogen with a little oxygen and carbon-dioxide at high temperatures, charged by electrical storms which synthesised amino acids in the sea evolving into organic substances, whose cells reproduced themselves producing through countless ages the myriad forms of life today. Such evolution must occur on all planets similar to Earth, while the inhabitants of some may live in a Stone Age the people of other worlds may have attained a technology transcending our own.

Throughout its history our Earth has been bombarded by rains of stones from the sky, most of these are incandesced into dust in the upper atmosphere, some siderites composed of iron and nickel litter the ocean floor, other aerolithes, non-metallic, are often mixed with terrestrial rocks; on rare occasions huge meteors have caused enormous craters all over the world. In 1836 the chemist, Berzelius, analysed stones fallen in France and was astonished to find the carbonacious substance contained considerable water, most surprising from space; later Berthelot examined fragments of the 1864 Orgueil meteorite and found organic substances. Suggestions that such discoveries evidence extra-terrestrial life were ridiculed by the astronomers, who argued that since science believed life could not exist in space therefore it did not exist. In 1961 prompted by current space-research, Professor Nagy and his colleagues re-examined pieces of the Orgueil meteorite and found their micro-structure to be of living origin containing hydrocarbons, which they later analysed as complicated chains of fatty substances, even sexual hormones, analogous but not completely identical to those of terrestrial metabolism.[28] Analysis of meteorites in museums all over the world found therein various minute but unmistakable traces of organic compounds. These meteorites may be fragments of the supposed planet, Maldek,[29] between Mars and Jupiter, which is believed to have exploded into the asteroids; such meteoritic showers must fall on Mars, Venus and our own Moon. In olden times shooting-stars had phallic significance, people believed they inseminated recumbent Earth. This may be true. Life may be carried on the currents of space from planet to planet. Our scientists now agree with the Ancients that life must exist everywhere.

Our largest optical telescopes are not powerful enough to detect whether any planets exist around Alpha Centauri, the nearest star, four light years away, until recently such detection appeared impossible. The radio-astronomers observed perturbations in signals from the Sun, when the planets Jupiter and Saturn occupied certain positions, suggesting that periodically their gravitation exercised greater influence on the Sun's radiation. Periodic perturbations in emanations from other non-binary stars inferred a similar phenomenon and there is reasonable certainty that Barnard's Star six light years distant has an invisible companion and that Tau Ceti, eleven light years away, also has planets. Russian astronomers believe that laser light flashes from the star, 61 Cygnus, in 1894 and 1908 were answers to an apparent signal from Earth, actually the Krakatoa eruption of 1883. Stars rotate quickly at the time of their creation, then, at a certain moment slow up, their energy being drained off by attendant planets. Observation infers that in order to know if a star had planets it suffices only to measure its speed of rotation; oscillation in the motion of a star may now be considered evidence of undetected planetary companions.

Biologists prove that the fundamental substance of all life-forms is de-oxyribonucleic acid, DNA, whose molecule in the form of a spiral contains in code all the information of heredity linked like a string of beads; this polymer is composed of sugar, phosphoric acid and nitrogenous bases. Discovery of DNA on another planet would be generally accepted as proof of life. The National Aeronautics Space Administration of America supporting its programme for an early landing by Man on the Moon and probes to Mars and Venus is devoting intensive research towards discovering life in space. A remarkable technique of absorption-spectroscopy could detect the presence of nitrogenous base hence life in soil samples, so the Americans have devised the multivator life detection system, a miniature biological laboratory weighing only one pound, which can perform fifteen separate experiments. On landing on a planet soil samples will be blown through the multivator, solvents injected into reaction-chambers, fluorescent lamps go on in sequence, the fluorescence is measured and the measurements telemetered to Earth for decoding. A Vidicon miscroscope will transmit photographs of micro-organisms from a planet's surface; Gulliver, a radio-isotope biochemical probe shaped like a small cone, will discharge three fifty-foot lines coated with a sticky substance, then reel them back into a culture broth; in four hours living organisms should begin to grow causing increase in radio-active gas, the radio-activity will be noted by a Geiger counter, whose information will be promptly telemetered back to Earth.[30]

Amino-acids, components of proteins, when heated to vapour, may be detected by spectrometry. NASA exobiologists propose to deposit miniaturised mass-spectrometers on a planet's surface, which would scan the spectrum of any biological molecule and telemeter it back to Earth; they say this experiment might detect a form of life not known to us. Another ingenious device is a Wolf Trap (not so ambitious as to snare wolves on Mars but being merely christened after its inventor, Professor Wolf Vishniac). This consists of a hollow tube intended to suck dust by vacuum which will be immersed into culture media. If bacteria grow, they will cause a change in light intensity on a photoelectric cell, whose varying signals will be transmitted to Earth. A further possibility is the landing of an ultra-violet spectro-photometer to compare the colours of the spectra of proteins and peptides to establish the presence of organic molecules; it is also hoped that living organisms in space may be detected by gas chromatography. Scientists propose to use a mixture of luciferin and lucifran, extracted from fireflies, whose glow is caused by their reaction with ATP (adenosin triphosphate), which is found in all living cells. When the mixture contacts any ATP the chemicals will glow and the result telemetered to Earth will be construed as encounter with living cells. These remarkable techniques show that the National Aeronautics and Space Administration recognise the possibility of extra-terrestrial life and will utilise every trick of science to prove its existence.

The Russian astronomer, Joseph Shklovsky, after brilliant analysis of our galaxy, supposes that if the distance between two civilisations is about ten light-years only three stars, Epsilon Eridani, Tau Ceti and Epsilon Indus are likely to possess intelligent Beings able to communicate with us. The Americans listening on the hydrogen-frequency of 1420 megacycles claim to have received strong impulses from these stars. The American professor, Robert N. Bracewell, supports Shklovsky and has produced graphs showing that if a technological civilisation lasts 10,000 years, then within the radius of a thousand light-years there are about 50,000 civilisations. At this distance radio-signals would be too feeble for detection; it is suggested that rockets with radio-sondes speeding at 100,000 miles a second could in a few centuries approach distant civilisations, emit signals, record and return signals received and perhaps televise to other worlds a map of the skies whence the sonde originated.[31]

At the beginning of April 1964 the Russians launched their Sonde 1 towards an unknown destination and in April 1965 Gennady Sholomitsky announced that they had discovered a new civilisation millions of miles away in space. Emissions of radio-waves from a mysterious source known as CTA-102 follow a regular pattern of flickerings every 100 days, suggesting control by intelligent Beings. Radio-astronomers at Jodrell Bank are quite sceptical and attribute the pulsations to a quasar, but Dr Nikolai Kardashev maintains that the emissions are extremely small and must be of intelligent origin. Scientists in Moscow now claim this as the most outstanding discovery in radio-astronomy. These signals are reminiscent of the pulsations from space monitored by Tesla and Marconi early this century.

The thousands, perhaps millions, of civilisations in our galaxy will surely advertise their existence to stars on the perimeter like our own Sun and will probably send radio-sondes to surveil our solar system. About thirty years ago Stormer and Van der Pol detected abnormal echoes, repetitions of signals from Earth several minutes after their emission; Bracewell believes they were repeated by an automatic extra-terrestrial sonde millions of miles away.

Shklovsky suggests that Supreme Intelligences may modify the stars themselves. He states that some stars of the rare spectral series S reveal faint traces of technetium, which is not found naturally on Earth, being a silvery-white powder produced in a nuclear-reactor. The life-period of radio-active technetium is only 200,000 years and it is difficult to understand how it can exist in stars thousands of millions of years old. Shklovsky speculates whether Supermen have manufactured millions of tons of technetium and impregnated the atmosphere of stars to manifest to the watching universe the reality of Intelligences in space. Such fantastic enterprise staggers us, yet who knows what technology is mastered by Supermen elsewhere?[32] The Russians speculate that the great Cosmic Intelligences may actually be stellar engineers able to modify and control the development of stars and with incredible laser-beams to explode them like super-novae.

Possible evidence of Intelligent Beings in our own solar system may exist in the moons of Mars: Phobos, 5,800 miles from the centre of Mars, and Deimos, 15,000 miles, are much closer to their planet than any known natural satellites. Shklovsky notes that the only celestial bodies in the solar system, which move around a planet faster than the latter turns on its own axis, are Phobos and Earth's artificial satellites; he stresses that Phobos, diameter 10 miles, Deimos, 5 miles, seem objects too small for a planetary system; neither has the classic red colour of Mars; the acceleration in the rotation of Phobos suggests retardation in the Martian atmosphere and eventual falling to the planet like our own artificial satellites. The density of the moons is too small for natural satellites and suggests hollow shells of steel, which André Avignon[33] calculates as only three inches thick, weightlessness in space would make the construction of such artificial moons technically possible. Shklovsky suggests that Phobos and Deimos are monuments to some race of Martians in ages past circling a dead planet as our own satellites may circle Earth after the last Man has perished. Photographs taken by the American Mariner IV space-probe suggest that the surface of Mars is apparently desert without the famous canals. At least one picture revealed a quadrangular structure, which encourages belief in intelligence on Mars.

While scientists are sceptic, alleged communications from Space Beings to sensitives on Earth insist that people like ourselves inhabit not only the planets around our own Sun but the worlds around countless stars. The whole universe throbs with life.

The greatest impediment to acceptance of Extra-terrestrials is Man's ignorance of Reality. Each Man is the centre of his own private universe cognised by his five senses, synthesised in a mind conditioned by education and experience. A Man's universe is the quintessence of his thoughts, some intuitives attempt in humility to transcend their egocentric view-point by aspiring to see the universe through the eyes of its Creator, only to realise they cannot escape the prison of Self and reduce God to their own image. Since all men have similar sensory faculties and at any time in history are conditioned by similar culture-patterns, it follows that general experience brings common agreement as to the apparent nature of the universe, whose appearance changes according to new knowledge. Our cosmology today differs vastly from the flat Earth and concentric celestial spheres postulated by Ptolemy, but in two thousand years our own conception of a finite expanding universe may appear ludicrous.

It is natural for Man to limit the universe to the evidence of his own sensory perceptions extended by ingenious instruments and to deny reality to domains outside immediate cognisance. Restricted observation may be paralleled by rigid attitude of mind; some people ignore phenomena such as the occult unacceptable to science, yet for thousands of years a vast literature has accumulated describing dimensions and states of existence outside normal cognisance.

The claim by the occultists of invisible worlds in astral realms and etherean planes inhabited by devas, faeries or the so-called dead, was long ridiculed by ordinary people believing in common-sense and by the materialist-minded scientists mesmerised by their own instruments. Research into the insubstantial atoms, the discovery of scores of sub-atomic particles, the new state of matter known as plasma, and increased awareness of vibratory fields, have revolutionised the scientific conception of matter to approach the teachings of the old Hermetic philosophers and the Yogis of Tibet. Physicists now admit that what we term the physical universe is just that spectrum of vibrations apprehended by our physical senses; it is logical to assume that there may be frequencies of matter beyond our tangibility, just as real as those dark stars we cannot see. Matter may exist in octaves co-spatial inside each other; within our own Earth may inter-penetrate other worlds inhabited by warm passionate Beings, who may manifest to our senses as apparitions or conversely Earthlings by mischance may vanish into another dimension. Occultists in fact claim another world co-spatial with Earth, whose capital is Shamballah, a glorious etherean city co-existent with our Gobi desert; some Adepts claim to visit this realm in their astral body.

The teachings of the once-derided occultists are now advanced by ultra-modern researchers, the Borderland Scientists,[34] who claim contact with Beings from etherean Venus enjoying a wondrous civilisation transcending our own. It is interesting to note that the *Secret Doctrine* and that profound work, *Oahspe*,[35] tell of Ethereans descending in fire-ships from their plane to our own material plane very many thousand years ago; the Hermetic philosophy taught that in time our Earth itself would become spiritualised to finer and finer vibrations passing from our present gross octave to an ethereal plane growing ever more refined until mergence with God.

Some Borderland Researchers believe that the sudden appearances and disappearances of UFOS are manifestations of spaceships from the invisible worlds, whose Masters are able to retard their bodily frequencies to materialise before us. A few sensitives claim the ability to travel in their etherean bodies; they report enlightening adventures on worlds beyond normal perception.

The reality of etherean planets daunts our minds conditioned to the materialist plane, yet their acceptance would readily explain much occult-phenomena, wondrous episodes in the Bible and religious literature, as well as many strange manifestations in history which still bewilder us. Perhaps some of the Gods in the past did 'descend' to Earth from 'heaven', those inner realms within our physical universe?

Until recently physicists believed that when God created the universe, He solemnly decided to build His atoms with a nucleus of positively charged protons and non-charged neutrons around which spin negatively charged electrons creating a positive universe inhabited by positive people, our positive selves. Why God should show such bias for the positive, when all Creation apparently functions on the balance of opposites, the duality of good and evil, right and wrong, light and dark, bothered certain philosophers, who reasoned that according to the universal fundamental principle of symmetry there must exist a negative universe, mirror to our own. This fanciful supposition appeared to be one of the lighter lunacies of science, like levitation and squaring the circle, and was frowned on by the Church. To accuse God of creating a left-handed universe was surely mortal sin.

In 1957 Madame Wu, uninhibited by our Christian theology, froze radio-active cobalt and was surprised to find its electrons emitted anti-symmetrically to the direction predicted; two Chinese-Americans, T. D. Lee and C. N.

Yang later discovered the spin of certain electrons was asymmetrical to the conventional matter, thereby implying the existence of matter negative to our own, like its reflection, as it were, in a mirror. Further researches into cosmic rays and particles, accelerated in cyclotrons, have revealed anti-protons, anti-neutrons, positive electrons or positrons, suggesting parallel anti-matter. At the moment of Creation, presumably a particle of positive matter and a particle of anti-matter would spring into co-existence and be immediately repelled by anti-gravity, since on touching these opposites annihilate each other into the primeval void. For the totality of Creation to be uniform, every atom of positive matter should be balanced by an equivalent atom of anti-matter, otherwise Creation would be unbalanced, such disequilibrium leading to its destruction, apart from offending our inate sense of harmony. In the universe of anti-matter our laws of physics might be reversed; anti-gravity will make apples 'fall' upwards, anti-cells will fabricate anti-men with fabulous anti-women.[36]

Astronomers now conjecture that some of the galaxies bejewelling the heavens may be made of anti-matter, their collisions with positive galaxies may cause those sudden bursts of energy rushing from space. Physicists are racing to isolate anti-matter, the winner can then make an anti-bomb to end everything.

In 1966, however, this principle of symmetry was seriously questioned. A team of physicists at Brookhaven, Long Island, led by Dr. Paolo Franzini with his wife, Dr. Juliet Lee-Franzini, Dr. Charles Balty and Dr. Lawrence Kirsch analysed half a million photographs of atomic collisions inside a tank of liquid heavy hydrogen. When a particle called the eta meson decays under an electromagnetic process they found unexpected differences in the speeds of the positive and negative particles. The mathematical foundations of modern physics based on the relativity theory and quantum mechanics are now open to question; our universe seems strangely lop-sided.[37]

In 1964 the Americans discovered that K-meson observations seemed to indicate the direction in which time is flying. Dr F. R. Stannard, a physicist of University College, London, in the August 1966 issue of *Nature* suggests that we may be surrounded by another, invisible universe in which time runs backwards. Our own apparently lopsided universe may be balanced by another governed by the same physical laws but in which time is reversed; the totality of Creation would thus by symmetrical after all. This theory postulates a faustian universe completely isolated from our own; a faustian man could walk right through us, faustian galaxies may exist in the sky which would appear to absorb light rather than emitting it. From our point of view inhabitants of the faustian universe would appear to live backwards growing younger towards their birth, such Beings would appear to be travelling as it were from our future. Interaction between these complementary universes may be suggested by the peculiar behaviour of the K-mesons, these decay rapidly into other particles yet a proportion seem to live much longer than they should. It is theorised that some K-mesons do a time-flip into the faustian universe, where they grow younger, then flip back again. Another elusive particle the quark hypothecates a new level of reality with odd ideas of space and time, even causality. In India photographs showed that a cosmic ray neutrino hitting an atomic nucleus in rock formed not one meson but two, suggesting that not just one muon had been produced but also a boson, which soon decayed into another muon; physicists with their tremendous accelerators now hope for revolutionary developments leading to the control of gravity. These esoteric conceptions confound our understanding. However, Extra-terrestrials with their advanced technologies have probably mastered nuclear techniques beyond our imagination.

Some researchers claim that the UFOS originate not from other planets but from the interior of our own Earth. Science ridicules pretensions that our Earth is hollow,[38] yet there are claims that vents at the North and South Poles open access to the fantastic civilisation of Agharta miles underground peopled by Lemurians and Atlanteans, whose continents perished millennia ago. These Subterraneans are said to reach our surface through secret tunnels and to surveil our world also from Flying Saucers; they are now more concerned than ever since our hydrogen-bombs which may destroy us would destroy them too.

Such a theory seems strange to our conditioned pattern of thought until we recall Greek legends of the Cyclops and their workshops underground, where they fashioned wonder-weapons for the War between the Gods and the Giants, also Mediaeval tales of Intruders from a twilight land, the Rosicrucian teachings of Lemurians living below Mt. Shasta in California, and the Shaver mystery alleging communication from Supermen inside our Earth. The discovery by Admiral Byrd of an ice-free region with mountains, forests, lakes and rivers apparently entered through an opening at the North Pole suggests startling evidence of a subterranean world. Quickened interest in the Antarctic and in those UFOS seen plunging to the depths of the seas hint at other fascinating realms within our surprising planet.[39]

Some mathematicians seriously theorise that the UFOS actually come like time-machines from our own Earth, from many thousands of years in the future. Our accepted Minkowskian concept of the universe, its space-time governed by Einstein's Theories of Relativity, is challenged by the intriguing models of Kurt Goedel, which while compatible with General Relativity nevertheless postulate the existence of the future with 'open' and 'closed' lines of time permitting the return of living Beings from the future.[40]

From whatever dimension the Spacemen originate, the legends of all countries seem to show that for thousands of years Beings with transcendent wisdom have intervened in human affairs. Man can learn much from the stars, more from history. What has been shall be again; the future lies in the past. The secret of Man's destiny may be found in the Ancient East.

CHAPTER THREE

Space Gods of Ancient India

The peoples of Antiquity dreamed their civilisations dawned in the East and marvelled at those enchanted lands of the sunrise where Emperors ruled in golden splendour, slave-girls rose to be jewelled Queens; holy men wrought miracles, and amid whose multitudes throughout long ages incarnated those divine Saviours to teach mankind the Love of God. Even today in our materialistic twentieth century despite our vaunted science and cynicism we find our souls stirred by the fabulous East and feel that veneer of sophistication which veils the age-old Mystery of Man himself.

The oldest source of wisdom in the world must surely spring from India, whose Initiates long ago probed the secrets of heaven, the story of Earth, the depths of Man's soul, and propounded those sublime thoughts which illumined the Magi of Babylon, inspired the philosophers of Greece and worked their subtle influence on the religions of the West. When the first Aryans invaded India from their unknown home in the North and about 2000 BC overcame remnants of a civilisation which traced descent down countless millennia from the Gods themselves, they inherited those occult traditions of Lemuria and Atlantis telling of cosmic intercourse with Teachers from Space. Centuries later waves of light-skinned Aryans migrated from the crowded plains of the Ganges and skirting the Himalayas swept northwards to Persia, westwards to Greece and on to Gaul bringing their culture and their Gods, and Sanskrit, the language of civilisation, root of the tongue we speak today. If Spacemen landed on Earth in ages past, as world-wide legends suggest, those Gods from the skies would surely dominate Ancient India.[41]

While scientists age our Earth as four and a half thousand million years and palaeontologists unearth human skulls a million years old, historians restrict civilisation to six millennia imagining that for vast tracts of time men lived in the limbo of a Stone Age in a suspended evolution until destiny suddenly pushed Homo Sapiens from darkness to light; archæologists occasionally discover artifacts which carbon-14 and potassium-argon techniques date with incredible antiquity, but in the absence of contemporary records these relics are ignored. Theologians preach that God created Man to praise His Wonders and vaguely accuse the Creator of waiting countless millions of years, amusing Himself meanwhile with watching geologic ages of brontosaurus bathe aimlessly in swamps, before placing His puppets on this earthly stage. If God really delayed such immensity of time before creating Man can we be as important in His Sight as the insects which He created first and which will infest our planet long after the last human has dissolved to dust? The lack of written records from far antiquity admittedly impedes scientific study, which follows its own discipline of facts, but the dearth of direct evidence subject to scrutiny does not wholly disprove civilisations long ago. Troy was lost for three millennia before Schliemann dug up the crown of Helen, the face that launched a thousand ships and burned the topless towers of Ilium; the Babylon of Nebuchadnezzar, King of Kings, sprawled a heap of rubble beneath Mesopotamian mud, fair Pompeii was lost to history until unearthed by the spade. Who knows what sunken cities once gay with life now moulder on the ocean bed, what teeming metropolis lies swallowed by desert[42] sands? In ten thousand years time cavemen may shamble forth from their underground shelters near the Thames to build a new London, totally ignorant of our own Capital blasted to dust by nuclear bombs. Future historians may question whether our proud civilisation could ever exist, of our twentieth century nothing may be left save distorted race-memories of flying machines and aerial wars with fantastic weapons haunting our descendants through centuries of darkness until human culture spiralled again. Only Adepts of the Secret Wisdom would preserve in their occult teachings traditions of our lost Age.

Evolution from the slime of the sea to thinking Man

preached by Darwin and all his disciples finds impressive proofs in natural history and is accepted generally by scientists everywhere, yet the failure to find the Missing Link after a century's search now leads to speculation whether Man was created in God's Image as the Scriptures[43] suggest, meaning that our Earth was possibly colonised by Beings from other planets, perhaps from the stars. In the fullness of time Earthlings may populate other worlds, for the destiny of Life is to people the entire universe as lichen creeps across the barren rocks. Yogis teach of a chain of worlds with waves of life passing from one planet to another, extra-terrestrial biology now makes this credible. Time in our universe is only relative; there seems no logical reason why our Earth was not first inhabited by colonists from other worlds millions of years ago. If the Planetary Empire dissolved and through cosmic cataclysm communication with the parent world ceased, the settlers marooned on Earth would be left to evolve by themselves with only a dim race-memory of their cosmic origin. Such speculation is not science-fiction but worth serious thought. Photographs taken by the American Mariner IV space-probe suggest that Mars may not be inhabited, although controversy regarding the Martians still exists; at the end of this century teams of men and women may land there. If the prophesied hydrogen-bomb war devastates our Earth, the marooned colonists on Mars will mate for survival leaving their descendants to people the planet. Could this be Man's origin on Earth?

The Sacred books of Dzyan teach that the first men on Earth were the progeny of the Celestial Men or the Pitris, meaning Fathers, Lunar Ancestors, who descended to Earth from the Moon, which is believed to exercise a subtle psychical and physical influence on our own world. These most ancient records are said to be the source of the sacred volumes of China, India, Egypt and Israel; traditions says the text in the secret sacerdotal tongue called Senzar was dictated by Divine Beings, presumably Space Men, to the Atlanteans. The Stanzas describe the evolution of Man from the First Race to our own Fifth Race stopping at the death of Krishna about 5,000 years ago. This doctrine of the Lords of the Flame directing human affairs and the Sons of the Wisdom sent from the Moon, stripped of its occult significance, may be a garbled race-memory of Venusians, who first landed on the Moon then colonised our Earth. The Gnani Yogis believe the First and Second Root races occupied tropical countries which are now covered by the ice at the North and South Poles, although the Secret Doctrine sites the Second Race in Hyperborea, the Land of Spring, sung by the Greeks, believed to be in the North-West of Europe. The Third Race of Lemurians about 18,000,000 years ago[44] (a chronology ridiculed by scientists ignorant of the occult wisdom), dwelled in a vast area comprising much of the present Indian and Pacific Oceans including Australasia.[45]

A Neanderthaloid skull of a hominid, half-ape, half-man, unearthed at Broken Hill, South Africa, appeared to have a bullet-hole in one side, the opposite side of the skull being shattered as by the bullet passing out.[46] In 1962 Russian palaentologists discovered in Yakuzia, a region of North-East Siberia, a perfectly preserved bison from prehistoric times, in its forehead was a circular hole, which the scientists believed to have been probably caused by a projectile from some firearm similar to our own weapons. In the opinion of Professor Konstantin Flerov the bison could not have been used as a target by some modern hunter, the animal did not die from the wound, examination showed the injury healed. Who shot it?[47]

The Lemurians during 'millions' of years made vast material progress and are said to have built aerial ships utilising forces we have not discovered; it seems likely that there was intercourse with the inner planets, particularly Venus. Many enlightened Lemurians forewarned of the cataclysm, which destroyed Mu, migrated to the continent of Atlantis. The Books of Dzyan describe the Divine Dynasties of early Atlantis stating the 'Kings of Light' occupied 'celestial thrones',[48] an apt description for an Extra-terrestrial in a spaceship. Atlantis too attained a most brilliant civilisation perverted to the Black Arts and about 9000 BC (some occultists interpret the date as 900,000 BC) this continent in turn became engulfed as narrated by Plato in *Timaeus*. Dzyan states that the 'Great King of the Dazzling Face' sent his air-vehicles (Viwan) to rescue the Chosen of Atlantis, suggesting that these Initiates were translated to Venus. This tradition probably inspired New

Testament prophecies that on Judgement Day the Heavens will open and the Son of Man will appear with His Angels to save His children from doomed Earth; surely a race-memory of celestial intervention on the Fall of Atlantis.

Many of the Lemurians fled to the tops of mountains, which after the convulsion became the Pacific Islands; later generations migrated to a new land to the north, which had arisen from the sea.[49] The Hindu epic, the 'Ramayana', states that the first people in India were Mayas, who left Lemuria and subsequently settled in the Deccan, eventually conquering the whole sub-continent.[50]

The most ancient Asiatic traditions tell of a vast inland sea ages ago north of the Himalayas in the centre of which was an island[51] of wonder ruled by the sons of God, the Elohim, possibly Spacemen, who controlled the elements, exercised domination over earth, water, air and fire, and mastered a psychic science, which they revealed to chosen Initiates. This arcane knowledge may have echoed the cosmic wisdom of the planets, whose fragments for countless millennia have been preserved in the garbled lore of weather-magicians, witch-doctors and shamans all over the world, who persist in confounding our scientists today.

Indian mythology believed the Earth to be the centre of a series of concentric spheres, corresponding to the Moon, Sun, Mercury, Venus, Mars, Jupiter and Saturn. The Hindus knew of a seventh planet, which may have been Uranus, re-discovered by Herschel in AD 1781; their intricate observations of the distant planets and stars resulted in fixing the calendar, inventing the Zodiac, calculating the Precession of the Equinox and the prediction of eclipses thousands of years before the Babylonians, who inherited their sciences, and suggests that the ancient astronomers of India possessed optical instruments lost to their descendants or derived their knowledge from Spacemen. Beyond the sky were Spheres of the Saints, the Sons of Brahm, and of the Deities, all enclosed by a cosmic shell. Around this were layers of water surrounded in turn by fire, air, the mind, all enclosed by Brahma, Himself, infinite, beyond space and time. This system of spheres was handed down to the Greeks, inspired the epicycles of Ptolemy, formed the cosmogony of Dante and the Church and of the Mediaeval scholars, persisting until the revolutionary discoveries of Copernicus and our modern astronomers.

The most ancient art of astrology practised since far antiquity seems to prove that early civilisations mastered a science in many respects more advanced than our modern astronomy, which must have developed through preceding millennia proving Man's cultural evolution through vast tracts of time, or this recondite wisdom must have been brought to Earth by Spacemen. The Ancients saw the universe as a Supreme Thought, a creation of mental fluid crystallising in the heavenly bodies, the phenomena of Nature and Man himself; all creation throughout all its planes visible and invisible were held in the Mind of the Creator in the Dream of Brahm. Astrologers believed that each star emitted potent rays influencing the mind of man—not so fanciful now our radio-astronomers measure electro-magnetic radiation from stars seen and unseen. When a man was born the particular constellations would imprint a certain pattern on his brain like the programme in a computer, which would direct the basic trend of his life just as the code of the chromosomes in his genes fashions his physical body or as the directions taped in a missile lock it unfailingly on to its target be it Mars or Moscow. The early peoples of India like the Tibetans believed that the reincarnating soul actually chooses the time and place for its rebirth, when the stellar influences prognosticate the future experience the individual needs for his new lessons in the training-school of Earth.[52]

The esoteric wisdom inspiring this belief presupposes an intelligence of the very highest order surpassing the average mind today, which sees the stars as convenient lamps in the sky and ridicules horoscopes mistaking the nonsense proferred by the newspaper columnists for the real science of astrology. The records of old Hindu astrology show its horoscopes romanticised more with fancy than fact yet the astrologers' art does reveal glimmerings of some ancient wisdom,[53] a world-wide psychic science of great antiquity far transcending our own.[54] Only now is ultra-modern physics with its fission of the atoms and its research into ultimate particles coming to the conclusion that so-called solid matter is merely a manifestation of a Supreme Thought, the radio-astronomers now record

emissions from stars seen and unseen, which affect [illegible]
ceivers, so these radio-waves or their more subtle fr[illegible]en-
cies must record indelibly on Man's subconscious mind. The extraordinary researches by Professor Giorgio Piccardi of Florence University into cosmic chemistry prove that energy-fields in space modify physical matter in chemical experiments and exercise a potent influence on living cells of brain and body, a fact long suspected by psychiatrists.

If our own scientists of acknowledged genius by empirical studies are turning towards the Cosmos and wonder if planetary radiations affect matter and Man, both accretions of energy, then the Initiates in ancient days who brought astrology to such mathematical and philosophical refinement must have developed a super-science enabling them to conquer space, control the elements, defy gravity, fly faster than light, to act as Gods, as Spacemen! Astrology, even in the sadly debased form practised today, proves millennia-old origin from Beings of transcendent wisdom, Men from Space, the Heroes of the Indian epics, the insight of our new knowledge, all give the Hindu legends wondrous meaning, their revelations become true.

The oldest literature in the world is probably the Rig-Veda, meaning 'verse-knowledge', comprising 10,000 invocations to the Gods written in Sanskrit about 1500 BC,[55] although certain astronomical data in the text suggest 4000 BC, the mythology depicts personifications of the Gods in a naturalism of immense antiquity recording celestial events many thousand years earlier.[56] Sanskrit scholars like the erudite Dr Max Müller, agree that the Vedas are far more ancient than Homer and form the real theogony of the Aryan race, in comparison the cosmogony and theogony of Hesiod and Genesis appear crude images of the Vedic sublimity. The early Aryans were joyful, playful people like the first Greeks worshipping Nature and the stars, conscious of the wonder of life. Not until many centuries later did their unsophisticated souls awaken to the religious problems of human existence; they seemed to dwell in natural innocence like Adam and Eve before they tasted the apple of knowledge and became self-conscious.

The Rig-Veda sings of the Nature worship with various

Gods, yet its refinement of thought reveals a mystic insight, which far transcends the unsophisticated culture of the Aryans and must emanate from a much earlier civilisation or from the Gods, that is, from the Spacemen themselves. In poetic language the Vedas preach an overshadowing Monism, the One God brooding over the Many. The universal essence, the Absolute, dreaming the universe into existence for a finite period of time, said to be 154 million, million years, was Brahma, Who sustained every star and every atom; the Father of the Gods, a personal Being, was Dyaus-Pitar, (Deva-God, Pitar-Father) hellenized to Zeus-Pater, in Latin, Jupiter, the Sky-Father worshipped under various names by Celts, Egyptians, Babylonians, Mexicans, Chinese and native peoples all over the world. Heaven was a physical realm in the sky, though esoteric thought generally assumed it to be composed of etherean vibrations finer than earthly matter. The Heavenly Father ('Our Father which art in Heaven' in our Lord's Prayer) was probably a Space King from some advanced planet in our own Solar System, an infinitesimal speck of the whole universe imagined by God, the Absolute Brahm. Dyaus-Pitar ruled the entire Earth in a Golden Age; the Hindus like the Japanese, Egyptians and Romans believed the early dynasties on Earth were divine.

The Rig-Veda describes Dyaus as 'a bull ruddy, and bellowing downwards', evoking the winged bulls of Babylon and Nineveh, which to the minds of a simple agrarian people possibly symbolised powerful spaceships. Dyaus is also compared to 'a black steed decked with pearls',[57] an allusion to the star-spangled sky, which recalls Pegasus, the Flying Horse of the Greeks on which Bellerophon waged celestial war, also symbolism for Space Beings. One poem refers to 'Dyaus smiling through the clouds'; in classical Sanskrit the word for 'smile' is associated with 'dazzling whiteness' and 'lightning', this lyricism could symbolise a shining spaceship speeding across the skies.[58]

A more powerful God from pre-Indian mythology mentioned in the Vedas, Varuna, was associated with heavenly bodies in the sky; he controlled the moon and the stars, the flight of birds, and had moral authority over men, but in the later poems he was overshadowed by the Warrior-God, Indra. There seems a striking parallel with the Greek legends; 'Varuna' meaning 'the encompassed sky' was 'Ouranos' (Uranus) supplanted by 'Indra', i.e. Saturn (Chronos). The comparison is strengthened by the fact that later Indra was dethroned and exiled in chains, while according to Ovid, Saturn was usurped by Zeus (Jupiter) and imprisoned in Britain. We can possibly interpret this as symbolising domination of our Earth in ages past by three successive invaders from space, as hinted in the Golden, Silver and Iron Ages of the Classical Poets.

Indra became the God of Battles flashing in an aerial car with the speed of thought drawn by steeds with[59] golden mane and shining skin; he waged war against the Asuras (Non-Gods) and destroyed their cities with thunderbolts like nuclear-bombs, reminiscent of the War between the Gods and the Giants described in Greek and Celtic mythologies suggesting conflict among Spacemen perhaps against Earth.

In his battles Indra was attended by the Maruts[60] or Storm Gods, depicted as youthful warriors, who rode on golden cars; they brandished darts of lightning in their hands and drove like the winds. Associated with Indra was Vayu, God of the Wind, who sped across the sky faster than light in a shining chariot drawn by a pair of ruddy steeds with eyes like the sun. Savitri, the Sun God, was borne by swift coursers spanning the heavens and beaming inspiration to men. Vishnu traversed the three worlds in three strides[61] and Pushan, 'the best pilot of the air', cut the void with dazzling swiftness for another solar-deity, Surya. In the Konarak, India, are found the finest carvings of the Eight Wheels described as a transportation for the Sun Goddess, Surya, to the sky. The most frequently invoked Gods were the twin Aswins,[62] who drove a ruddy, tawny car, bright as burnished gold, armed with thunderbolts; sometimes they 'floated over the ocean, keeping out of the water' in a vehicle oddly described as 'tri-columnar, triangular and tri-wheeled, well-constructed' on which they rescued Bhujya from the sea in a ship which flew from space. The Aswins, Sons of Heaven, were eternally young, bounding in a flash to the Sun in the twinkling of an eye accompanied by the fair Surya; the pair often descended to Earth delivering people from distress and acted as divine physicians. The deeds of the two

Aswins and their general popularity make them identical with the Greek, Dioskouroi, Castor and Pollux, St Michael and St George, celestial cavaliers coming to the aid of men. These Celestial Beings invoked in the Vedas dwelled in the skies not as insubstantial Spirits but as real Spacemen from a near planet, who winged down in their gleaming spaceships and consorted with the peoples of old India.

The hymns of the Rig-Veda extol lesser Celestials, who occasionally descended to Earth for love or war, just like the Gods and Goddesses of Greece. The Gandharvas, according to the Vishnu Purana, were followers of Indra, the Storm King; they defeated the Nagas, the Serpent Men from Lemuria, seized their jewels and usurped their Kingdom in the Deccan; their home in the realms of space survives in the expression 'City of the Gandharvas', as one of the Sanskrit names for 'mirage'. The Apsaras, alluring wives of the Gods, were seductive nymphs from the 'waters' of space. The Indian poets lyricised the Apsaras smiling at their beloved in the highest heaven; beautiful and voluptuous these aerial nymphs were Mistresses of the Gandharvas and formed the rewards in India's heaven held out to heroes who fell in battle, just as the Houris in Paradise allured the fanatical Moslem Faithful of Mahomet. Sometimes an Apsara would wing down to Earth and become enamoured of mortal man, like Urvasi, who according to the Satapatha Brahmana married her earthly lover, Pururavas, and bore him a son, only to return to the skies. This romance formed the theme of *Vikramarvasi* or *Urvasi won by Valour,* the brilliant and poignant play by the fifth century classical dramatist, Kalidasa.[63] It intrigues us to read in the mediaeval chronicle *De Nugis Curialium* by Walter de Mapes[64] about the Saxon patriot, Edric the Wild, who in AD 1070 fell in love with a beautiful damsel from space, whom he married and presented at the Court of William the Conqueror; their son, Alnodus, became renowned for his wisdom and piety. Unhappily the Space-bride vanished to the skies leaving the heartbroken Edric to pine away; unlike Urvasi who later returned to her husband and lived in blest content. We recall the 'succubi', female 'demons' of the Middle Ages seducing mortal men, and the ravishing Spacewomen like Aura Rhanes, who charmed Truman Bethuram[65] in

America. Perhaps the Apsaras were real women from other planets who married heroes of old India? The Rig-Veda mentions a race of priests called the Bhrigus to whom Matarishvan brought the secret fire stolen from heaven. This Indian version of Prometheus suggests with similar legends akin to Greece, a world-wide conflict in far antiquity between the peoples of Earth and the Spacemen.

Viewed with our modern insight the wonderful hymns of the Vedas reveal remarkable affinity with those glorious manifestations in the skies entrancing us today.

CHAPTER FOUR

Space Heroes of Old India

The 'Ramayana' telling in magic imagery the quest of Rama for his stolen wife, Sita, has thrilled the people of India for thousands of years; generations of wandering story-tellers have recited its 24,000 verses to marvelling audiences captivated by this brilliant panorama of the fantastic past, the passions of heroic love, tragedies of dark revenge, aerial battles between Gods and Demons waged with nuclear bombs; the glory of noble deeds; the thrilling poetry of life, the philosophy of destiny and death. These wonderful tales were narrated by the Sage, Narada, to the historian, Valmiki, who wove the colourful incidents into an enthralling epic poem studded with pearls of wisdom, whose perennial inspiration cheers Indians today. Some scholars date the 'Ramayana' before 500 BC, others before 3000 BC, though since the stories were sung by minstrels down the ages the actual events probably occurred in far antiquity.

Rama, son of Dasaratha, King of Ayodha (Oudh) in Northern India was married to the chaste Sita, still the idol of Indian women. The King was about to make Rama his heir-apparent, when the Queen persuaded him to appoint his other son, Bharata, instead, and to banish Rama for fourteen years. Rama lived happily with Sita in the forest of Dandaka; on the King's death Bharata nobly offered the throne to Rama, who refused and crusaded against the giants and demons infesting the forest. The giant chief, Ravana, carried off Sita to the island of Lanka, (Ceylon) where she was found by Rama's friend, Hanuman, Lord of the Monkeys; Rama and his followers aided by Hanuman with his monkey-hordes, launched aerial invasion of Lanka. Rama duelled with Ravana in celestial cars fighting in the sky and destroyed him with annihilating missiles to win back Sita. Her fidelity suspected, Sita purified herself by the ordeal of fire and returned with Rama to Ayodha, where they ruled in a glorious Golden Age.

In his wonderful translation of the 'Ramayana'[66] Romesh Dutt describes Rama's father, King Dasaratha, as 'sprung of ancient Solar Race', a descendant of Kings of the Sun, Spacebeings, who ruled India, a title still bestowed on the Mikado of Japan. While Rama and Lakshman were in the forest hunting an enchanted deer, Ravan seized the helpless Sita.

> 'Seat her on his car celestial yoked with asses winged with speed
> Golden in its shape and radiance, fleet as Indra's heavenly steed
> Then arose the car celestial o'er the hill and wooded vale.
> Like a snake in eagle's talons Sita writhed with piteous wail.'

During the flight they were attacked by Jatayu in a giant 'bird' like a fighter-plane.

The giant Ravan imprisoned Sita in his fortress in Ceylon. Hanuman flew across the straits to the island and gave her a token from Rama, who marshalled a great army to storm the citadel, aided by the Celestials he launched aerial assault.

> 'Brave Matali drove the chariot drawn by steeds like solar ray,
> Where the true and righteous Rama sought his foe in fatal fray.
> Shining arms and heavenly weapons he to lofty Rama gave,
> When the righteous strive and struggle, Gods assist the true and brave
> "Take this car!" so said Matali "Which the helping Gods provide
> Rama take these steeds celestial, Indra's golden chariot ride".'

Ravan speeding on his chariot and Rama on the heavenly car fought an epic duel in long and wild fury, the winds were hushed in voiceless terror and the livid sun turned pale.

'Still the dubious battle lasted, until Rama in his ire
Wielded Brahma's deathful weapon flaming with celestial fire,
Weapon which the Saint Agostya had unto her hero given,
Winged as lightning dart of Indra, fatal as the bolt from heaven.
Wrapped in smoke and flowing flashes, speeding from the circled bow
Pierced the iron heart of Ravan, lain the lifeless hero low.
Voice of blessing from the bright sky fell on Raghni's valiant son.
"Champion of the true and righteous! Now thy noble task is done".'

After her purification in the flames, Rama took Sita home by aerial car, an enormous, beautifully painted two-storied car, furnished with windows adorned with flags and colours, and several apartments for passengers and crew; the vehicle emitted a melodious sound heard on the ground.

'Mark, My Love!' so Rama uttered, as on flying Pushpa car,
Born by swans, the home-returning exiles left the field of war.

The happy pair, reunited, flew from Ceylon across India over the Ganges, home to Ayodha, as Rama gave a colourful description of the historic landscape of hills and rivers gliding swiftly below.

'Sailing o'er the cloudless ether Rama's Pushpa chariot came
And ten thousand jocund voices shouted Rama's joyous name.
Silver swans by Rama's bidding soft descended from the air
And on earth the chariot lighted—car of flowers divinely fair.'

(To marvelling mortals spaceships gleaming in the sunshine would resemble silver swans.)

Suspicion that Sita had yielded to Ravan's seduction haunted Rama; he exiled his pregnant wife to the forest, where she founded a hermitage and gave birth to twin boys. Years later Rama discovered her and his sons and torn with remorse implored her to return to Ayodha to prove her virtue.

'Gods and Spirits, bright Immortals to that royal Yajna came,
Men of every race and nation, King's and Chiefs of righteous fame.
Sita saw the bright Celestials, monarchs gathered from afar.
Saw her royal Lord and husband, bright as heaven ascending star.'

Sita's steadfast faithfulness amid darkest suspicion and dire tribulations still make her the inspiration of Indian womanhood, who for centuries have submissively followed her selfless example.

Heartbroken, the faithful Sita would not plead her cause, asserting her innocence, she asked Mother Earth to relieve the burden of her life.

'Then the Earth was rent and parted and a golden throne arose,
Held aloft by jewelled Nagas as the leaves unfold the rose.'

Rama lived on more lonely than ever. He held a secret conference with a heavenly Messenger (We think of the Biblical Prophets meeting the 'Lord'). His brother, Lakshman, unwittingly intervened and in penance lost his life. Years later Rama left Ayodha and entered heaven. Like Elijah he may have been translated to the skies.

The *Drona Parva*, p. 171, rejoices that when Rama ruled his kingdom, the Rishis, Gods and men, all lived together on the Earth; the world became extremely beautiful. Rama (and presumably his descendants) reigned in his kingdom for eleven thousand years. In this Golden Age Celestials from other planets trod our Earth as mentioned in the Egyptian and Greek texts.

The name of Rama is blessed throughout India. The assassinated Gandhi died invoking 'Rama!' Every autumn the Tale of Rama and Sita is enacted in ten-day festivals all over India.

There is striking resemblance between the 'Ramayana' and the 'Iliad'; both deal with the husband's quest for his captured wife, whose rape launches fierce wars and sets the world aflame. The heroes are inspired by the Gods, who intervene in human affairs and direct the destiny of men. It intrigues us to learn that both the 'Ramayana' and the 'Iliad' have a fascinating affinity with an epic poem found in ancient Ugaritic texts as Ras Shamra, wherein about fourteenth century BC a Semitic hero, King Kret, (suggestive of Minoan Crete) loses his bride to an enemy whose city he storms to regain her. Perhaps civilisation thousands of years ago was world-wide; this epic in many countries of the Prince and his ravished bride provoking war and the destruction of a great city appears to have a common historical origin.[67]

This wonderful epic of the 'Ramayana', the inspiration of the world's great classic literature, intrigues us most today by its frequent allusions to aerial vehicles and annihilating bombs, which we consider to be inventions of our own twentieth century impossible in the far past. Students of Sanskrit literature soon revise their preconceived ideas and find that the heroes of Ancient India were apparently equipped with aircraft and missiles more sophisticated than those we boast today. The thirty-first chapter of the *Samaranganasutradhara,*[68] ascribed to King Bhojadira in the eleventh century, contains descriptions of remarkable flying ships such as the elephant-machine, wooden-bird-machine travelling in the sky, wooden-vimana-machine flying in the air, door-keeper-machine, soldier-machine, etc. denoting different types of craft for different purposes. The poet had not described methods of constructing the machines; 'any person not initiated in art of building machines will cause trouble.' Surely the understatement of the century!

Ramachandra Dikshitar[69] in his fascinating *War in Ancient India* translates the *Samar* as saying that these flying machines could attack visible and invisible objects, ascending, cruising thousands of miles in different directions in the atmosphere, even mounting to the solar and stellar regions. 'The aerial cars are made of light wood looking like a great bird with a durable and well-formed body having mercury inside and fire at the bottom. It has two resplendent wings and is propelled by air. It flies in the atmospheric regions for a great distance and carries several persons with it. The inside construction resembles heaven created by Brahma himself. Iron, copper, lead and other metals are also used for these machines.' Despite their apparent simplicity the *Samar* stresses that these vimanas were costly to make and were the exclusive privilege of the aristocrats, who fought celestial duels. Today we associate such craft with Spacemen.

The most fascinating tales of war in the air waged with fantastic weapons transcending our own science-fiction today are narrated in the 'Mahabharata', a wonderful poem of 200,000 lines, eight times as long as the 'Iliad' and 'Odyssey' combined, a veritable world in literature. This epic concerning the great Bharata War in Northern India fought about 1400 BC paints in glorious colour a great and noble civilisation, where kings and priests, princes and philosophers, warriors and fair women, mingled in a brilliant society, perhaps the most glittering period in all history. The multitudinous incidents from duels in the skies to the storming of cities, councils of war to cattle-stealing, tournaments to star-crossed weddings, were sung by wandering minstrels with all the magic of the East until centuries later poets enshrined them in those strange Sanskrit symbols to form an inexhaustible treasure-house of wisdom inspiring Indians for thousands of years to dominate their culture even today. The brilliant characterisation of the noble prince, Arjuna, his peerless bride, Draupadi, the God, Krishna, the host of Celestials and warrior-knights, transcend the bucolic creations of Homer and the colourful pageant is studded with human personages, whose fallings from sublimity to despair are revealed with an insight unsurpassed by genius in our Western world. Transmuting the martial adventures and exquisite passions brood the sublime teachings of the *Bhagavad Gita* with their incalculable influence on the Greek philosophers and the great Thinkers of the West. We today are more intrigued by the aerial craft and wonder weapons suggesting some secret science inspired by Beings from Space.

The 'Mahabharata' describes the eighteen days war between Duryghodana, Chief of the Kurus, and his cousin, Yudhishthira, Leader of the neighbouring Pandus, tribes on the Upper Ganges, which is said to have occurred fourteen centuries before Christ. Within this narrative is a fantastic collection of legends, tales of the Gods and Kings, and lengthy disquisitions on religion, philosophy, social customs, mingled with stirring tales of battle and tender love stories, which make the work a veritable quintessence of Indian culture. The discourses between the hero, Arjuna, and the Lord Krishna, as the warrior hesitates to fight his own kinsfolk form the lofty *Bhagavad Gita, The Song of the Lord,* wherein Krishna reveals the meaning of the universe, the wisdom of Brahma and the duty of men, expounding the religion of the Hindus.

It is difficult to believe that this sublime epic actually portrays the civilisation of 1400 BC, when the nomadic Aryans were pouring through the Northern passes to invade the Indian plain, a time probably contemporaneous with Moses. Churchward in *The Children of Mu*[70] claims the 'Mahabharata' includes history from temple records referring to times 20,000 years earlier, which may have coincided with that Golden Age, when Ouranos, a Spaceman, ruled the world, extolled by Ovid and the Classical Poets; the war in the air evokes the Greek legends and Hesiod's *Theogony* describing celestial war between the Gods and men.

Madame H. P. Blavatsky in *The Secret Doctrine* insists the 'Mahabharata' refers to the historical strife between the Suryavansas (Worshippers of the Sun) and the Indavansas (Worshippers of the Moon), a conflict of great esoteric significance, which the less occult-minded may possibly interpret as a struggle between two races of Extra-terrestrials from Space.

In his very fine translation from the Sanskrit Romesh Dutt describes how suitors from all India contended for the hand of Draupadi, the Princess of Panchala.

> 'And the Gods in cloud-borne chariots came to view the scene so fair,
> Bright Adityas in their splendour, Maruts in the moving car.'
> 'Bright Immortals gaily crowding viewed the scene surpassing fair,
> Heavenly blossoms soft descending with a perfume filled the air.'
> 'Bright celestial cars in concourse sailed upon the cloudless sky,
> Drum and flute and harp and tabor sounded deep and sounded high.'
>
> (Book One, Chapter 4)

Yudihishthir summoned an assembly to proclaim his supremacy over all the Kings of Ancient India.

'Bright Immortals robed in sunlight sailed across the liquid sky
And their gleaming cloud-borne chariots rested on the turrets high.
'Ida, adja, homa offerings pleased the "Shining Ones" on high,
Brahmans pleased with costly presents with their blessings filled the sky.' (Book Three, Chapter 2)

'And he saw in them embodied beings of the upper sky,
And in lotus-eyed Krishna saw the Highest on the High.'
(Book Three, Chapter 3)

Through passion for gambling Yudihisthir staked his kingdom, his brothers, himself, then fair Draupadi, all he lost to his jealous enemy, Duryodhan, and went into exile. His usurper, Duryodhan, quarrelled with Ghandharvas, Celestial Beings, and was taken prisoner but was rescued from his aerial captors by the Pandav brothers. After twelve years penance Yudihishthir led an army to regain his throne, aided by Arjuna and Krishna.

'Devas from their cloud-borne chariots, and Ghandarvas from the sky
Gazed in mute and speechless wonder on the human chiefs from high.' (Book Eight, Chapter 2)

Duryodhan's famous General, Bhisma, smashed all attacks.

'Vainly too the Pandav brothers on the peerless Bhisma fell,
Gods in sky nor earthly warriors Bhisma's matchless might could quell.' (Book Eight, Chapter 8)

Finally Duryodhan was killed, Bhisma died. Yudihishthir, crowned King, performed the ancient Hindu custom of Sacrifice of the Horse to assert his kingship; the festival was attended by Celestials and all India's Princes.

'Devas, rishis, viewed the feasting, sweet Ghandarvas woke the song,
Asparas like gleams of sunlight on the green sward tripped along.'

Yudihishthir stood triumphant, receiving homage from Gods and men.

'And he stands amid his brothers, brightly beaming, pure and high.

Even as Indra stands encircled by the dwellers of the sky.'

The battle between Arjuna and the giant Rakshasas soared from the plains of India to the skies. The *Samsaptakabadha Parva,* p. 58, describes Arjuna and Krishna borne in a car.

> '. . . exceedingly resplendent like a celestial car. O, King, in the battle between the Gods and the Asuras in the days of old, it displayed a circular, forward, backward and diverse other kinds of motion. . . . The Son of Pandu blew his prodigious conch call, Devadotta. And then he shot the weapon called Tashtva, that is capable of slaying large bodies of foes together.'

The *Drona Parva,*[71] p. 661 comments:

> 'In that dreadful battle those shafts, O King, like the very rays of the Sun, in a moment shrouded all the parts of the compass, the welkin and the troops. Innumerable iron balls also, O King, then appeared like resplendent luminaries in the clear firmament. Shataghnis, some equipped with four and some with two wheels and innumerable maces and disci with edges sharp as razors and resplendent like the Sun also appeared there.'

This description fits a fleet of Spaceships in the sky.

In poetical language the *Drona Parva,* p. 497, describes an apparent Spaceship as:

> 'Beholding that mountain like a mass of antimony with countless weapons falling from it, Drona's son was not at all moved. The latter invoked into existence the Vajra weapon. That Prince of mountains, struck with that weapon, was quickly destroyed. Then this Rakshasa becoming a mass of blue clouds in the firmament, decked with a rainbow, began to furiously shower upon Drona's son in that battle a downpour of stones and rocks. Then that foremost of all persons, acquainted with weapons, viz. Ashwatthaman, aiming the Vayarya weapon destroyed that blue cloud, which had risen on the firmament.'

This somewhat garbled account suggests a bombing attack by spaceships, one of which was destroyed by a ground-to-air missile.

> 'A headless trunk and mace appeared on the face of the sun.' (*Drona Parva,* p. 209)

Students of UFOS may be struck by this resemblance to

the sightings chronicled by Livy and Julius Obsequens over Ancient Rome.[72]

Reference in the 'Mahabharata' to fantastic weapons no longer evokes ridicule but becomes of intense interest to our twentieth century minds haunted by nuclear bombs. The *Bhisma Parva*, p. 44, describing the conflict between Arjuna and Bhisma states the enemy invoked a celestial weapon resembling fire in effulgence and energy. Chandra Roy in his masterly translation notes, 'This Brahma-danda, meaning Brahma's Rod, is infinitely more powerful than even Indra's bolt. The latter can strike only once, but the former can smite whole countries and entire races from generation to generation.' For thousands of years scholars assumed this to be a figment of the Poet's imagination; we at once are struck by the ominous resemblance to our hydrogen-bomb, whose radiations mutate generations unborn.

Arjuna and his contemporaries appeared to possess an arsenal of diverse, sophisticated nuclear weapons, equal to, perhaps surpassing, the missiles of the Americans and Russians today. The *Badha Parva*, p. 97, mentions the Vaishnava weapon conferring invisibility, able to destroy all the Gods in all the worlds. The *Drona Parva*, p. 383, refers to an annihilating mace or missile.

> 'Encompassed by them (bowmen), O Bharata, Bhisma smiting the while and uttering a leonine roar, took up and hurled at them with great force a fierce mace of destruction of hostile ranks. That mace of adamantine strength, hurled like Indra's thunder by Indra himself, crushed, O King, thy soldiers in battle. And it seemed to fill, O King, the whole Earth with a loud noise. And blazing forth in splendour, that fierce mace inspired thy sons with fear. Beholding that mace of impetuous course and endowed with lightning flashes coursing towards them, thy warriors fled away uttering frightful cries. And at the unbelievable sound, O Sire, of that fierce mace, many men fell down where they stood and many car-warriors also fell down from their cars.'

Atomic warfare with defenders vainly launching anti-missiles to counter nuclear rockets startles us by its uncanny resemblance to future wars, when our Earth's capital may be blasted with bombs of anti-matter launched from space-satellites. The *Drona Parva*, p. 592, describes:

'On one occasion assailed by Valadeva, Jarasandha, excited with wrath, hurled for our destruction a mace capable of slaying all creatures. Endued with the splendour of fire, that mace coursed towards us dividing the welkin (Creation) like the line on the head that parts the tresses of a woman and with the impetuosity of the thunder, hurled by Shukra. Beholding that mace thus coursing towards us, the Son of Rohimi hurled the weapon called Sthunakarma for baffling it. Its force destroyed by the energy of Valadeva's weapon, that mace fell down on Earth splitting her (with its might) and making the very mountains tremble.'

Descriptions of 'splitting the Earth' evoke occult teachings of the destruction of the tenth planet, Maldek,[73] between Mars and Jupiter, by its evil inhabitants into fragments we call the asteroids.

A fantastic account is given in the *Drona Parva,* p. 690, concerning the destruction of three 'cities' in the sky, possibly immense mother-ships, which some sensitives believe to patrol space today.

'Formerly the valiant Asuras had in heaven three cities. Each of these cities was excellent and large. One was made of iron, another of silver and a third of gold. The golden city belonged to Kamaloksha, the silver city to Tarakaksha and the third made of iron had Vidyunmalin for its Lord. . . . When however the three cities came together in the firmament, the Lord Mahadeva pierced them with that terrible shaft of his consisting of three knots. The Danavas were unable to gaze at that shaft inspired with the Yuga fire and composed of Vishnu and Soma.'

Selective missiles like the Narayana weapon, called 'scorcher of foes' were probably utilised against troops on the battlefield. The ultimate weapon was the Agneya, reminiscent of the Atlantean mash-mak, said to utilise some sidereal force, mercifully undiscovered by us today. The *Drona Parva,* p. 677, holds us spellbound.

'The valiant Adwatthaman, then staying resolutely on his car touched water and invoked the Agneya weapon, incapable of being resisted by the very Gods. Aiming at all his visible and invisible foes, the preceptor's son, that Slayer of hostile heroes, inspired with mantras a blazing shaft of the effulgence of a smokeless fire and let it off on all sides, filled with rage. Dense showers of arrows then issued from it in the welkin. Endued with fiery flames those arrows encompassed Parthie on all sides. Meteors flashed down from the firmament. A thick gloom suddenly shrouded the (Pandava) host. All points of the compass also were enveloped by that darkness. Rakshashas and Vicochas crowding together uttered fierce cries. Inauspicious winds began to blow. The Sun himself no longer gave any heat. Ravens fiercely croaked on all sides. Clouds roared in the welkin, showering blood. Birds and beasts and kine and Munis of high vows and souls under complete control became exceedingly uneasy. The very elements seemed to be perturbed. The Sun seemd to turn round. The universe scorched with heats seemed to be in a fever. The elephants and other creatures of the land scorched by the energy of that weapon, ran in fright, breathing heavily and desirous of protection against that terrible force. The very water being heated, the creatures residing in that element, O Bharata, became exceedingly uneasy and seemed to burn. From all the points of the compass, cardinal and subsidiary, from the firmament and the very Earth, showers of sharp and fierce arrows fell and issued with the impetuosity of Garuda (spaceship?) on the wind. Struck and burnt by those shafts of Ashwattam that were all endued with the impetuosity of the thunder, the hostile warriors fell down like trees burnt down by a raging fire.

'Huge elephants burnt by that weapon, fell down on the Earth all around, uttering fierce cries loud as those of the clouds. Other huge elephants, scorched by that fire, ran hither and thither, roared aloud in fear, as if in the midst of a forest conflagration. The steeds, O King, and the cars also burnt by the energy of that weapon, looked, O Sire, like the tops of trees burnt in a forest fire. Thousands of cars fell down on all sides. Indeed, O Bharata, it seemed that the divine Lord Agni burnt the (Pandava) host in that battle like the Somvarta fire destroying everything at the end of the Yuga.' (Celestial fire destroying civilisation at the end of a World-Age.)

Could this marvellous description of a nuclear-like blast related by that simple Indian thousands of years ago be surpassed by our scientific reporters today? Such gripping narrative in homely words reminds us of the eye-witness accounts of the people of Hiroshima. This tale is stamped with the hall-marks of truth; it can be no aery-fairy science-fiction, long ago in our world's tortured history this frightful catastrophe must have happened.

Such fantastic warfare must have baffled Chandra Roy as he translated the *Drona Parva* in those leisurely days of 1888, when battles were won by cavalry charges and heroes waving banners; today we understand too well the titanic horrors of atomic war. Remembering the five year effort of the finest scientists of America and Britain, backed by immense industrial technique, required to manufacture the primitive bomb which devastated Hiroshima, we naturally feel somewhat sceptical at suggestions that sophisticated nuclear-weapons of colossal force were wielded by warriors in India millennia ago; apart from the advanced science involved, the delivery of such missiles demands intricate electronic guidance-systems, and most complex defences, the perfection of an anti-missile missile defeats our scientists of genius today. Conventional history denies any high technology to the peoples of antiquity, who are believed to have lived in a static culture for thousands of years in agricultural communities waiting for James Watt to wake up one day and invent the steam-engine.

Already new techniques are slashing the costs of manufacture; backward China has hydrogen-bombs, Indonesia and Israel threaten to follow her, soon we are promised that any enterprising community with a 'Do-It-Yourself' kit will be able to make bombs enough to blow their neighbours sky high. The existence of nuclear bombs in Ancient India presupposes this period followed an advanced civilisation of thousands of years, possibly the Lemuria and the Atlantis described by the occultists.

What if science in Antiquity developed by different techniques from our physics today? The Agneya weapon which shattered the Pandava hosts in Old India evokes the destruction of Sodom and Gomorrah,[74] the annihilation of Sennacherib's[75] army besieging Pelusium(?) in 670 BC (?), and the fire from heaven which blasted Vortigern's castle in fourth century Britain.[76] Man has suffered other Hiroshimas long ago; humanity always learns enough to make the same sorry mistakes.

The Indian Prometheus, Matarishnan, stole the hidden Agni, the secret fire, from heaven. Perhaps the Indians learned their nuclear techniques from Spacemen?[77]

The 'Ramayana' and the 'Mahabharata' written so

many millennia ago show that our remote ancestors were not barbarians but lived and loved in a gay and glittering culture[78] with a spiritual insight into cosmic mysteries transcending our own. Perhaps in that distant past we discern our future. In a few decades our Earth may be graced again by Spacemen, the Gods of Old India.

CHAPTER FIVE

Space Stories in Sanskrit

Legends from every country in the world describe in far Antiquity intercourse between Celestials from the skies and the peoples of Earth. The simple folk of Greece and Israel worshipped the Spacemen as Gods with fearful superstition but a thousand miles distant in India the sophisticated nobles treated the Visitants as equals, unawed by their heavenly guests. Sanskrit literature delighted in ravishing tales of the rivalry of Gods and mortals for the love of some alluring damsel, gallants from the upper world winged down to Earth and laid siege to some proud beauty in amorous exploit transcending the coarse lusts of Zeus seducing the women of Greece. Heroes soared to the skies in celestial cars and fought aerial duels blasting their rivals with explosive darts or annihilated armies with nuclear bombs. These enchanting stories of old India, more fascinating than our own science-fiction, told of a warm, colourful land of culture, its society sparkling with bejewelled splendour, where princes and poets, saints and scoundrels, mystics and magicians, lived with an exhilaration unequalled until the glittering Renaissance awoke the genius of Italy to life; in those exotic kingdoms beyond the Himalayas the Spacemen felt at home in a sophistication they could never find amid the stark austerity of the Peloponnese or the proud intolerance of Palestine. The Sanskrit tales glow with a humanism and humour distilled in bewitching poetry, depicting a genial, cultured society ages old, surely inspired by some wondrous, resplendent civilisation from the stars.

The poets and storytellers seemed impressed by the tales they told; in their unsophisticated fashion they likened the aerial craft to the birds and animals they knew best, calling an airship a flying horse just as many centuries later

Red Indians saw a railway-engine as an iron horse. Subishmanya rode a peacock, Brahma a swan, Vishnu and Krishna flew through the heavens on the giant bird, Garuda; occultists teach that this monstrous half-man and half-bird, the Indian phoenix, the Egyptian man-lion or Sphinx, is an esoteric symbolism for Solar and cyclic time. Unrepentent we wonder whether Garuda was a Spaceship? The Asura (Non-God) called Maya owned an animated golden car with four strong wheels and having a circumference of 12,000 cubits, which possessed the wonderful power of flying at will to any place. Dikshitar[79] states this car was equipped with various weapons and bore huge standards in the battle between the Devas and the Asuras in which Maya distinguished himself; several warriors were said to have ridden birds. The *Drona Parva*, p. 145, narrates:

> 'Bowless and car-less with an eye however to his duty as a warrior, the handsome Abhinanya, taking up a sword and shield jumped into the sky. Displaying great strength and great activity and describing the tracks called Krucika and others, the son of Arjuna fiercely coursed through the sky like the Prince of winged creatures (Garuda).'

The *Badha Parva*, p. 546, referring to the battle between Rama and the Rakshasas states:

> 'Thy son, Dasaratha, proceeded against that mighty car warrior, Prativindhya, who was advancing (against Drona) scorching his foes in battle. The encounter that took place between them, O King, looked beautiful like that of Mercury and Venus in the cloudless firmament.'

This quotation is particularly fascinating since it reveals that the ancient Indians knew of Mercury and Venus and some possible conflict between them, knowledge we tend to associate only with the Greeks.

King Satrugit was presented by a Brahman, Gotava, with a horse named Kirvelaya, which conveyed him to any place on Earth, reminiscent of the Greek hero, Bellerophon, and his flying horse, Pegasus.

The Buddhist monk, Gunavarman,[80] in the fourth century AD claimed to have flown from Ceylon to Java in order to convert its King to the Wisdom of the 'Way of the Eight Paths'. The day before his landing, the King's mother dreamed that a great Master had descended from the sky in a flying ship. As the dawn sun illumined the Earth, Gunavarman arrived; believed to be a Messenger from the Gods he was treated with immense respect. All the beholders marvelled to see a glittering vessel glide and land without the slightest sound. Another Jataka told of a King in Benares who owned a vehicle decked with jewels which flew in the air; the dramatist Bhavabhuti in the fifth century AD wrote about a flying vehicle used for general work in the community by local council officials. In his remarkable *War in Ancient India* Ramachandra Dikshitar recalls that in the Vikramarvastya (*Drona,* p. 176) King Puruvravas rode in an aerial car to rescue Urvasi in pursuit of the Danava, who was carrying her away.

Intriguing references to air-travel appear in the *Budhasvamin Brihat Katha Shlokasamgraha,*[81] a Sanskrit romance written in beautiful old script of a type well known in Nepal of the twelfth century, a reproduction of a very old manuscript. This was translated into French by Felix Lacote in 1908.

The tyrant, Mahasena, King of the Avanti people in Northern India, ruled in Uijayani, a city surrounded by moats as wide as the sea, immense as the hills; he was deposed by his elder son, Gopala, who one day chanced to hear . . .

> '. . . a Lover complaining to his Mistress that she torments him. The Mistress suggests he kills her husband, "Laws are despised, drunk by appetite for power the son killed the King, his father".'

Gopala, who had led a wild life hitherto, decided to become an ascetic, he abdicated the throne to his younger brother, Palche, the latter after a long reign left it to his young nephew, Avantwardhava. One day Avantwardhava became enamoured of a young woman, whom he saw in a swing on a tree, afterwards his elephant ran amok then knelt down at the feet of this maiden, who had stolen the young King's heart.

> 'She was Surasamanjari, daughter of Chief Upalastaka of the Matangos. Avantwardha married Surasamanjari. She said her father was really Siddhamatanjavidya, who had promised her to a villain called Ipploha. "One day as

my father was travelling in the air, his crown of flame, surrounded by swarms of bees, yellow with pollen, he was enchanted by the wind." He was cursed by Narada sitting on the Ganges bank but the curse would be lifted when his daughter married the son of Gopala. She said the King of the Vidyaharas and other Celestial Beings, established as a rule that a King even in the wrong should not be disturbed when he is in his harem. Ipploha fuming with rage kidnapped him. Hermits fixing their eyes on the sky saw come with a sword and shield resplendent in the light a Divine Being. He descended by way of the winds holding Ipploha in chains.

'The Divine Being said, "From Naravashanadotta, King of the Vidyaharas, know that I am thy cherished Servant. I am called Divaskavadeva. As I was traversing the airs of the Himavit at Mount Malaya on passing above Avanti, I saw the Sandala who was fleeing kidnapping the King and his wife. . . . I fought with him and conquered him. I led him to the Cakravartim (Emperor) who interrogated him and sends him to the Court of Justice of the Kashyupe. . . . He will come to see you tomorrow with his wives."

'After this speech of Divaskavadeva, the Rishis bathed with tears of joy, found the night long. In the morning in the cloudless sky, the ascetics heard a rolling, which filled the atmosphere. "What is it?" they asked the Aerial Being. "It is the noise of the drums of the aerial voyagers, as they are enclosed in the bosom of the chariots, one hears them like a rolling of thunder. Here comes our Master, the King of Kings of the Vidyaharas with the storm of drums rumbling by the paths of heaven. Look!" Like a troupe of clouds that the rainbow illuminates, the lightnings and the cranes reclothed in golden splendour, filling all the spaces of the firmament, a troupe of chariots, stupefied by the enormous splendour of varied jewels, appeared to the Ascetics in the distance arriving from the sky. The chariots descended, that of Shakravatan halted at the door of the hermitage, the others in the gorges, on the backs and the tops of mountains. The chariot of the supreme King of the Vidyaharas had the form of a lotus-flower ornamented with twenty-six petals, which were of ruby. He himself was standing in the middle of the pericarp, formed by an emerald and on the petals were posed his wives marvellously attired.

'At the Court trial before the Celestials, Ipploho claimed that Surasamanjari had been promised to him but King Upalastaka said it was indeed true that Ipploha had renounced her saying she was the daughter of man accursed (by Narada on the Ganges). He had then promised her to the King of the Avantis. Kacyopa then sentenced Ipploha to go to Benares, to sink the corpses in the Ganges, to live in a charnel-house dressed in garlands of criminals, he would live on alms. At the end of a year he would be free of the curse.

'At last to Ujyayami by all means people hurried. Even old men, blind and the newly blind, simple souls and young children, eager to see the son of the King of the Vatsas, and the forest of the hermitage was filled by the joyous crowd.'

This charming tale tells of the days when the Space People consorted with men in mutual pleasure. The 'noise of drums of the aerial voyagers' reminds us today of aeroplanes breaking the sound-barrier; the likeness of the spaceships to jewels is surely reminiscent of the Prophet Ezekiel, who described his Visitants in chariots of precious stones; the trial before the Celestials evokes the Gods of the Greek playwrights who gave judgement to men.

The *Brihat Katha* continues with an entrancing tale which reminds us today of science-fiction, although the Sanskrit writer penned it as truth.

'King Padmavati and Queen Vasavadotta greatly desired a child, finally she became pregnant. One day while she was musing anxiously over the coming event her Mother-in-law told of how when she herself was pregnant, she was standing on the terrace of the palace regarding the heavens. Then a "bird" swooped down and carried her off through the air and set her down in a far land. It was going to devour her but she was rescued by two young Rishis, they were slim, a luminous circle spread a golden light on their limbs, their tresses bloomed in beauty. They said to me "Queen, have no fear. This is the hermitage of Vasistha situated in a pure place at the foot of Mount Oriental." There she gave birth to Udayana. When he grew up, Udayana journeyed from the hermitage. In a lake full of lotus and all kinds of birds, he saw young people, who had no human form disporting. He closed his eyes and they took him to the abode of the Serpent People without sun, moon, planets nor constellations nor star, but the splendour of sun-stones and moon-stones which dissipated the darkness. In the town there was no old age, no sickness, no moral or physical deformity but delightful palaces and in that splendour the sound of cymbals. It was the City of the Serpents, Bhagavata, where dwelled Beings, who lived a Kalpa. Reluctantly Udayana had to leave, so they escorted him back to the top of the lake.'

Supporters of the hollow-earth theory would say Udayana had been translated to that wonderful civilisation of Agharta[82] alleged to exist hundreds of miles beneath our feet. The 'Serpent People'[83] are known esoterically as a non-human race of wondrous Beings with immense cosmic wisdom; it is interesting to find they were apparently known to the writers of Old India.

Greek mythology abounds with stories of the Gods (Spacemen?) who descended to Earth to seduce some desirable wench. The *Brihat*, Book Five, p. 179, enchants us with:

> 'At Mathura Manorama, wife of powerful King Ujrasena, wandered in the charming garden of her house to breathe the perfume of the kadambas. "She was in the first day of her month." A Danava, named Drumba, was passing in the air, the beauty of the garden attracted his look; he saw Manorama there and by a spirit of malice took the form of Ujrasena (her husband), united with her, immediately she found herself pregnant.'

The *Brihat Katha*, p. 190-199, later gives more direct information about flying.

> 'Thereupon Padmavit explained that Vasavadotta desired to mount in an aerial chariot and to visit thus all the Earth. Vasantoke, Master of Sports, exclaimed bursting out laughing, "The wives of the King's servants had exactly the same desire. I said the same to all of them. Suspend a swing from long perches, climb on them, then come and go in the air. For other means to satisfy you, your husbands know nothing of them! If *she* has a desire to travel in the air let her be contented in the same fashion!" All began to laugh. "Leave the joke!" said Rumanvit, "and come to the question!" "What is the use of dreaming about it?" said Yongandharayame. "It is exclusively the business of artisans." Rumanavat convoked the carpenters and enjoined them to fabricate a machine which moves in the air, without delay. They went out and the corps of artisans held a long conference then they came to find Rumanavat, they stammered with fright. "We know," they said, "four kinds of machines, water-machines, stone-machines, dust-machines and those made from a mass of pieces. As for flying machines, the Yavanas (the Greeks) know them but we have never had occasion to see any."

'A Brahmin then told about a carpenter named Pukrasaka who was told by his King about Vicvita, who mounted on a mechanical cock. Foreign ambassadors said, "One must never reveal to anyone, artisan or anyone else, the secret of aerial machines difficult to acquire for anyone who is not Greek." Rumanavat said the King was trying to drag from him the secret of the flying-machines, that it was his duty to hide like misers their treasures. Artisans could be put in irons, whipped, tortured, without revealing the secret.

'Suddenly a stranger appeared, asked Rumanavat for necessary materials and made a flying chariot in the form of Garuda, adorned by mandara flowers.

'The Queen and her husband travelled in the air around the Earth and returned to the city of the Avantis.

'On a wondrous Spring Day, the Queen gave birth to a son.'

The peoples of Ancient India considered all Westerners from the Mediterranean to be 'Yavanas' or Greeks, just as the Arabs centuries later called Crusaders 'Franks', whatever their country of origin. Possibly they would use the word 'Yavana' to denote any person of lighter skin, even a Spaceman. Who was this 'stranger' who appeared to Rumanavat and built that aerial chariot? Was he a Spaceman?

Further reference to Yavanas and their flying-machines was made in the 'Harscha Charita'[84] of Bana, a Brahmanical Vatsyayenas, who lived in Thanesar in Northern India at the beginning of the seventh century AD. Bana's historical romance took his own King, Shri Harscha as his hero and was based on an actual event in the latter's reign. A Chinese Buddhist traveller, Hinan Throng, visited Shri Harscha's court about AD 630 and left a vivid account. Bana's own fascinating work provides a wonderful picture of seventh-century India.

The brilliant translation by E. B. Cowell and F. W. Thomas describes the varied fortunes of Harscha, his loves, asceticism, treacheries, battles, until he becomes King. He vowed immediate vengeance on the King of Ganda and called upon his Commander of Elephants, Shandagupta, to mobilise. Shandagupta thereupon burdened him with a long harangue on disasters due to mistaken carelessness, which, while not particularly relevant to Spacemen, is certainly worthy of salutary interest like most of these tales of old India.

> 'Shandagupta replied, ". . . Dismiss therefore this universal confidingness, so agreeable to the habits of your own land and springing from innate frankness of Spirit. Of disasters due to mistaken carelessness frequent reports come daily to your Majesty's hearing. In Padmavati there was the fall of Najasena heir to the Naga house, whose policy was published by a sharika bird. In Sharavasti faded the glory of Shutavarman whose secret a parrot heard. In Mittikarati a discourse of counsel in sleep was the death of Suvanaranda.
>
> '"The fate of a Yavana King was encompassed by the holder of his golden chariot, who read the letters of a document reflected in his crest jewel. By slashes of drawn swords Viduratha's army minced the avaricious Mathura, King Brihadratha while he was digging treasure at dead of night. Vatsapati who was wont to take his pleasure in elephant forests was imprisoned by Prahasena's soldiers issuing from the belly of a sham elephant (? Trojan horse?) Sumitri, son of Wjnimita being over fond of the drama was attacked by Mitradeva in the midst of actors and with a scimitar shorn like a lotus stalk of his head. Sharabha, the Ashmaka King, being attached to string music, his enemy's emissaries disguised as students of music cut off his head with sharp knives hidden in the space between the vinga and its gourd. A base-born General, Prispantri, murdered his foolish Maurya master, Brihadratha, having displayed his whole army on the pretext of manifesting his power. Kakavarma, being curious of marvels, was carried away, no one knows whither, on an artificial aerial car made by a Yavana condemned to death".'

This Sanskrit story of a King whisked away in an aerial car recalls the tale of the Enchanted Horse in the *Arabian Nights*. Was this a kidnapping to another planet or the first aerial accident recorded in history?

Shandagupta continued to depress King Harscha with accounts of misfortune; these may have little reference to Spacemen yet these fascinating stories should perhaps be resurrected from the neglected Sanskrit and presented now for the enlightenment of our modern readers. We, too, may find salutory enlightenment from the following incidents in old India.

'The son of Shushumaya was at the instance of his Minister, Vasudeva, reft of his life by a daughter of Devabhuti's slave-woman disguised as his Queen. By means of a mine in Mount Godhama, joyous with the tinkle of numerous women's jewelled anklets, the Maghadha King, who had a penchant for treasure-caves, was carried away by the King of Makabo's Ministers to their own country. Kumavasene, the Pannytha Prince, younger brother to Prodyota, having an infatuation for stories about selling human flesh, was slain at the feast of Mahakabe by the vampire Tabajongha. By drugs, whose virtues had been celebrated through many different individuals, some professed physicians brought on atrophy upon Ganyapati, son of the King of Vidaha, who was mad for the elixir of life. Confiding in women, the Kalinga, Bhorasena, met his death at the hands of his brother, Virasena, who secretly found access to the wall of the Chief Queen's apartments. Lying on a mattress in his Mother's bed, a son of Dodhra, Lord of the Karusas, encompassed the death of his Father, who proposed to anoint another son, Bandrakaba, Lord of the Sokones, being attached to his Chamberlain, he was with his Minister deprived of life by an emissary of Shudsoka. The life of the chase-loving Pushnava, King of Cammidi, was sipped, while he was extirpating rhinoceroses of the Lord of Campas's soldiers ensconced in a grove of tall-stemmed reeds. Carried away by a fondness for troubadours, the Markhari fool, Ksatravarman was cut down by bards, his enemy's emissaries, with the cry of "Victory" echoing on their lips. In his enemy's city the King of the Shakos, while courting another's wife, was butchered by Cantragupta, concealed in his mistress's dress. The blunders of heedless men arising from women have been brought sufficiently to my Lord's hearing. Thus, to secure her son's succession, Suprabha with poisoned gnats killed Mahasena, the sweet-toothed King of Kashi. Rotnavati pretending a frenzy of love, slew the victorious Jarutha of Ayodhya with a mirror having a razor edge. Dbaki, being in love with a younger brother employed against the Souhouza Devasena an ear-lotus whose juice was touched with poisoned powder. A jealous Queen killed Rantideva of Vranti with a jewelled anklet emitting an infection of magic powder; Vindumati, the Vishnu Vidmatha with a dagger hidden in her braided hair, Hamsavati the Sauviva King, Virasena, with a girdle ornament having a drug-poisoned centre; Pauravi the Paurava Lord Somaka by making him drink a mouthful of poisoned wine, her own mouth being smeared with an invisible antidote.

> 'So much he said and went forth to execute his Master's order.'

In no way daunted by this melancholy recital, Harscha led his army forth to defeat the King of Ganda.

Surely these wonderful tales of Old India, so reminiscent of Renaissance Italy and the brood of Borgias would provide plots for dramatists today and would inspire our jaded television scriptwriters to much-needed brilliance.

The Gods of Ancient Greece revelled in amorous delights with any beauty, married or single, who attracted their lustful eyes, on occasion it would seem that those same celestial deities disported over Ancient India. The *Boital Pachis* or *The Twenty-five Tales of a Sprite*, translated from Hindi by J. Platts,[85] tells of Hariswami who was 'as beautiful as Cupid, equalled Brihaspati in his knowledge of scientific and religious treatises and was as wealthy as Kuvera'. He wedded and brought home a Brahman's daughter whose name was Levenyavata.

> 'To be brief, one night in the hot season they were both sleeping sound on the flat roof of a summer-house. The woman's veil accidentally slipped off her face while a demi-god seated on a car was proceeding somewhere through the air. His gaze suddenly falling upon her, he lowered the car and placing her asleep on the car flew off with her. After some time the Brahman also awoke and, lo! his wife was not (beside him). On this he became alarmed and coming down from thence searched throughout the house. When he did not find her there, he went about seeking her throughout all the streets and lanes of the city but did not find her. Thereupon he began to say to himself "Who has carried her off and whither has she gone?" His sorrow proved fatal, after much misery, he ate rice, which had been poisoned by a snake and he died.'

Somehow we lack sympathy, we feel that any man who sleeps with his wife on a flat roof with spaceships hovering overhead simply deserves to lose her. The moral for us today in this age of UFOS is to sleep indoors.

The Twenty-five Stories of a Vetala[86] written in the seventh century AD tells of a carpenter who built an aerial car camouflaged like a huge bird enabling a young man to rescue his betrothed from the harem of a powerful King.

The tales of the *Panchatantra*[87] in the Sanskrit of old

India have been told by wandering story-tellers down the generations across the whole world. These magical romances from realms of wonder inspired the *Golden Ass* of Apuleius, the fabulous *Arabian Nights,* the chivalrous *Gesta Romanorum,* Boccacio's saucy *Decameron,* the fables of La Fontaine and those delightful tales of Grimm and Hans Anderson, which entrance us today. Those faery stories enchanting our childhood still evoke a world of magic, which we feel must be the true reality beyond our limited cognisance, perhaps those transcendent realms where Wondrous Beings manipulate the secret forces of the universe; some mythologists believe the fairies were former Gods, today we confuse them with Spacemen.

The tale of *The Weaver as Vishnu* translated most charmingly by Alfred Williams, tells how in the country of the Gandas in a city named Pundravardhanam, a young weaver and a carpenter arrayed in their best clothes wandered through the crowd celebrating a great festival. Seated before an upper window of the royal palace, they beheld the Princess whose matchless beauty transfixed the Weaver's heart. So distraught was he for love that his friend, the Carpenter, made him a wonderful machine shaped and painted like a bird, modelled on the divine Garuda, to ascend to the Princess, who slept alone on her balcony. The Weaver bathed, dressed himself in fine attire, scented his breath and mounted his machine. The Princess alone on her balcony was sighing at the moon, when she saw the Weaver in the form of Vishnu on a huge bird coming from the sky.

The Weaver told the maiden, who believed him to be Vishnu, that she was his former wife and that they could be wedded under the stars. Every night he visited the Princess and as dawn illumined their love-making, he bade a fond farewell and ascended to the heavens. Eventually the King found out the Princess's secret and vowed her lover must die; the Princess then revealed she was courted by Vishnu himself. Both the King and Queen were delighted at the God making love to their daughter and the King boasted that with Vishnu as son-in-law he would conquer the Earth. Thus emboldened he defied the mighty Vikramasena, King of the South, and refused to pay his usual tribute; Vikramasena then invaded the country with a great army of elephants, so the King asked his daughter to tell the blessed Vishnu to annihilate the enemy. The Weaver promised to do so and the delighted King vowed that whoever killed Vikramasena would have all the latter's immense treasures.

At first the Weaver was alarmed at the prospect of battle but life without his beloved Princess was death; he would challenge Vikramasena, who might imagine him to be the real Vishnu after all.

In heaven the God, Vishnu, who had watched this impersonation with generous amusement, suddenly realised his image would greatly suffer were the Weaver, believed to be Vishnu, slain by mortals, so he entered the Weaver's body and mounted on the Bird hurled his discus at Vikramasena, cutting him in twain. The invading army surrendered in panic. The inspired Weaver claimed all the possessions of the defeated King and in victory showed true nobility of soul. The King paid him the highest honour, all the people greatly rejoiced, so the Weaver and the Princess lived happily ever after.

It intrigues to speculate as to whether if a UFO enthusiast today impersonated a Spaceman some blonde Venusian would come to his rescue? Perhaps we should try?

Another entertaining story from the *Panchatantra* describes how the exiled King Putraka obtained a pair of magic boots and flew high above cities, rivers and mountain-tops to vanquish his enemies.

Scientists in many countries are now studying the ancient Sanskrit texts minutely to rediscover secrets of space-flight. A most remarkable translation has been made by Maharshi Bharadwaja called *Aeronautics,* described as *A Manuscript from the Prehistoric Past,* contains fascinating, almost incredible data quoted in the following sample extracts published by the International Academy of Sanskrit Research, Mysore, India.

Against chosen verses of Sanskrit are these intriguing interpretations which astound us.

> 'In this book are described in eight pregnant and captivating chapters, the art of manufacturing various types of Aeroplanes of smooth and comfortable travel in the sky, as a unifying force for the Universe, contributive to the well-being of mankind. That which can go by its own

force like a bird, on earth, or water, or in air, is called "Vimana". That which can travel in the sky, from place to place, land to land, or globe to globe, is called "Vimana" by scientists in Aeronautics.

'The secret of constructing aeroplanes, which will not break, which cannot be cut, will not catch fire, and cannot be destroyed. The secret of making planes motionless. The secret of making planes invisible. The secret of hearing conversations and other sounds in enemy planes. The secret of receiving photographs of the interior of enemy planes. The secret of ascertaining the direction of enemy planes' approach. The secret of making persons in enemy planes lose consciousness. The secret of destroying enemy planes.

'Just as our body if complete in all its limbs, can achieve all things, so an Aeroplane should be complete in all its parts in order to be effective. Commencing from the photographing-mirror underneath, an aeroplane should have thirty-one parts. The pilot should be provided with different materials of clothing according to differences in seasons, as prescribed by Agnimitra.

'Three varieties of food should be given to pilots, varying with the seasons of the year, as per Kalpa-Shastra. Twenty-five kinds of poisons which arise in the seasons are destroyed by the above changes of diet. Food is of five forms, cooked grain, gruel, paste, bread and essence. All of them are wholesome and body-building.

'Metals suitable for Aeroplanes, light and heat-absorbing, are of sixteen kinds, according to Shownaka. Great sages have declared that these sixteen metals alone are the best for aeroplane construction.'

This is not science-fiction or secrets of the American Air Command; these "revelations" are extracts from the Sanskrit Classics penned in that tatalising, beautiful script, many thousand years ago. Do such disclosures not suggest a technology, aerodynamics, electronics, engineering, metallurgy, communications, space-medicine, all centuries in advance of our own?[88]

The great Sanskrit grammarian, Panini, who lived about 400 AD is said to have written a fascinating work called *The Travels of Panini* in which he describes visits to the Inner Planets claiming that the Extra-terrestrials frequently took the Initiated on jaunts to Mercury and Venus. Shades of Adamski! Did George read Sanskrit? It is facetious perhaps to ridicule Adamski since phenomena now seen by our cosmonauts tend to substantiate his claims to have travelled in a spaceship;[89] likewise the learned Panini may have told the truth to an unbelieving posterity. A few decades earlier in AD 312[90] Constantine and all his army beheld a 'Fiery Cross', an apparent Spaceship in the heavens on his march to Rome, confirming that Extra-terrestrials were haunting our Earth in that century; moreover the ruins of an old temple at Borobodura in Java dating from that period bear frescoes showing apparent Spacemen and astronomical symbols suggesting Visitants from Venus.

While our Western civilisation is based on the Graeco-Judaic cultures, it is seldom realised that the Greeks and the Jews derived many of their fundamental concepts from old India especially after the invasion of Alexander the Great in 327 BC promoted commerce and enlightenment between India and the Middle East. About this time according to Livy, while Spacemen were visiting Rome it would surely be likely that they would surveil other parts of the Earth too. Frank Edwards,[91] the American UFO investigator, writes that two shining silvery shields spitting fire around the rims dived repeatedly on the Greek columns descending the mountain-passes into the Punjab, stampeding horses and elephants then they returned to the skies. This incident cannot be confirmed from contemporary histories by Arrian, Ptolemy, Megasthenes or Strabo, yet there is a striking parallel with those flaming shields from the skies, which in AD 776 rescued Charlemagne's Knights in Sigiburg from the besieging Saxons, so vividly described in *Annales Laurissenses* in Migne's *Patrologiae,* Saeculum IX.

Kananda and the Gnani Yogis speculated on the atom five hundred years before Democritus, Aryabatha in the sixth century before Christ taught the rotation of the Earth, the scientific principles of medicine, botany and chemistry were established as early as 1300 BC in India, while Indian astronomy dates from remote Antiquity.

The Creation in Genesis seems a primitive version of the profound teaching of the Days and Nights of Brahm; the tale of Noah an echo of Vaivasvata warned by Vishnu to build a ship for the coming Flood; the Jewish Kabbala and various events in the Bible can be traced to Hindu scriptures written many centuries earlier.

To minds conditioned by two thousand years of Christianity, the lives and teachings of Krishna and Buddha throw so much doubt on the historicity of Jesus, that we dare to wonder if the whole Christian Legend is but a plagiarism of Hinduism[92] and Buddhism. Such apparent blasphemy outrages all our feelings, to doubt the reality of Jesus seems mortal sin, yet if we honestly study the teachings of Krishna, hellenized to Chrestus hence Christ, and compare the fundamental dogmas of Virgin Birth, Miracles, Ritual Death on a Tree or Cross, Immortality, we find ourselves speculating whether Jesus was a myth based on the earlier historical Krishna. Some intuitives claim that the Hindu teachings were brought from India by that truly wonderful ascetic, Apollonius of Tyana, who is said to have been the Man we worship as Jesus. Such contention baffles our comprehension today, perhaps we may compromise and turn our studies to the inspired Apollonius and his youthful companion, Damis, treading the narrow streets of Taxila eager to learn TRUTH from the lips of Indian Sages, who possibly inherited their wisdom from Spacemen.

Many scholars believe that Old India was the source not only of civilisation, the arts and sciences, but also of all the great religions of Antiquity. Some Orientalists suggest that the Vedas reflect foreign influence of most ancient date. Occultists state that India's culture originated from the drowned continent of Lemuria; this may be so, but our new insight into the inhabited universe arouses speculation as to whether India's teachers descended from the stars.

The earliest legends tell of India's first Dynasty of Divine Kings, the Race of the Sun, who reigned in Ayodha (now Oudh); the second, the Race of the Moon, who reigned in Pruyag (Allahabad); an intriguing parallel with the Divine Dynasties of Egypt listed by Manetho and the Gods of the Golden Age of Greece, sung by Hesiod and Ovid, all agreeing the ancient domination of Earth by Supermen from Space.

Admittedly the evidence from the remote past is scarce and confused, although M. Agrest, the Soviet physicist, has recently stated that in the famous Cave of Bohistan are inscriptions showing Earth and Venus joined by an arrow.[93] Who knows what revelations may be found by archæologists unearthing the baffling ruins of Mohenjo Daro and Harappa?[94] Will some new 'Rosetta Stone' throw dazzling illumination on Spacemen in Ancient India?

If we now view those fascinating Hindu Classics with their traditions of flying-machines, fantastic bombs and wondrous Heroes in the light of our modern space knowledge we feel the growing thrill that Ancient India was ruled by Spacemen.

CHAPTER SIX

Spacemen in Old Tibet

The glorious Sun enchanted the Earth to splendour inspiring the Giants with the joy of life, the thrill of basking in the beauty of this wonderful world, living almost for ever like the golden Sky Gods. Sunbeams danced on the wavelets washing this Tibetan shore and caressed the crowds sporting on the beach; children played and splashed in the sea pausing to stare wide-eyed as a gleaming vimana glided down towards the gilded towers of Lhasa, the Celestial City, whose translucent temples and flowery parks reminded the Venusians of their own fair planet. Young lovers frolicked in joyous abandonment to music conjured from the air; some gazed mutely at their mates lost in love's sweet mystery, while their friends gaily prattled of holidays in the forests at the South Pole, climbing those snow-capped mountains of Atlantis, or even tripping to Proserpine, the newly discovered planet beyond Pluto, whose alluring witches promised tempting delights. Women in exotic gowns, which matched their moods, flaunted a beauty of body and soul; in feminine glee they gossipped about the latest scandal intriguing the gay Tibetans. Talor, the young High Priest, whose fantastic but wayward genius amazed even the renowned scientists of that Asiatic island, had materialised from etherean realms a blond maiden whom he meant to marry. The ladies protested in indignation, brides from the stars might be welcome perhaps but a demoness from the astral world surely offered unfair competition, especially if her face was really fairer than the Sun, her eyes more magic than the Moon; her vivacious charms were seducing the virile High Priest, perversely immune to all the Beauties in Tibet. Some ladies defended the gallant. After millennia of peace, men were bored; space no longer thrilled; one planet seemed like any other; telepathy with the animals proved disappointing; even sex was losing its savour; this demoness brought new ideas; her strange, exciting revelations of the etherean world would revolutionise life on Earth, the future shone with promise.

On a rock nearby some blond Giants sat listening to Yellus, the psycho-scientist, whose bronze features showed concern unusual for the cheery Tibetans. He was explaining that astronomers on Saturn had detected a celestial body approaching the Solar System; observers believed the intruder to be an errant asteroid but sensitives swore it was a missile from Sirius, whose Lords directed the destinies of Earth. Man had now reached the end of a world-age; the time was come for human souls to spiral to a new octave of evolution; civilisation must be destroyed to rise again to splendour. The Giants stared in disbelief, the Sun shone, Earth rejoiced; Zeus, their Divine King, would save his people; yet all remembered the Prophets foretold destruction this century.

Forebodings were soon confirmed. All the nations of the Earth mobilised to withstand the shock. Shelters were tunnelled in mountains and stored with provisions and equipment for those few who survived. Initiates secreted time-capsules with the Ancient Wisdom for generations unborn; space-fleets from Venus rescued the Chosen; some scientists in nuclear submarines sought refuge at sea, but as the fearsome asteroid filled the sky its gravitational pull threatened to shatter Earth itself.

The world-defence Chiefs counselled Zeus to lead a space armada to disintegrate the onrushing monster with nuclear missiles; the distortion of spatial tensions fused the electronic navigational devices and most of the fleet was wrecked.

Electrical storms convulsed the atmosphere blacking out power-supplies, radio-communications and grounding all aerial craft. Forests flared into flames, titanic winds toppled cities to ruin, the boiling oceans swept from Pole to Pole, volcanoes belched forth floods of molten lava burying villages and towns in fire. Huge chasms yawned and closed again, mountains shook and slithered to the depths, the dusty steaming air choked men and beasts to suffocation. The blazing asteroid crashed in the north-west displacing Earth's axis sending the planet reeling out into space. Dense palls of smoke and dust blotted out the sun and noxious gases polluted the atmosphere; most creatures yet living gasped to frantic death.

Months later the few gaunt survivors crawled from their caves and stared on a terrifying desolation which shocked their stricken minds in fantasy. Lands had become seas, seas had become lands; the old familiar world had gone. Earth glowed with a raw newness like the Day of Creation. The solitary Giants left in Tibet shuddered with sudden cold; when at last the red sun loomed through the mist its crimson light revealed a weird landscape, the friendly seas were vapourised, the Celestial Island had become elevated to a lofty plateau high in the clouds ringed by great mountain peaks, the proud buildings of Lhasa sprawled in mud.

The forlorn survivors implored the Gods to aid Earth again, a few Extra-terrestrials descended in their ships of light to teach Man civilisation. The hungry generations fighting grimly for life under savage conditions remembered the Golden Age of their ancestors as a vague dream, only solitary Initiates preserved the Ancient Wisdom of the past; the world must suffer for many millennia before Man could spiral again to new splendour.

The Sacred Books of Dzyan refer to the Lhas who 'revolve, driving their chariots around their Lord, the One Eye', a curious description suggesting the Eye of Horus, the Egyptian symbol for a Spaceship. An occult Stanza describes how 'the flames came, fires with sparks, the Lhas of the High (Dragons of Wisdom) fought the goat-men, and the dog-headed men and the men with fishes' bodies', reminiscent of Oannes, the Babylonian half-fish, half-human, an Extra-terrestrial wearing a space suit. This perplexing symbolism may be some garbled memory of the classical War in the Heavens between the Gods and the Giants. The Lhas, the ancient Asiatic 'Spirits' built the Celestial City called Lhasa,[95] probably on that legendary island in Central Asia inhabited by the Sons of God, who worked magic dominating Earth and Sky with wonders. Tibetans believe that before the Himalayas appeared, their country was flat and fertile surrounded by sea[96] and peopled by survivors of the drowned Continent of Mu,

Empire of the Sun. The Himalayas were probably not actually elevated from the Earth's crust, the seas were drained away leaving the mountains with Tibet poised in the air, exactly as in South America the former sea-port of Tiahuanaco was left stranded thousands of feet up the newly-appeared Andes. Tibetan traditions assert that the Void gave birth to a wonderful Egg, which burst giving forth space, fire, ocean, mountains and Man himself. This strange conception may be a confused memory of the rebirth of the shattered world following some cosmic catastrophe.

Tibetan history is veiled in myth and legend. The first King, Shipuye, was followed by Seven Heavenly Khri (Thrones) and Two Upper Teng (High Ones) analogous to the Divine Dynasties of Vietnam, India, China, Japan, Egypt and Greece. These Rulers were succeeded by Six Middle Lags (Good Ones), Eight Earthly De (Worldly Monarchs), Four Lower Tsan (Mighty Kings), similar perhaps to the Age of Heroes recalled in most countries. The first historic ruler, Nami Sontson, in the seventh century led Tibetan armies in triumphant campaigns from China to Persia.[97]

The original religion of Tibet, the Bon cult, is a universal animism, where stars and stones, trees and rivers, possess Guardian Spirits, propitiated by sacrifices lest they influence humans.[98] The Gods if angered send hailstorms and plagues but may be humoured into blessing the world with sunshine and fertility. The heavens are linked closely to Earth; spirits descend to rebirth passing the souls of the dead ascending to astral realms. The Lords of Light wage eternal war with the Powers of Darkness as in the Semitic theologies; this celestial conflict common to most religions may be some spiritualisation of the War in the Heavens waged by the Gods or Spacemen. The lives of the Tibetans are ruled by omens casting baleful shadows which may be averted only by the exorcism by Lamas, the turning of prayer-wheels[99] or the waving of prayer-flags. Modern science and formal Christianity scorn the Bon beliefs as primitive superstition, although many are shared by the Catholic Church, but comparison with world-wide native cults suggests that all may be debased remnants of a transcendent universal Wisdom from far Antiquity, probably brought to Earth by Teachers from Space. Recent study of sub-atomic particles, the revelations of the Spiritualists and the researches of Borderland Scientists into etherean matter, suggest the co-existence of invisible realms peopled by Beings of more subtle matter than ourselves, who may intrude into our plane of Earth and produce strange phenomena long known to the Bons of Tibet and to ancient cults all over the world. Though the official religion of Tibet is[100] Buddhism with its sublime Message of compassion for all sentient creatures, the Lamas acknowledge many beneficent and malignant Gods and Goddesses ruling every detail of daily life, worshipped in the intricate ritual formulated in the Tantric texts. All Tibetans believe in transcendental realms from which Avatars, Bodhisattvas, return to teach mankind on the cosmic pilgrimage to Union with God. The Great Soul, Chenrezi,[101] incarnates as the Dalai Lama; the next Saviour, the Lord Maitreya, awaits in the Tushita Heaven preparing to descend to Earth.[102]

Until invasion by the Chinese Communists Tibet was generally regarded as a land of magic and mystery ruled by a God, where Lamas developed supernatural powers practising a sorcery confounding our logical science. A few Europeans have lived among the Tibetan magicians and give awed testimony to bewildering phenomena which flout our Laws of Physics. Madame Alexandra David-Neel,[103] an inspired Student of the occult, records the materialisation of thought-forms into persons or things, men who out-run horses, naked hermits who warm themselves amid mountain snows, telepathic communication across vast distances, transmigration of souls, translation of the ethereal Self, astral travelling, intercourse with the so-called dead, corpses who dance, conflicts with demons, and many other fantasies beyond belief though confirmed by other reliable observers. The noted scholar, Dr W. Y. Evans-Wentz,[104] devoted his life to the study of Tibetan Yoga and the Secret Doctrines revealing a vast field of esoteric knowledge utterly alien to our own conventional thought-patterns; other researchers verify levitation, suspended animation by Yogis buried alive, exact prophecies and many startling prodigies unknown to our cynical Western world. It is salutary to realise that avant-garde researchers into parapsychology, precognition, telepathy, occultism, even nuclear-physics, are transmuting our materialistic science into esoteric studies slowly fringing on to the psychism long practised by the Tibetan Lamas.[105] The Ancient Wisdom of Tibet must surely have been inherited from some lost civilisation of the past or taught by Spacemen from an advanced planet.

The vast literature of Tibet is hardly known in the West; the assembled archives of the lamaseries must rival in wisdom the Vatican Library. The *Kanjur* comprises 1,083 distinct works, the *Tanjur* consists of 225 volumes of folio, each weighing from four to five pounds, the *Batam-Hgym* is a compilation of Tibetan literary works in 225 volumes[106] dealing with literature, science, astronomy and tantric ceremonies. For fifteen hundred years Tibetan monks have studied the human soul, the heavens and the invisible realms around[107] us; many of these scholars must have been men of genius with millennia of tradition and experience, they must surely have discovered many facets of this amazing universe beyond our cognisance. The *Bardö Thödol,*[108] often compared with the Egyptian *The Book of the Dead* describes life after death, the trials of the soul in the astral worlds and the process of rebirth with a spiritual insight transcending our Western philosophies. It is believed that as in the Sanskrit texts of old India these ancient books of Tibet may somewhere explain the secrets of anti-gravity, teleportation, psycho-kinesis, and sidereal forces beyond our knowledge; they must surely contain fascinating records about the Spacemen not revealed to the West. Some researchers think that the existence of these ancient records with their wonderful secrets of arcane technologies actually prompted the Chinese invasion of Tibet, a somewhat extravagant claim perhaps, but a concern which can hardly be dismissed. The unexpectedly swift development by the Chinese of the hydrogen-bomb proves their fearsome potential in nuclear science, which might be enhanced by knowledge gleaned from old Tibet.

Folk tales from Tibet delight in the supernatural common to every country in the world. A well-known story tells of a boy with a deformed head, who married the daughter of the Fairy King dwelling among the Gods in heaven but occasionally descending to Earth in the form of a white duck. The daughter lived with the youth for nine years then suddenly returned to the skies. Lost in anguish the disconsolate husband roamed far and wide seeking his vanished wife; one day he saved a holy Gryphon from a Dragon, in reward he was flown to the skies where he met his wife. The Gods were so moved at their mutual love that finally they permitted the celestial wife to descend and live with her mortal husband in happiness on Earth.[109] An identical story the *Sudhana Avadana* tells of the celestial maiden, the Kinnari, Manohara, captured with a magic chain by the hunter, Philoka, while bathing with her companions in a lake; her beauty kindled the passion of Prince Sudhana and she became his bride. Years later she returned to her own folk among the 'Spirits' followed by her devoted husband, who after severe trials was finally reunited with his wife for ever. A similar theme recalls the myths of the 'Knights of the Swan' in the Middle Ages, which probably inspired Wagner's *Lohengrin* and Tschaikovsky's popular *Swan Lake* ballet. Such stories do suggest that people centuries ago believed in intercourse with other realms with the same credulity we today accord to the Spacemen.

A colourful Tibetan tale describes Sudarsoma, the City of thirty-three Gods in the skies, which was 2,500 yojanas in length, as many in breadth, with seven rows of golden walls 22 yojanas high having 999 gates, each guarded by 500 Yakahas in blue robes and coats-of-mail armed with bows and arrows. The architecture glowed with gold, silver, beryl and crystal; wishing-trees blossomed with blue, yellow, red and white raiment; the Gods imagined any clothing they desired and these trees obligingly grew it; a fanciful explanation perhaps for the materialisation of thought-forms, which some sensitives today allege to be the process of manufacture used by the Masters on advanced planets. King Mandhotar after conquering the whole world ascended to this celestial city and shared the throne of Indra until ambition drove him to aspire to domination of both Heaven and Earth, such arrogance the outraged Gods could not permit, so he was cast down and died. While Mandhotar was in the skies the Celestial City was attacked by the Asuras; the war-chariots of the Gods and the Asuras clashed in aerial battle; the King out-fought them all and routed the enemy back to their own fortress far in space. The Tibetans believed the Gods dwelled on the summit of Mount Meru, where one day was equal to a hundred years on Earth; since the Gods lived one thousand celestial years, their age equalled thirty-six million of the years of men. A long, long time but only a moment in the infinite Universe. Death comes at last, even to the Gods![110]

The long chivalrous, magical *Epic of Gesar of Ling*[111] is the 'Iliad' of Central Asia ranking with the 'Ramayana' and Virgil's 'Aeneid'. Gesar, sometimes identified with Kuan-ti, the War-God of the Manchu Emperors, is said to have lived in Eastern Tibet between the seventh and eighth centuries, although his fabulous adventures probably mention incidents in ancient popular legends. The Guru Rinpoche, the Previous Spiritual Master of Tibet, known under his Sanskrit name, Padma Sambhava, persuaded a God to incarnate as the hero, Gesar of Ling, in order to destroy the Demon-Kings who were perverting the Earth with evil and attacking the good people of Tibet.

Padma Sambhava rode through the clouds on a winged horse; after one visit to the young Gesar he 'shut himself into his marvellous tent and slowly rose into the sky; for a few moments the light that surrounded him traced a luminous path amid the clouds, then faded in the distance'. Surely a wonderful description of a UFO! The Master entrusted Gesar with a magic 'dorje' or vril rod with which to open the subterranean palace that contained treasures; in Gesar's battles against the demons, Padma Sambhava appeared in the sky surrounded by numerous Gods and Fairies, who waved flags, carried umbrellas and rained down flowers and rice upon the Victor; reminiscent of the celebrations after Rama's defeat of Ravan described so brilliantly in the 'Ramayana'. In his fantastic campaign Gesar employed magic weapons, sticks of invisibility, conjured apparitions, rode flying horses, used enchanted dolls, aided by the Celestials and their fair Dakinis in a most wondrous and entertaining epic far transcending our cold science-fiction today. The fabulous exploits of Gesar of Ling in seventh-century Tibet amaze us by their sophistication and exotic extravagance transporting us far beyond that icy plateau in the Himalayas to a wonderland of Gods and Demons, Wizards and Faeries, casting their spells in breathless enchantment, where physical laws are held in miraculous suspense, dimensions transcending space and time, perhaps the real universe, suggesting the wondrous technology we attribute to the Spacemen.

Those intriguing trails in the snows of the Himalayas ascribed to the Yeti or Abominable Snowmen may actually be caused by radiation from the Spaceships like the shining oval aeroform seen high over the peaks by the explorer Nicholas Roerich in 1921[112] and the glistening silver object miles above Everest observed by the climber, F. S. Smythe, during his 1933 expedition.

That controversial Lama, Lobsang Rampa, son of a Tibetan noble, whose revelations bewilder and embarrass all the experts on Tibet, claims that Flying Saucers have visited Tibet[113] for thousands of years; he has seen them in the sky and on the ground and tells a highly diverting tale of a trip in one rivalling Adamski.[114] Writing in 1957 before the first Sputnik this intriguing Lama described the brilliant panorama of star-encrusted Space and the appearance of our Earth exactly like the future cosmonauts. Adamski! Lobsang Rampa! Again we wonder?

Is Tibet still the Home of the Gods?

CHAPTER SEVEN

Spacemen in Old China

The Chinese are believed to have inherited their unique civilisation from the ancient Empire of the Uighurs, the greatest colony of the Children of the Sun, of lost Lemuria.[115] Traditions assert that the old Lemurian ideals still formed the political and philosophical basis of Chinese culture about 2000 BC; veneration of their original Motherland, drowned millennia earlier, developed into ancestor-worship, codified into the State religion by the Emperor Yao in the year 1550 BC.

The oldest records state that in most ancient times China was ruled for 18,000 years by a race of Divine Kings, according to the manuscript Tchi, a fascinating parallel with similar revelations for India, Japan, Egypt and Greece, chronicled in the 'Ramayana', the *Kojiki*, the *History* of Manetho and the *Theogony* of Hesiod. The classic *Huai-nan-tzu,* (Chapter 8) describes an idyllic Age, when men and animals lived in peace and beauty in a Garden of Eden, body and soul united in cosmic understanding; the climate was benevolent, there were no natural calamities, 'the planets did not deviate from their courses', injury and crime were unknown, Earth and humanity prospered.[116] Later men fell from Grace and filled the world with discord. The 'Spirits' frequently descended among men and taught them divine wisdom, then mankind degenerated to lust and perversions. The *Shan-hai-Ching* (Book Seventeen) mentions a troublesome human race with wings called the Miao, who about 2400 BC lost the power to fly and after quarrelling with the 'Lord on High' were exiled.

The *Shoo-King* (Part Four, Chapter 27, p. 291) referring to the Fourth Root Race (The Atlanteans) states:

'When the Mao-tse (that antidiluvian and perverted race which had retired in the days of old to the rocky caves and the descendants of whom are said to be still found in the neighbourhood of Canton) according to our ancient documents, had, owing to the beguilements of Tchy-Yeoo, troubled all the Earth, it became full of brigands —The Lord Chang-ty (A King of the Divine Dynasty) saw that his people had lost the last vestiges of virtue. Then he commanded Tchang and Lhy (two lower Dhyan Chohans) to cut away every communication between Heaven and Earth. Since then there was no more "going up and coming down".'[117]

The Miao, like the Nine Li before them, fostered new rebellion, so the Emperor Yao requested the descendants of Tchang and Lhy to quell the disorder. It was said that 'Tchang lifted Heaven up and Lhy pressed Earth down'; the communication between Heaven and Earth ceased.[118]

In the *Kuo-yiu*, King Chao of Chu (500 BC) wondered if this 'communication' had not been cut, whether mortals could still ascend to heaven. His advisers, equally confused, offered the interpretation later propounded by our theologians in the West and vaguely hinted that the 'Spirits' like the 'Angels' were disembodied entities, although actually the context of these Chinese texts like the Bible suggests that those Visitants from the skies above were surely Spacemen.

Students of mythology at once recognise the familiar story repeated in traditions from most countries of the world, how in far ancient times the Gods, Wondrous Beings from Space, ruled Earth in a glorious Golden Age; mankind rebelled, catastrophes ravaged our planet, the Space Kings returned to the stars leaving Man to build civilisation again. Thousands of years ago there was apparently constant communication between our Earth and other worlds, now there remain only vague memories, which our conditioned minds will not accept.

As with most ancient peoples Chinese chronology is conjectural and most confused. Almost all the ancient records were destroyed on the orders of the Emperor Che Hwang-te in 213 BC,[119] just as in the West a few centuries later most priceless documents of the past were put to the flames by megalomaniac Roman Emperors and fanatical Christians, copied in the seventeenth century by the bigoted Spanish priests in Mexico, who systematically smashed the priceless archives of the Aztecs. The almost total loss of the records of Antiquity can never be replaced by archaeology; revelations from occult sources are scorned by the modern scientific mind, which interprets discoveries unearthed by the spade to suit our own conditioned ideas; so it is exceedingly doubtful whether the Golden Age of the Gods can ever be reconstructed except from the legends and ancient epics. The unexpected discovery of the Dead Sea Scrolls is now fundamentally influencing our conception of Christianity, perhaps some future Champollion will salvage some Rosetta Stone from lost Atlantis or decipher some inscription in the Gobi Desert and revolutionise our knowledge of the past.

Some Sinologists speculate that the Chinese originated in Akkadia[120] and construe a possible affinity with the early Babylonians, which is hardly surprising since there is evidence of massive migrations across Europe and Asia millennia ago, caused perhaps by world-shaking catastrophes. Philologists state that 'Sumerian was unique amongst the languages of the ancient Middle East in being agglutinative, it belonged in this respect to the same group as Chinese'; the Chinese syllabary even of the present day is based on signs fundamentally similar to the pictographs used by the Sumerians.

The Bible, the Talmud and the Babylonian legends suggest that Spacemen landed in the Middle East a few centuries before Christ, so it is probable they visited China too. The Chinese themselves vaguely believe that there was an age of magic followed by an heroic age, which agrees with the classic traditions of a divine Golden Age, then an era of wars and calamities degenerating to world-barbarism slowly ascending to a civilisation far inferior to that wonderful culture of the past. The earliest written evidence is found in bone and tortoise-shell texts from Honan attributed to the Shang-Yin Dynasty about 1700 BC,[121] the script reveals such elegance and technical skill that it had obviously developed throughout many centuries. Inscriptions on exquisite bronze vessels unearthed at Anyang, 200 miles south of Peiping, suggest a highly developed civilisation possibly 2000 BC or even earlier;[122] the first dated texts however only go back to the Emperor

Wu Ting in the fourteenth century BC, thus reliable Chinese records date back only three millennia and are therefore not very helpful in studying the remote past.

The ancient Chinese believed in astrology, which taught that influences from the stars affected the human psyche and motivated terrestrial events. Recent discoveries by the sputniks and cosmic-ray physicists prove that our universe appears to be a vast radiation-field, while Professor Piccardi in Florence cogently demonstrates in exquisitely delicate chemical experiments that the variations in subtle spatial tensions as our Solar System sweeps onwards through space do exercise detectable influence here on Earth. The much ridiculed astrology of the Ancients seems to be a remnant of a vast world-wide psychic science taught by Spacemen. In China as in Ancient Rome men watched the portents in the heavens with foreboding, a falling star was feared as an ill omen; it is said that about 2000 BC a Chinese Emperor put to death his two chief astronomers for not predicting an eclipse of the sun; today would any King care?[123]

Chinese astronomy in ancient times was astonishingly precise, particularly as regards to the fixing of the Calendar, accurate calendars existed from the Hsia, Yin and Chou Dynasties of the second millennium BC, probably earlier. Professor Tung-Stso-pin in a report to the United Nations in 1951 asserts that the Shang-Dynasty (1700-1100 BC possibly earlier) used the Ssu-Fen mixed lunar-solar calendar, whose month consisted of either 29 or 30 days with an exact length of 29.5305106 days approximating our modern calculation of 29.530585 days; the year consisted of 365.25 days almost in exact agreement with our own.[124] In very early time the intercalary day was placed at the end of the year, later seven intercalary months were inserted in each period of nineteen years to reconcile the solar year of 365¼ days with the 'common' year of 365 days. This period of nineteen years when the sun and moon occupy nearly the same place in the Zodiac as they did at the commencement of the period was not known in the West until it was discovered by Meton, who described it in a book called *Enneades Caterides*; this Meton Cycle was adopted by the Athenians in 432 BC and engraved in letters of gold on the walls of the Temple of Minerva, Diodorus Siculus alleged that a God visited Britain every nineteen years, danced and sang then returned to the stars. Perhaps on his periodic trip this Spaceman paused in China?

An oracle bone unearthed at Anyang bears an inscription recording an eclipse of the moon 'on the fifteenth day of the twelfth moon of the twenty-ninth year of King Wu-Ting', i.e. on November 23rd, 1311 BC. 'In the Chou Dynasty in the thirty-eighth year of the Shang Emperor Ti-hsin (1137 BC) the Chou ruler Chou-wen-wang ordered a sacrifice to be offered because the eclipse happened not on the right day, it occurred on the sixteenth day of the month, according to the calendar, instead of on the fifteenth.' The fact that the Chinese astronomers more than three thousand years ago could prognosticate eclipses with such accuracy surely suggests advanced technical knowledge developed throughout many millennia or perhaps taught by Extra-terrestrials.

Intriguing texts from the Chou Dynasty for the year 2346 BC record the appearance of ten suns in the sky, which at once recall those extra suns over Ancient Rome chronicled by Julius Obsequens, the celestial prodigies mentioned in the Middle Ages by Matthew of Paris,[125] and similar sightings reported by UFO students today. The ancient manuscripts, *Chuang-tzu* (Ch. 2), *Liu-Shi, ch'un-ch'iu* (Ch. 22, 5), and *Hua-non-tzu* (Ch. 8), probably written centuries later, vividly described how the Earth in the reign of the Emperor Yao was afflicted by terrible calamities, intense heat parched the land, the crops died, fierce storms lashed towns and countryside, the seas quaked and boiled drowning the fields in floods, huge monsters roamed and ravaged, mankind dreaded Doomsday, the end of a world-age.[126]

The Emperor Yao consulted his priests and wise men, who, as usual when needed most, were not particularly helpful, so in exasperation he called upon his divine archer, Tzu-yu, who could fly in the air and lived only on flowers, an intriguing affinity with those Spacemen today, said to live on fruit and sunflower seeds. This hero promptly shot down the nine false suns, thoughtfully leaving the real sun to shine on the follies of mankind, he also slew all the monsters and generally saved the Earth for an ungrateful posterity.

Tzu-yu's chivalrous enterprise failed to impress his wife, Heng-O; while her husband was killing dragons and no doubt rescuing damsels in distress, she took an anti-gravity pill and flew to the moon, which she found to be luminous and icy-cold; the sole vegetation being cinnamon-trees; braving the discomfort there she stayed. On returning from his crusade, Tzu-yu, often known as Shen I, the divine archer, showing space-science ate a magic cake to counteract heat and mounting an enchanted Bird flew to the sun, where he basked in bliss; suddenly remembering his wife he sped on a beam of light to the moon. Heng-O showed little enthusiasm at seeing her wandering husband; he built her a palace of cinnamon-trees, this failed to cheer her, so Tzu-yu returned to the Sun, built himself a wonderful palace and lived in blessed happiness.[127] This legend may perpetuate most ancient teachings that both sun and moon were inhabited; a belief shared thousands of years later by the astronomer, Sir William Herschel, who thought the sun was cold, a theory seriously advanced by some revolutionaries today.

It is difficult to evaluate this story of Tzu-yu satisfactorily; many myths appear to have several sub-strata of truth; frequently in the course of time race-memory fuses a few separate incidents into one and offers a garbled tale not easily disentangled. The ten suns may be a fancied explanation to account for the fantastic heat scorching the Earth, and the culture-hero shooting down nine of them a naïve invention explaining how the cataclysm was averted; today if some celestial intruder threatened the Earth our own 'archers' would launch nuclear-missiles to bring it down. The concept of more than one sun in the sky was clearly acceptable to ancient Chinese thought, which leads to the supposition that celestial discs chronicled in old Egypt and Rome also visisted China. Polynesian, Red Indian and Siberian legends tell of several suns burning the Earth, which some warrior or animal later destroyed. The Greeks accuse Phaeton of mis-driving the sun-chariot scorching whole countries aflame; there is geological and historical evidence to suggest that four or five thousand years ago some cosmic cataclysm did menace our planet.

This devastation of China was possibly the same catastrophe overwhelming Hyperborea, the Lands of the West, mentioned in the Greek Classics.[128]

Divinities in the sun and moon were worshipped as part of the State Religion, changes in their colour or eclipses were feared as portents of misfortune; like the Egyptians the Chinese paid superstitious veneration to Tien-Kou, Sirius, the Dog Star; perhaps the Secret Wisdom of the Priests taught that Sirius was inhabited by Great Souls, Guardians of our Solar System, as believed by sensitives today. The famous text 'Hsio-hsiao-chieng', a calendar for farmers showing the twelve lunations in fourth century BC was later incorporated into Chapter 47 of the *To-tai-Li-chi*, this comprised the earliest stellar catalogue compiled from the *Shih-Shen, Kan-Te* and *Wu-Hsien*, which are now lost. In the eighth century AD, the astronomer, Ch'u-t'-an-Hsi-Tu in his work *Kai-yuan-chang-ching* mentioned observations made in fourth century BC leading to the construction of a stellar catalogue containing 1,464 stars divided into 284 constellations. The chapter on astronomy (T'ien-Kuan') in the *Shih-chi* of Ssuma-Chien, about 90 BC, contains a list of constellations and describes the celestial movements and conjunctions and offers interpretations of unusual phenomena. In the first century BC the *Shan-shu-wei-kao* advanced the theory that the Earth moved 30,000 li to the west after the winter solstice and 30,000 li to the east after the summer solstice, remaining still only at the equinoxes.[129] All the stars were believed to be possessed by 'Spirits', some beneficent, others malevolent; which influenced man for good or evil; oddly enough our modern astronomers now teach life on countless planets, our UFO enthusiasts are eagerly awaiting 'Spirits' from the stars. The belief in influences from the stars shared by all the peoples of Antiquity may be remnants of some ancient cosmic science of Spacemen versed in knowledge of the emanations of radiation and electrical tensions charging space. The Chinese knew of Mercury, Venus, Mars, Jupiter and Saturn, which had characteristic colours; they influenced terrestrial events and were homes of the Gods.

In the excavations at Anyang remarkable bronze astrolabes have been discovered showing how the ancient Chinese astronomers plotted the stars. Chou-li about 175

BC attributed the first observation of the summer-solstice to the Duke of Chou as early as the ninth century BC; Liu-Hsiang in 20 BC mentioned in his *Wu-ching-t'ung* that the true causes of eclipses of the sun were known as early as the fourth century BC; the same astronomer in 7 BC published the 'Sou-t'ung' calendar based on a cycle of 135 months containing 23 eclipses. The explosion of a supernova recorded in 134 BC was also observed in Greece by Hipparchus and inspired him to compile his stellar catalogue preserved by Ptolemy. The Chinese astronomers recorded their observations in meticulous detail showing the exact position, time, duration, brightness and colour of phenomena, all catalogued with scientific method. It is generally recognised that the star-lists of the Chinese are the most accurate coming to us from Antiquity. The fourth century BC *Chi-nitzu* showed that the Chinese also took meticulous observations of meteors, unusual phenomena, floods and droughts. It would appear that these astronomers on ancient China had inherited remarkable mathematical and observational techniques either from millennia of development or from Extra-terrestrials.

Chinese literature does not glory in a great national epic like the 'Ramayana' or the 'Iliad' to inspire men's pride, lowly mortals basked in the brilliance of the divine Emperor, Son of Heaven, denoting descent from the skies. The Chinese believed their Emperor derived his powers from the God at the Celestial North Pole; the Emperor's throne and the sun-temples therefore always looked southwards, while their subjects gazed at them northwards. It is interesting to note that this veneration for the Pole Star also found in Ancient Egypt may have some relation to our modern belief that the spaceships visiting us now apparently approach from the North through the polar opening in the Van Allen radiation-belts. Like the native Siberians, the Chinese worshipped the Constellation of the Great Bear, which may perhaps be traced to the appearance of Spacemen from the direction of that constellation.

The myths of China are not so dramatic as the classic tales of India or Greece; their characters lack the heroic passions of Rama and Apollo, mainly because during the long Chou Dynasty (1027-221 BC) the practical Chinese mind tended to rationalise their Gods from Supermen to the conventional personage of their own Emperor. Scholars trained in the humanistic precepts of Confucius stripped the old tales of the supernatural and presented them in every-day social terms, just as any Marxist today rewriting the Bible would omit God and submit the 'Book' as the class-struggle of the Jews. In reaction the Han Dynasty and its successors turned to folk-lore of the ordinary people and conjured forth an amazing profusion of Gods and Demons apparently dwelling in astral realms with a social organisation paralleled to Earth's, almost every object, living or dead became animated with its own personal God. Popular legends immortalised persons of local interest and elevated them as Gods, just as in the West certain characters became canonised as Saints. It is difficult therefore to equate many of the multitudinous Chinese deities with Spacemen from the skies.

Our present-day astronomers, who reject the theory of continuous creation for expansion of the universe from the explosion of the infinitely dense primeval atom, may find some dubious encouragement in the old Chinese belief of Panku hatched as from an egg creating Heaven and Earth from Chaos, a myth which like their account of the Flood, the Chinese probably borrowed from the Indians and Babylonians. Taoist and Buddhist philosophers speculated further and taught the universe originated from Spirit, the Known from the Unknown, a conclusion which our own Science accepts.

Legends in the *Feng-shen-yen-i* tell of an Age of Wonder four thousand years ago narrated like fantasies of science-fiction in terms outside our present experience, approximating the air battles of the 'Mahabharata'. Rival factions fought for domination of China aided by Celestials, who took sides just like the Gods supporting the Greeks or the Trojans during the Siege of Troy. In modern terms we might imagine the Martians backing the Americans and the Venusians counselling the Russians in any future conflict of tomorrow; this prospect may not be quite so fantastic as it seems; awareness of the advent of the Spaceships today from at least two planets makes Extra-terrestrial interference in our partisan politics of Earth a fascinating possibility. Our science-fiction writers today with all their dazzling imagination developing the amazing scientific inventions transforming the world, would find their futuristic fantasies eclipsed by the enchanting wizardry of the old Chinese tales.

The Gods wielded marvellous weapons more sophisticated than our modern armaments today. No-Cha used his Heaven-and-Earth bracelet to defeat Feng-Lin, who vainly plunged into protective smoke-screen; later the hero on his Wind-Fire-Wheel vanquished Chang-Kuei-Feng summoning to his aid hosts of silver flying-dragons. Weng-Chung lashed Chi'ih with a magic whip but was routed by an irresistable yin-yang mirror radiating some deadly force. Wars were waged with the technology we credit to Spacemen; the combatants flashed dazzling beams of light, released poisonous gases, launched fire-dragons and globes of flame, hurled lightning-darts and thunderbolts; they practised biological warfare dropping capsules of microbes from celestial umbrellas, protected themselves by veils of invisibility and apparently possessed radar detection-images able to see and hear objects hundreds of miles away; almost identical technology to the weaponry detailed in the Sanskrit verses of the 'Mahabharata'.[130]

The ancient Chinese anticipated our modern chemists by compounding pills conferring immortality, rejuvenating tablets giving eternal youth; other drugs produced a state of hibernation with the body in suspended animation, which our space-medicine hopes to devise for immobilisation of our cosmonauts on years-long journey to the stars. The old alchemists are said to have produced a pill to annul the effects of gravity, powders turning rice-water into wine, and incense magically restoring aged people's sight. Such bio-chemical compounds with wondrous effects are also mentioned in the Sanskrit Classics. It is difficult to believe that a primitive agricultural community could acquire pharmaceutical knowledge surpassing our own chemists' today; such marvellous drugs surely hint at some transcendent science possibly from Spacemen?

China chose as her national emblem the Dragon, a symbol of profound significance. In antidiluvian times during the days of Atlantis, the night sky looked different; the Pole of the Heavens being Alpha-Draconis in the constellation of Draco not our present pole-star in Ursa Minor, the Little Bear; the Spacemen, Celestials with transcendent wisdom, who descended from the stars to teach mankind, were known to the Ancients as the Dragons or Serpent People. Serpents were worshipped by the Lemurians and Atlanteans as symbolising divine wisdom, millennia later this worship degenerated into serpent cults among native peoples all over the world. By some paradoxical inversion of thought, possibly a theological misinterpretation of the Serpent in the Garden of Eden, the serpent became associated with Satan and Emblem of Evil. Neolithic temples were approached by serpentine rows of columns, from Babylonia to Japan drawings of fiery dragons are found on baked tiles and silken tissues, flying fiery serpents were mentioned by Prophets in the Bible and were venerated in old Mexico. Welsh traditions assert that in the days of sun-worship in the reign of Prydain, Son of Aedd the Great, dragons carried the Children of the Goddess, Keridwen, to their home in the skies. Initiates in Egypt and India associated the Dragon King with Saturn, Father of the Gods; he had some mystical connection with King Arthur and the religion of the Celts.

More than any other nation the Chinese made the dragon a symbol of their civilisation; they believed the Celestial Dragon to be Father of their First Dynasty of Divine Emperors; the dragon's pictorial emblem closely influenced that uniquely fascinating Chinese art and in popular consciousness was regarded as inspiring divine beneficence to its Children in this Land of the Sun.

Zoologists doubt whether dragons ever existed; many million years ago the toothy pterodactyl appeared to resemble our concept of a flying dragon, none of those fearsome birds survived to historic times. Even our educated people today find it difficult to picture something they have never seen; all of us can describe an aeroplane with general agreement, but could we agree on a description had it not been invented? Tales from Antiquity all over the world correspond in uncanny similarity detailing the fire-breathing dragons roaming Earth, sea and sky. No people give such colourful descriptions, even drawings of dragons, as the Chinese. The ancient texts describe fantastic monsters, bodies covered with scales like armour, eyes flashing lightning, jaws belching flames, the great beasts roared on the winds to the heavens, plunged down to the ocean depths; their fiery breath shrivelled towns to ash; sometimes a dragon kidnapped a damsel and carried her off to its lair in the clouds.[131] Are we not reminded of those frightening tales of UFOS told by terrified peasants in South America today?

The Dragon Kings exercised supernatural powers, practised mesmerism and telepathy, were invulnerable to mortal weapons, lived and loved in eternal youth; they were said to dwell in enchanted palaces at the bottom of the sea but all owed allegiance to their Lord in the stars; they soared to the skies like flashing lights on rushing winds causing storms until the Earth roared. Seas could have meant the Waters of Space, although we are reminded of the many Spaceships today said to plunge to bases in our ocean depths. The Gods rode on dragons so did Emperors and holy men. Yu, the Founder of the Hero Dynasty, had a carriage drawn by two dragons; the Emperor Yoan claimed to be the Son of a Red Dragon. Ghosts wearing blue hats sometimes appeared on dragons. The souls of the Dead were conveyed to Heaven by the winged Gods. A Dragon is said to have appeared at the birth of Confucius. Could the illiterate Chinese of Antiquity imagine a dragon, could its concept permeate his consciousness, inspire his religion and art, impress his daily life, if this 'flying object' never existed?[132]

To students of UFOS these ancient descriptions of fiery flying-dragons viewed with our modern eyes seem strangely familiar; the fantasy fades and the picturesque dragon materialises into a spaceship. The texts of Ancient China tell in wonderful imagery of UFOS streaking through the skies, plunging the seas, terrifying peasants, scorched fortifications, shrivelling countrysides, kidnapping people or landing divine Strangers to inspire mankind. We are promptly reminded of the luminous flying object which on November 4th 1957 hovered over the Brazilian fort of Itaipu[133] and paralysed soldiers and electrical circuits with heat-rays, of the numerous individuals whose mysterious disappearances suggest celestial abduction, and of Orthon, the Venusian, who spoke to Adamski. The Celestials, the Dragons, the Sons of the Sun, the Spirits of Old China, were surely Spacemen.

Historical references to Chinese sightings are admittedly

scarce. That erudite researcher, Yusuke J. Matsumura, in the Cosmic Brotherhood Association's fascinating magazine, *Brothers*, Vol. 1, No. 2, states:

> 'You can also find the record of a kind in Wen Hien Tsung Kwao Encyclopaedia edited by the Ma Tsuanling Publishing Corporation saying that a comet-like substance was seen for two months in the era of the Former Han in the year 12 BC. There is another wheel of flame reported just in the Chinese way in the *Picture Dictionary of Foreign Affairs* compiled in 1932. It says that the wheels were attached to the coach at the angle of degrees toward the movement direction, quite different from those of ordinary carriages. A unique energy starting is hinted in the picture. It is said that a kind of vehicle called Kiryao available in the era of Yin was a white speckled animal-shaped flying device whose mane was red, eyes were gold, head looked like that of a rooster. It is said that if a man ride on its back he will live for 1,000 years. "The Book of the Mountains and the Seas", one of the famous Chinese mythical stories, tells that an androgyne who had only one arm and three eyes flew in a flying vehicle to the far away countries on the wind.'[134]

A Chinese Wood-cut from Tu Shu tsi Chang depicts Kikung's Flying Chariot.

The Chinese Emperor was believed to be a Descendant of the Sun God; Genghis Khan in crises prayed to the Sun for aid; for centuries the Mongolian Empire worshipped the Sun. Some early Christians are said to have believed that Christ was a Celestial from the Sun; a similar belief was held by the Chinese who probably originally worshipped Wondrous Beings from the Sun rather than the physical Sun itself. Yusuke J. Matsumura recalls:

> 'A personified sun was called a golden god in India, while the Chinese classics *Shi-Chi* and *Han-Shu* have a description of the "gold-coloured heavenly man" who had been heard of as long as 500 years between the age of Han and that of Tang. It is very significant that they used not "god" but "gold-coloured heavenly man".'

The tales of old China glow with magic, the legends suggest Wondrous Strangers with marvellous science living and loving and imparting their wisdom to those slant-eyed Children of the Sun.

CHAPTER EIGHT

Spacemen in Old Japan

The smiling Japanese bask in the belief that their earliest ancestors came from 'The Abode of the Gods' and worship their Mikado as direct descendant of Amaterasu, the shining Goddess of the Sun, Ruler of the High Plains of Heaven. Conscious of their divine origin, the Children of the Gods developed their exotic culture in splendid isolation, today beneath that astonishing westernisation transforming Japan the spirit of Bushido, a peculiar chivalry, still inspires superiority over lesser mortals of the world. These Sons of the Sun may never gain military dominance yet more than any other race they feel in their souls an affinity with Celestials, transcending the commoners of Earth, in their secret hearts the Japanese imagine themselves as Spacemen.

Ancient traditions teach that many thousand years ago the islands of Japan formed a distant colony of Lemuria,[135] Empire of the Sun; the early colonists, a white-skinned race, brought with them from the Motherland a highly developed civilisation, which preserved the basic Lemurian culture until the advent of the Europeans only a century ago. The Japanese flag, the Rising Sun, still symbolises the sacred emblem of drowned Lemuria. Like the Hindus, Chinese and Egyptians, the Japanese too boast twelve dynasties of Divine Kings reigning 18,000 years, suggesting domination by Spacemen.

Ethnologists agree that the first ancestors of the Japanese were the white-skinned Yamato,[136] who conquered the neolithic aborigines, the hairy Ainu, a primitive decadent race, who today are almost extinct. Millennia of inter-marriage with the yellow-skinned, high-cheek-boned, slant-eyed Mongols have produced that characteristic mutation we style as Japanese, but a surprising number look almost European. Linguistic analysis hazards the suggestion that the Japanese language has affinities with Babylonian and that the ideographic script exactly resembles Assyrian leading to speculation regarding the Tower of Babel and the Lost Tribes of Israel. Survivors of some great cataclysm in the Middle East three or four thousand years ago crossed Central Asia and sailed down the long Siberian rivers to those fragrant islands off the China coast; other Caucasians and Semites came by way of India, Malaysia and the Pacific. It has even been alleged that Jesus survived the Cross and died in Northern Japan, suggested by some curious Christian Sect existing centuries before the Portuguese missionaries landed there. Ancient tombs sometimes hold relics characteristic of the Mayas in Mexico, hardly surprising since there must have been some communications with the American Continent. Admittedly at this late date it is difficult to present solid facts but the accumulated evidence does tend to support the conclusion that about three thousand years ago, the age of Solomon, Troy, the 'Mahabharata' in India, King Bladud in Britain, Japan formed part of a world-wide culture, ruled and inspired by Men from Space.

Excavations of ancient dolmens and grave-mounds show that during the third millennium BC, the Yamato enjoyed a sophisticated culture displaying an artistry in delicate ceramics, resplendent armour and weapons of bronze and iron wrought with technical skill, exquisite mirrors and magnificent jewels rivalling the contemporary treasures of Ninth Dynasty Egypt. In Britain the sun saw no Stonehenge, a thousand years would roll by before Helen's beauty launched a thousand ships to burn the topless towers of Troy; near the city of Ur in Chaldea Abraham tended his flocks and talked to 'God', to Yahweh, who was to inspire his son, Israel, and the Children of Israel, through forty centuries of suffering. While 'Angels' (Spacemen?) saved Lot from the Sodom and Gomorrah they destroyed, spoke with Moses and the Prophets, the Yamato in their island of cherry-blossom continuing the civilisation of Lemuria, lost Empire of the Sun, must surely have welcomed these Men from the Stars.

In the prehistoric tombs are found 'haniwa', clay-figures of curious little people, these terra-cotta figurines called

Jomon Dogus have faces of Caucasian nobility not of oriental Mongol; archaeologists once believed them ceremonial substitutes for human sacrifice, lately their resemblance to the celebrated 'Martian' of the Tassili rock-paintings in the Sahara, to questionable petroglyphs in a cave near Ferghana in Uzbekistan,[137] and to Aztec figurines in old Mexico, suggests that these little men wore space-suits and helmets like Oannes, who according to Berossus taught the people of Babylon. Admittedly such Neolithic inscriptions may have been representations of the Sun God, however they might just as easily have been portrayals of actual Spacemen. The brilliant Japanese investigator, Yusuke J. Matsumura and his learned Colleagues of the Cosmic Brotherhood Association of Yokohama have made a profound study of the Jomon statuettes, reported in Vol. 2, Nos. 1-4 of their magazine *Brothers*.[138] Isao Washio in a convincing study notes that in the Tohuku Area statues appeared to be wearing 'Sun Glasses', those found in the Aomori Prefecture apparently had helmets and divers' suits; which closely resembled the suits worn by the American cosmonauts today. Yusuke J. Matsumura compared these statuettes with rock-paintings and carvings found in Fukuoka, Prefecture, Kyushu, Hokkaido, and in many other parts of Japan; similar reports were given by Dr Alexander Kasantzev, the noted Soviet investigator, who insisted 'Highly advanced creatures from Mars have visited the Earth many times until today'.

Evidence of Space Visitors in Antiquity may stare us in the face but some curious warp in our thought-patterns frustrates recognition, just as scientists with conditioned minds cannot accept the spaceships, so clearly seen by their own eyes. In a Chip-San tomb in the suburbs of Yamaga City, Kumamoto, Pref. Kyushu, a wall-painting dated about 2000 BC shows an ancient Japanese King holding up his hands to welcome seven Sun Discs, similar to prehistoric murals found in Etruria, India and Iran; another picture shows seven people holding hands in a large circle looking up at the sky evoking the Flying Saucers to appear in Izumizaki, Fukushima. Archaeologists had supposed such scenes symbolical of sun-worship but the new illumination of Extra-terrestrialism now suggests that these resplendent orbs represent spaceships revolutionising our conception of the past. The very word 'Chip-san' in the pre-Ainu language is said to have meant 'the place where the Sun came down'.

C.B.A. Scientific Research Division report in *Brothers*, Vol. 2, Nos. 1-4 that:

> 'The Bay of Yatsushiro-kai in Kyushu, Japan, has been called the Shiranuhi-kai Sea or the Sea of Unknown Fire from ancient times, and a mysterious fire which has never been understood appears there on a specific day, or towards daybreak on August 1st by the old calendar.'

Modern research suggests that this 'Unknown Fire' is a magnetic fire lighted from Space and is completely controlled by the Flying Saucers and is connected with those Wheels of Fire visiting our Earth throughout history.

In a special study of sun-disks, winged and wingless, Yusuke J. Matsumura draws convincing comparison with sun-disks of Ancient Egypt, Iran and Israel, proving apparently that the disks represented not the sun but the Flying Saucers. It is intriguing to note that the sun-disks found in ancient tombs had remarkable similarity to the circular symbols of the world's air-forces today, a truly prophetic coincidence. Dr Yoshiyuki Tange states in *Brothers*, Vol. 2, Nos. 1-4:

> 'It was found that those Sun Marks drawn inside ornamented ancient tombs in Kyushu are the symbol of Flying Saucers thousands of years ago. In the meanwhile, a legend of the Ainu people in Hokkaido says that Okikurumi-kamui (Ancient Ainu God) descended from the heavens and landed at Haiopira in Hokkaido aboard a shining Shinta (Ainu cradle) on which we discovered the same Sun Mark. He had taught a righteous way of life to the Ainu people and destroyed an evil God; he was a Space Brother himself who visited from outer Space aboard a Flying Saucer called Shinta by Ainu people in those days.'

The Cosmic Brotherhood Association of Yokohama offer a revolutionary interpretation of the stone circles found all over the world.

> 'As can be seen on the Cosmic ruins of ground pictures of twofold or threefold circles found at Kawagoe City in Saitama Prefecture in Japan or Glatley, Little Cursus,

Dorchester of England; and the Stonehenges also in England, or the Stone Circle at Oyu, Akita Pref. in Japan, the CIRCLE and SPACE are closely connected with each other.'

The earliest literature of Japan, the *Kojiki*[139] or *Record of Ancient Matters* in archaic Japanese characters based on centuries-old tales preserved by bards and public-reciters was composed in AD 712 by an imaginative Court Chamberlain, Hiyeda-No-Are, a man of marvellous memory and infinite invention; he dictated a confusion of myths and legends to a noble O-No-Yasumaro, who dedicated his masterpiece to the formidable Empress Gemmyo. Shortly afterwards in AD 720 the same traditions were revised and rewritten in classical Chinese, the language of scholars, in thirty books known as the *Nihongi* by Prince Toneri and Yasumara-Futo-No-Ason, and duly dedicated to the Empress proving for all posterity her divine descent from Amaterasu, Goddess of the Sun.

The Japanese treasure these old Chronicles but we in the West are hardly impressed. Imagine our Western culture without any written records until the eighth century, the age of Charlemagne! No Bible, no Homer, no Aeschylus, no Aristotle, no Virgil, no Cicero, no Pliny, none of those classical philosophers who have shaped our arts, our science, our politics, our civilisation! The glory of Greece, the splendour of Rome, would be but a dream, a haunting memory, half-forgotten like Atlantis. The ancient tombs of Japan reveal no hieroglyphics, no Rosetta Stone as unlocked the Wonders of Egypt, the cherry-blossom does not fall on tablets of clay like that cuneiform library describing the deeds of Assyria; civilisations must have risen and fallen of which no memory remains. How many great Kings, noble philosophers and ladies of beauty lived and loved in old Nippon; what bloody wars stained their sun-drenched soil, whose ghosts paused for life's brief hour then flitted down the dusty corridors of time never to return? For the Japanese today Antiquity bequeathes no legacy to match our heritage from Greece and Rome, no revelation comes from God to rival our Christianity, no words from wise philosophers to copy our democracy; the writings of Japan go back only twelve centuries, to the

Japanese mind the Ancient World remains a Realm of Myth.

The Japanese may retort that England's earliest literature apparently dates from the same time as their own with 'Beowulf' and the 'Histories' of Bede; the whole world forgets that the Druids of Britain were said to have stored centuries-old manuscripts in Ogham script in the great Library at Bangor, destroyed in AD 607,[140] when the Archbishop and his Culdee priests were massacred by the Saxons allegedly on encouragement from Rome. Geologists believe our Earth to be about 4,500,000,000 years old, palaentologists now credit Man with an existence of twenty million years, it would seem likely therefore that civilised communities inhabited the flower-decked islands of Japan many thousand years ago. The Yogis teach of Four Root Races prior to our own; traditions of all nations hint at recurrent cycles of humanity destroyed by cataclysms, then mankind reborn spirals higher in the chain of evolution until periodically halted by further catastrophes, preludes to still higher rebirth. Though basically true this cosmic progression is retarded by temporary regression in evolution, for some of our primitive peoples in Africa and America now seem to be degenerate descendants of great nations whose civilisation millennia ago transcended our own today; the fragmentary wisdom of witch-doctors and weather-magicians appears to be remnants of world-wide psychic science far in advance of our twentieth-century.

If our own civilisation is destroyed by some nuclear war, all the world's books might perish in the holocaust, in five thousand years' time of our arrogant century nothing might remain except a few garbled race-memories telling of ancestors who misused the forces within the atom and encompassed their own destruction. Today we gaze baffled at the inscriptions of the Etruscans, the hieroglyphics of Mexico, the Linear 'A' script of Knossus, the curious symbols of Mohenjo-Daro; maybe tomorrow archaeologists will discover pictographs of old Japan, which some computer can interpret to illume in wonder a glorious panorama of the past?

The Japanese myths in the *Kojiki* were doubtlessly modified by prevailing Chinese influence, these traditions of former ages being compiled to glorify the reigning Dynasty and promote national unity. The *Nihongi* or *Chronicles of Japan* shortly afterwards interpolated pure Chinese elements and a vague chronology but the proximity of Japan to the Chinese mainland makes it almost certain that the two countries shared similar experiences with Spacemen. Contributory sources were the *Kogushui* or *Gleanings from Ancient Stories* compiled in AD 807, supplemented by the *Norito,* very ancient liturgies, collected in AD 927 in the *Engi-shiki* or *Ceremonies of the Engi Period.* Secondary material of particular fascination were the *Fudoki* or *Provincial Gazeteers* begun in AD 713, which collated the legends and folk-lore of local regions in colourful profusion, literary and romantic edification was added by the *Manyoshu,* an assembly of poetry made in the eighth century containing poems recited hundreds of years earlier. All these sources combine to furnish the intrancing but bewildering mythology of Japan.

The *Kojiki* states that in the Beginning Chaos was in the form of an Egg containing all the germs for Creation; a remarkable resemblance to our own cosmological theory of the expansion of the universe from the original superatom. On the Plain of High Heaven were born the Deities, Master-of-the-August-Centre-of-Heaven, the High-August-Producing-Wondrous-Deity and the Divine-Producing-Wondrous-Deity, after this Holy Trinity appeared several Celestial Divinities. From a reed-shoot which sprang up when the Earth was young and drifted like a jellyfish more Deities evolved. The Celestial Divinities command Izanagi and Izanami standing together on the Floating Bridge of Heaven (a Spaceship?) to plunge a heavenly jewelled Spear into the chaotic brine, which they stirred until the liquor curled and thickened and drops of brine dropping back into the ocean self-condensed into the island of Onogoro. Izanagi and Izanami descended on the island making it the centre of the land and erected a Heavenly-August-Pillar and a Hall-of-Eight-Fathoms. The Celestial Pair longed to unite to bring forth people for their island but to their mutual embarrassment found themselves ignorant of the delectable art of intercourse, hardly surprising since the natural method had not been attempted. Somewhat frustrated the two Divinities watched a wagtail jerking its head and tail to and fro', thus inspired Izanagi and Izanami invented the joys of sexual intercourse for the delight of future lovers; they copulated incessantly producing numerous deities, also islands, seas and mountains, even fire. The birth of the God of Fire so burned the private parts of the August Female that Izanami died leaving Izanagi the joyless task of creation alone; from his left eye was born the Sun Goddess, Amaterasu, the Heaven Shining, from his right eye, the Moon God, Tsuki-Yami, and from his nose, Susanowo, the Impetuous Male.

Izanagi made Amaterasu Ruler of the High Plain of Heaven and gave Susanowo domination over the Sea. The Impetuous Male in disappointment demanded to meet his Mother, Izanami, in the Nether Distance, when his Father refused permission and banished him Susanowo ascended to Heaven to take an uproarious farewell of his Sister. Alarmed at his boisterous approach, Amaterasu drew her bow and sun-tipped arrows, the sight of this lovely Amazon aroused romantic emotions in the Impetuous Male, who amicably suggested they swear an oath to avoid contention and disport their energies in getting together in the pleasant pursuit of procreating posterity, a suggestion which appealed to Amaterasu, who gave birth to more Divinities. The behaviour of the Impetuous Male grew worse, he trampled down the neat division of the rice-fields in heaven, filled in the irrigation ditches and defiled the Royal Palace with excrement. Finally this outrageous God flayed a heavenly piebald colt which fell backwards, breaking a hole through the palace roof on to women weaving heavenly garments, causing the flying shuttle to wound them fatally in their private parts causing their deaths. Susanowo was censured by the High Council of the Gods, heavily fined, the nails of his fingers and toes were torn out and he was cast down on to Korea, then he crossed to Izumo bent on more misadventures. The outraged Sun Goddess retired to a cave leaving the world to darkness and disaster until at last the other Deities somewhat alarmed seduced her out with a mirror, so light returned to the Plains of High Heaven and the Cherry Blossom Land below. This diverting tale is the Japanese version of the War in Heaven between the Gods and the subsequent cataclysm on Earth; a much more charming description than the horrific conflict in the skies depicted by the Chinese.[141]

In this mythological age of the Gods Japan was known as Toyo-ashi-hara-no-chio-aki-no-mizuho-no-kuni, Land-of-Fertile-Reed-Plains-, Of-Bounteous-Harvests-and-Full-Rice-Ears.[142] For centuries the country was called Yamato; the province where the first Emperor Jimmu built his Capital in 660 BC; the Chinese character 'Wa' representing 'Yamato' also meant 'dwarf' so in AD 670 the Japanese asked the Chinese to refer to their country as 'Nippon' or 'Nihon', 'Sun Origin' or 'Place of the Sunrise', the Chinese and Koreans rendered the characters for 'Nihon' as 'Jih-pen', later westernised as 'Japan', still symbolising the basic Japanese belief of their celestial origin from the Sun, which we today construe as originating from Spacemen.

Susanowo, the 'Fallen God' banished from Heaven for his impetuosity, rescued a Princess from an eight-headed, eight-tailed dragon; he built a fine palace at Suga in Izuma married her and had many children; other Deities descended to Earth and mated with the daughters of men, confirming similar traditions of celestial intercourse with mortals mentioned in 'Genesis' and the Sanskrit and Greek classics. The most famous son of Susanowo, called Okuninushu became Ruler of the Land, outraging the Gods in Heaven by ignoring their authority and following his own plans for Empire. The Gods aggrieved at this rebellion sent down various Deities to restore their sovereignty without success; these emissaries were overcome by the insurgents on Earth. Finally the Sun Goddess in Takama-ga-haro, the Plain of High Heaven, commanded her grandson, Ninigi-no-Mikoto, to take possession of the Land of the Reed Plains and restore celestial rule. Prince Ninigi and Ame-no-Koyana, the ancestor of the courtier families, carried in the Floating Bridge of Heaven (a Spaceship?) descended on the peak of Takachiho of Hyuga in Kyushu opposite the land of Kara (Korea). With him Ninigi brought from Amaterasu, the Sun Goddess, the Sword, the Mirror, and the Jewel, the three symbols of sovereignty; he soon conquered surrounding regions and established rule in Japan, of the divine Dynasty.

A fascinating account of the descent of the Celestials in spaceships to conquer the Earth abandoned to iniquity and sin is given in the *Nihongi*[143] or *Chronicles of Japan* from earliest times to AD 697. The following brilliant translation by W. G. Aston, Book One, p. 110, seems vaguely similar to Genesis, Hesiod's *Theogony* and conflict between Gods and mortals suggested in the 'Mahabharata'.

In 667 BC the *Nihongi* describes the Emperor Kami-Yamato-Ihare-Biko.

'When he reached the age of forty-five, he (the Emperor) addressed his elder brothers and his children saying, "Of old our Heavenly Deities, Taka-mi-musuli-no-Mikoto and Oho-hiru-me-no-Mikoto, pointing to this Land of Fair Rice Ears of the Fertile Reed Plain gave it to our Heavenly Ancestor, Hiko-ho-no-ninigi-no-Mikoto. Thereupon Hiko-ho-no-ninigi-no-Mikoto throwing open the barrier of heaven and clearing a cloud-path urged on his superhuman course until he came to rest. At this time the world was given over to widespread desolation. In this gloom therefore, he fostered justice and so governed this western border (Kyushiu). Our Imperial ancestors and Imperial parent, like Gods, like Sages, accumulated happiness and amassed glory. Many years elapsed. From the date when our Heavenly Ancestor descended until now is over 1,792,470 years. But the remote regions do not yet enjoy the blessings of Imperial rule. Every town has always been allowed to have its Lord and every village its chief, who each one for himself makes division of territory and practises mutual aggression and conflict.

'"Now I have heard from the Ancient of the Sea, (Shiho-Tsutsu-no-Ogi) that in the East there is a fair land encircled on all sides by mountains. Moreover there is there One who flew down riding in a Heavenly Rockboat. I think that this land will undoubtedly be suitable for the extension of the Heavenly task (i.e. for the further development of the Imperial power) so that its glory should fill the universe. It is doubtless the centre of the world. The Person, who flew down, was, I believe, Nigi-hoye-lu' (means 'Soft-swift-sun') Why should we not proceed thither and make it our Capital?

'"All the Imperial Princes answered and said 'The truth of this is manifest. This thought is constantly present to our minds also. Let us go thither quickly.' This was the year Kinoye Tora (51st) of the Great Year".'

The claim that Heavenly Ancestors descended from the skies in a Heavenly Rocking-Boat nearly two million years ago will certainly amuse the scientists who believe civilisation was evolved by Man himself a few thousand years since, yet the landing of Spacemen in remote Antiquity is confirmed by occult teachings, the sacred Books of Dzyan and legends all over the world.

Before Ninigi departed for Earth he was told that at the crossroads of heaven was a strange Deity, whose nose was seven hands long and from whose mouth and posterior a light shone. This odd description may refer to a Celestial in a spaceship from another Galaxy since none of the Gods knew anything about him. The Goddess, Uzume-hime, approached the Stranger, who said his name was Saruto-hiko; he, too, was proposing to land in Japan and offered to make the Goddess a Flying Bridge or Heavenly Bird-Boat.

Prince Ninigi's great grandson, the Emperor Jimmu, invaded Naniwa (Osaka) to conquer the Yamato but at first was repulsed by the Tsuchi-gumo, the 'Earth-Spiders', who were the original hairy Ainu aborigines not descended from the Gods. After final conquest the Emperor climbed a mountain and gazing at the fair scene exclaimed, 'Umashi kunizo Akitan-no-toname-suru ni nitari!' ('Beautiful country! It looks like copulating dragonflies!') So to the Spacemen looking down Japan must be 'Akitsushima'—'Land of the Dragonfly.'[144]

The Japanese believe that in 660 BC the Heavenly Deities came to the assistance of the Emperor Jimmu to vanquish his foes, reminiscent of those Heavenly Twins, Castor and Pollux, who in 498 BC aided the Romans to defeat the Tusculans at Lake Regillus.[145] The support of the Deities to Jimmu was hardly decisive, for history adds that the Emperor invited eighty 'Earth Spiders' to a banquet and had them assassinated before conquest was complete.

In 9 BC, according to Yusuke J. Matsamura,[146] 'Japanese aborigines called Kumaso were prospering in Kyushu, exceeding the Yamato Dynasty in influence, when there appeared nine suns in the sky depicting signs of much chaos in the land on February 10th and the Yamato Dynasty was thrown into an uproar in the eighteenth year of the Emperor Suinin. These nine suns, or Sun Disks as the Ancients called them, were Flying Saucers.'

The nine suns over Japan in 9 BC parallel the ten suns

over China in 2346 BC when nine were shot down by the 'Divine Archer', Tzu-yu. On both occasions Earth was torn with discord; the appearance of the nine 'Saucers' in 9 BC was believed by the peaceful aborigines, who worshipped the Sun Disks, to be a sign of heavenly displeasure against the Yamato Dynasty for their mental and physical enslavement of their subjects.

The *Nihongi,* Book One, p. 226 states about AD 200:

> 'Moreover there was in the village of Notorita a man named Hashiro-Kuma-Washi ('Feather-White Beer-Eagle'). He was a fellow of powerful frame, and had wings on his body, so that he could fly and with them soar aloft. Therefore he would not obey the Imperial commands but habitually plundered the people.'

Even the divine Leonardo da Vinci failed to master the problem of human flight. Could this fellow have been a Spaceman?

During the early centuries when 'Angels' were aiding King Arthur and Merlin, later St Patrick and St Germanus in their struggles with the Saxons invading Britain, on the other side of the world the Gods assisted the Japanese. About AD 220 the famous Empress Jingo invaded Korea, the Deities went before and after the expedition. The King of Silla (Korea) was overwhelmed by these divine invaders and promptly surrendered.

An intriguing reference to an apparent Spaceman in AD 460 appears in the *Nihongi,* Book One, p. 342.

> '4th Spring. 2nd month. The Emperor (Oho-hatsuse-Waka-Taka) (*Note:* 'Hatuse' is a place in Yamato, 'Waka-taka' means 'young, brave') went a hunting with bows and arrows on Mount Katsuraki. Of a sudden a tall man appeared, who came and stood over the vermilion valley. In face and demeanour he resembled the Emperor. The Emperor knew that he was a God and therefore proceeded to inquire of him saying, "Of what place art thou, Lord?" The tall man answered and said, "I am a God of visible men (i.e. One who has assumed mortal form). Do thou first tell thy princely name and then in turn I will inform thee of mine." The emperor answered and said, "We are the Waka-taka-no-Mikoto". The tall man next gave his name saying, "Thy Servant is the God, Hito-Koto-Mushi" (Literally 'One Word Master. The Deity who dispels with a word the evil and with a word the good). He finally joined him in the diversion of the chase. They

pursued a deer and each declined in favour of the other to let fly an arrow at him. They galloped on hit to hit, using to one another reverent and respectful language as if in the company of Genii. Herewith the sun went down and the hunt came to an end. The God attended on the Emperor and escorted him as far as the water of Kume. At this time, the people all said, "An Emperor of great virtue!".'

Is this tale not evocative of the Celestials and Princes of Ancient India, the Gods and Mortals of Greece, the Angels and Kings of the Old Testament? Are there not faint echoes of those congenial meetings between Spacemen and their 'Contacts' alleged today?

This Visitation in AD 460 was mentioned again about a hundred years later in the *Nihongi* in AD 556 during the reign of the Emperor Ame-Kuni-Oshi-Hiroki-Hiro-Niha.

'The Minister, Soga, said, "Formerly in the reign of the Emperor Oho-hatsuse, thy country was hard-pressed by Koryö (Korea) and was in an extremely critical position like that of a pile of eggs." Thereupon the Emperor commanded the Minister of the Shinto religion reverently to take counsel of the Gods. Accordingly the priests by divine inspiration answered and said, "If after humble prayer to the Deity, the Founder of the Land (Oho-na-mochi-no-Kami) thou goest to the assistance of the Ruler who is threatened with destruction, there will surely be tranquillity to the State and peace to the people." Prayer was therefore offered to the God, aid was rendered, and the peace of the country was consequently assured. Now the God who originally founded the country is the God who descended from Heaven and established this State in the period when Heaven and Earth became separated, and when trees and herbs had speech. I have recently been informed that your country has ceased to worship him. But if you now repent your former errors, if you build a shrine to the God and perform sacrifice in honour of his divine spirit, your country will prosper. Thou must not forget this".'

The *Tau-shö* commentator here quotes the following curious statement from a work called *Sei-to-ki*.

'In the reign of the Emperor Kwammu (AD 782-806) we (Japan) and Korea had writings of the same kind. The Emperor disliking this burned them and said, "These speak of the God who founded the country and do not mention the Gods, our ancestors." But possibly this only refers to the legend of Ton-kun, which the "Tongkom" gives as follows: "In the Eastern Region (Korea) there was at first no chief. Then there was a Divine Man, who descended under a sandal-tree, the people of the Land established him as their Lord. He was called Tan-kun (Sandal-Lord) while the country received the name 'Choson' (meaning 'freshness'). This was in the reign of the Chinese Emperor, Tong-Yao (2357-2258 BC) the year Mon-Shem. The capital was at first Phyong-yong; it was afterwards named Pek-ok (the white hill). In the 8th year (1317 BC) of the reign of Wu-Ting of the Shang Dynasty he entered Mount Asatai and became a God".'

This Divine Being was believed to have lived a thousand years in Korea, then was apparently translated to the skies. We are reminded of the mysterious Count St Germain, who is said to have visited Earth during several centuries, returning periodically to the planet Venus. We wonder?

The only Star God mentioned in Japanese myth is Kagase-Wo, described as a conquered rebel, possibly referring somewhat vaguely to some conflict in Space; he is stripped of the titles Kami (Deity) and Mikoto (August) affixed to the names of other Gods. The only stars mentioned in the *Kojiki* or *Nihongi* are Venus, Mars, Jupiter, the Pleiades and the Weaver or the Star Alpha Lyrae, the latter being connected with a Chinese legend.

The *Nihongi*, Book Two, p. 122 intrigues us with the tale of a remarkable infant prodigy born on the 10th day of the fourth month AD 593 during the reign of the Empress Toyo-Mike-Koshiki-Yo-Hime.

'The Imperial Prince Mumayodo-no-Toyo-Sumi was appointed Prince Imperial. He had general control of the Government, and was entrusted with all the details of administration. He was the second child of the Emperor Tochibane-no-Toyo-hi. The Empress-Consort, his Mother's name, was the Imperial Princess Anahohe-Hashito. The Empress Consort on the day of the dissolution of her pregnancy went round the forbidden precinct inspecting the different offices. When she came to the Horse Department and had just reached the door of the stable she was suddenly delivered of him without effort. He was able to speak as soon as he was born and was so wise when he grew up that he could attend to the law-suits of ten men at once and decide them all without error. He knew beforehand what was going to happen. Moreover he learnt the Inner Doctrine (Buddhism) from a Korean Priest named Hye-Cha and studied the Outer Classics (Chinese Classics) with a Doctor called Hok-ka. In both of these branches of study he became thoroughly proficient. The Emperor, his father, loved him and made him occupy the Upper Hall, South of the Palace. Therefore he was styled the "Senior Prince Kamu-tou-miya-Mumaya-do-Toyo-to-mimi" (The Honourable-Upper-Palace-Stable-Door-Off-spring-Of-The-Empress-Toyo).'

While his name might have been apt, the Prince must surely have needed all his serene philosophy to tolerate such a title!

AD 619: A bright object like a human figure was seen over the Gamo River, Central Japan. (*Brothers*, Vol. 3, No. 1)

Like the Romans, Mayas and Chinese the old Japanese paid superstitious respect to prodigies in earth and sky, which the soothsayers prognosticated as heralding fateful events.

AD 650: According to the *Nihongi*, Book Two, p. 241, the Emperor Ame-Yorudzu-Toyo-Lu declared:

'When a Sage Ruler appears in the world and rules, the Empire is responsive to him and manifests favourable omens. In ancient times during the reign of Changwong of the Chou Dynasty, a ruler of the Western Land (China) and again in the time of Ming-Ti of the Han Dynasty, white pheasants were seen. In our Land of Japan during the reign of the Emperor Hamuto a white crow made its nest in the Palace. In the time of the Emperor Oho-sazaki (Ojinn Tenno AD 271) a Dragon-horse appeared in the west.'

A dragon-horse had wings on its head; it crossed water without sinking and appeared when an illustrious sovereign was on the throne. This may have been a UFO but was probably a comet like 'a long star' seen in the south in AD 634 during the reign of Emperor Okinaga-Tohashi-hi-Hiro-Nuka, which the people called a besom-star. Three years later in AD 637 the *Nihongi*, Book Two, p. 168, reported:

'A great-star floated from East to West and there was a noise like that of thunder. The people of that day said it was the sound of a falling star. Others said that it was earth-thunder. Hereupon the Buddhist Priest, Bin, said, "It is not the falling star but the Celestial Dog, the sound of whose barking is like thunder".'

A week later there was an eclipse of the Sun.

The learned Priest Bin was doubtlessly misled by *The Classics of the Mountains and Seas,* a very ancient Chinese book which said:

> 'At the Heaven-Gate mountain there is a red dog called the Celestial Dog. Its lustre flies through Heaven and as it floats along becomes a star of several tens of rods in length. It is swift as the wind. Its voice is like thunder and its radiance like lightning.'

This description suggests a cigar-shaped spaceship!

The Celestial Dog was Sirius but this classical reference to a star which floated, elongated, glowed red, moved swiftly, sounded like thunder and flashed radiation, parallels the great Mother-Ships seen high in our own skies today.

A commentary in the *Nihongi* states:

> 'The Celestial Dog or Tengu of modern Japanese superstition is a winged creature in human form with an exceedingly long nose, which haunts mountain-tops and other secluded places.'

Students of UFOS at once recognise the resemblance of this apparition to the Spacemen mentioned in the Classics and which are alleged to scare peasants in France, America and Brazil today. Spaceships in Biblical times landed among the mountains, whither the 'Angels' summoned Moses and the Prophets to receive divine revelations; most countries have at least one sacred mountain associated with the manifestations of the Gods.

The 'exceedingly long nose' of the 'winged creature in human form' no doubt referred to some headpiece with breathing apparatus, for to some Extra-terrestriala our oxygenated atmosphere may be poisonous; we are reminded of Oannes, a Being with the body of a fish, who according to Berossus taught the Babylonians the arts of civilisation, his likeness to a fish probably denoted the Stranger was wearing a Spacesuit, perhaps one of those Jomon Dogu 'pressure suits' reproduced in the various statuettes found all over Japan? Since the long-nosed winged creature gave rise to a superstition it would suggest that his manifestations in the mountains of Japan were not infrequent throughout several centuries showing regular surveillance of the Children of the Sun.

In November AD 1837 'an intruder, an uncatchable monster of superhuman powers, was prowling the lanes of Middlesex in England. According to J. Vyner in his fascinating article in the *Flying Saucer Review*, May-June 1961:

> 'The intruder was tall, thin and powerful. He had a prominent nose and bony fingers of immense power which resembled claws. He was incredibly agile. He wore a long flowing cloak of the sort affected by opera-goers, soldiers, and strolling actors. On his head was a tall, metallic-seeming helmet. Beneath the cloak were close-fitting garments of some glittering material like oilskin or metal mesh. There was a lamp strapped to his chest. Oddest of all: the creature's ears were cropped or pointed like those of an animal.'

The old Duke of Wellington, who had routed Napoleon at Waterloo, took a couple of pistols and in true fox-hunting style set out to snare this Springheeled Jack who jumped over hedges and houses with effortless ease, but after a few months tantalising the honest gentry, scaring wenches with eyes like red balls of fire, the apparition vanished to re-appear in 1880, 1948, 1953 and in America.

Perhaps the winged creature of the ancient Japanese Classics had wearied of the cherry-blossom and sought the more exciting suburbs of the West?

> AD 638: 'On the 26th day of the first month of Spring a long star appeared in the north-west. Priest Bin said that it was a besom-star. When it appeared there was a famine.'

Astrologer Bin probably saw a comet. The *Nihongi*, Book two, p. 169, delights future UFO students by recording in

> AD 640: 'On the 7th day of the second month of Spring, a star entered the moon.'
> AD 642: 'In Autumn, 9th day, 7th month, during the reign of the Empress Ame-Toyo-Tokaro-Ikashi-hi-Tarashi-Hime a guest star entered the moon.'

Chinese history records that Venus entering the moon was looked upon by the diviners as portending mortality among the people. It is significant that Venus was the only star worshipped by the Aztecs in Mexico with great veneration to which the bleeding hearts of captives were offered in sacrifice. Association of Venus with malevolence towards Earth may have been some half-hidden race-memory of War with Invaders from that lovely planet mentioned in the Greek and Sanskrit Classics.

The Japanese believed in Demons similar to the Asuras or 'Rebel Gods' described in the 'Rig Veda'; the Gandharvas—Celestial Warriors, Garudha—the monstrous 'man-bird', sky-ship of Indra, and Aerial Beings resembling those 'proud Demons in glass ships' mentioned in 'Orlando Furioso', Canto 1, Stanza 8, by Ariosto, Poet of the Italian Renaissance. *Nihongi,* Book Two, p. 272, mentions:

> AD 661: 'In Autumn, 1st day, 8th month. The Prince Imperial in attendance on the Empress's remains returned as far as the Palace of Ihase. That evening on the top of Mount Asakura there was a Demon (note, or "Spirit") wearing a great hat, who looked down on the funeral proceedings. All the people uttered exclamations of wonder.'

This manifestation recalls AD 1099 when the Crusaders were besieging Jerusalem. Matthew of Paris in *Historia Anglorum* wrote that a radiant Knight waving shining shield suddenly appeared on the Mount of Olives and beckoned the discouraged Crusaders to launch a new attack. Students of UFOS will at once remember the amazing incident on June 26th, 1959 in New Guinea when the Rev. William Booth Gill,[147] an Anglican Missionary, beheld a huge disc with two pairs of legs pointing diagonally downwards, four men on the 'deck' waved back to him. AD 661 Japan, AD 1099 Jerusalem, AD 1959 New Guinea! Are these friendly Spacemen always watching us?

Three years after this sighting in Japan in AD 664 according to Bede's *Ecclesiastical History,* Book Four, Chapter 7,[148] a light from heaven shone on the Nuns in the cemetery of the Monastery at Barking on the River Thames, then moved over to the other side, shone on the Monks, then withdrew to the skies.

August 11 AD 671: 'Flaming object was seen flying to north from many countries in Japan, one year before the war of the Jinshin.'
October 1 AD 679: 'Cotton-like matter ("Angel Hair") about 5 to 6 foot long fell over Naniwa, former name of Osaka, and was drifted by the wind here and there.' (*Brothers*, Vol. 3, No. 1).

The seventh century apparently witnessed world-wide UFO activity. The celestial lights recorded by the Anglo-Saxons appeared over Japan. The compilers of the *Nihongi* anticipated our own Charles Fort[149] and quoted many fascinating phenomena.

AD 680: '11th month, 1st day. There was an eclipse of the Sun. On the 3rd day there was a brightness in the East from the hour of the Dog to the hour of the Rat. (8 p.m. to midnight.)'
AD 681: '9th month, 16th day. A Comet appeared, on the 17th day the planet Mars entered the moon.'
AD 682: '8th month, 3rd day. The Korea guests were entertained in Tsukushi. On this evening at twilight a great star passed from the East to the West.'
AD 682: '8th month, 11th day. A thing appeared in shape like a Buddhist baptismal flag and of a flame colour. It floated through the Void towards the north and was seen by all the provinces. Some said that it sank into the sea off Koshi. On this day a white vapour arose on the Eastern Mountain four fathoms in size.

'On the 12th day there was a great earthquake.

'A day later the Viceroy of Tsukushi reported a sparrow with three legs. On the 17th day there was another earthquake. On this day there was a rainbow at dawn right in the middle of the sky and opposite the sun.'

It is noteworthy that in 'Prodigiorum Libellus' Julius Obsequens records bright lights over Ancient Rome shortly preceding earthquakes, and since 1947 observers have noted UFOS in the heavens prior to earthquake activity, confirming reports by alleged Spacemen that their Spaceships monitor Earth's magnetic field and show great concern over apparent fault zones in our Earth's crust.

AD 684: 'Autumn, 7th month, 23rd day. A comet appeared in the North-west more than ten feet long.'
AD 684: '11th month, 21st day. At dusk seven stars drifted together to the North-east and sank.

'11th month, 23rd day. At sunset a star fell in the quarter of the East as large as a jar. At the hour of the Dog (7-9 p.m.) the Constellations were wholly disordered and stars fell like rain.

'11th month. During this month there was a star which shot up in the zenith and proceeded along with Pleiades until the end of the month when it disappeared.'

AD 692: Autumn. '7th month, 28th day. Reign of Empress Tokama-No-Hara-Hiro-No-Hime. The Imperial car returned to the Palace. On this night Mars and Jupiter approached and receded from one another four times in the room of one pace, alternately shining and disappearing.'

The sightings chronicled in the *Nihongi* have continued through the Middle Ages until modern times. The Cosmic Brotherhood Association of Yokohama record at least seventy intriguing celestial phenomena from AD 858-1832. In the nineteenth and twentieth centuries these mysterious visitations have increased until today the serene skies of Japan seem haunted by Spaceships; sensitives claim friendly communication with Extra-terrestrials like their ancestors in Antiquity.

The Japanese *Historical Records* tell how the Emperor Hwang desiring to bring down a dragon to ride on its back, first gathered copper, a metal associated with the planet Venus, on a mountain, then cast a tripod. Immediately a dragon winged down to him; after the Monarch had used the 'God' as an airship, seventy of his subjects went for a flight in it too.[150]

Shinto, or Kami-no-Michi, the Way of the Gods, permeates practically every aspect of Japanese life, although Buddhism, particularly the enlightenment of Zen, profoundly influences the arts and sciences, inspiring all Seekers for Truth.[151] There are many thousands of Gods in Shintoism, which embraces ancestor-worship and the cult of nature-spirits making the Japanese mind receptive to the existence of life throughout the universe, dwellers in other dimensions and Spacemen from the stars. The Shinto system has remarkable affinities with the Druidism of Ancient Britain. The Japanese like the Celts believed in the sanctity of royal ancestral Beings, memories of the Golden Age of the Space Kings. Even today most Japanese will venerate their Mikado as Descendant of Amaterasu, Goddess of the Sun.

Today the Japanese treasure the glorious past and

through their Cosmic Brotherhood Association are planning the golden future, when sunny Japan will lead all humanity to wondrous friendship again with our Brothers from Space.

CHAPTER NINE

Space Kings in Ancient Egypt

Egypt! Land of wonder, mystery and magic. For unknown centuries the massive Pyramids, the inscrutable Sphinx and those mighty temples down the Nile, have dominated the minds of men; their silent grandeur evoking echoes of a glorious, grandiose Antiquity, the presence of proud Immortals, that Golden Age of the Gods when Earth was young. Those colossal ruins from a past far remote intrude into our present like symbols of some Galactic Race, their aura of power and spiritual strength radiate a message men cannot read; solitary they stand in alien isolation lording the sands beyond space and time waiting for Man to raise himself to understanding. Such awesome majesty reveals a greater, nobler race of Beings transcending mortal man, the Celestials, who taught civilisation to Earth, those Spacemen from the stars.

Today our sophisticated world has lost its sense of wonder, that divine expectancy of soul transmuting the cold relics of the past to warm and passionate life. Our soulless twentieth century conditioned by science and socialism to esteem our age with all its faults as the highest peak in human endeavour, derides Antiquity as dismal ignorance, forgetting that true civilisation matures within the soul not by super-bombs. We, who ring the Moon with rockets and challenge the stars, scorn the Sages of the past. What if the secrets of Ancient Egypt spell some dazzling revelation transforming Man's future? Suppose conventional views are wrong? Our world cries out for compassion. Should we not seek inspiration from the stars?

The few millennia which we imagine to mark the history of Man upon our Earth, are determined by the various objects discovered by archaeologists, dated by radiocarbon potassium-argon or other techniques, confirmed by contemporary records, if any exist; of the vast aeons of human evolution preached by the palaeontologists nothing is known. Scientists now concede that civilisations on other planets are not synchronous with our own; in some star-systems people may be thousands, even millions of years more advanced than we are; it is possible that in ages past Spacemen exploring our edge of the Galaxy landed on Earth and obedient to the Cosmic Law taught primitive Man the beginnings of culture, perhaps ruled as Kings, then left to sow the seeds of civilisation elsewhere. Such a claim is hardly science-fiction since in the centuries to come it is the intention of future cosmonauts to scatter the doubtful blessings of Earth on every star in sight.

Egyptologists have dedicated their lives to studying the sands of the Nile, archaeologists of genius subjecting their finds to scholarly insight have revealed a brilliant panorama of Ancient Egypt, the splendour of the Pharaohs, the wisdom of the priests, the wondrous heritage bequeathed to Greece and Rome, profoundly influencing our civilisation today. Champollion's decipherment of the Rosetta Stone illumined a lost world. Sir Flinders Petrie with his spade unearthed proud history; scholars from a dozen countries patiently resurrected a glowing living picture for seven thousand years of civilisation. Seven thousand years! Herodotus wrote the Egyptians believed themselves to be the most ancient of mankind. What happened in Egypt before history?

Occult traditions preserve esoteric knowledge handed down by countless Adepts from remotest Antiquity illuminating vast epochs of Man's evolution far beyond the limited range of factual archaeology. Such revelations are not acceptable to science, which must follow its own strict methodology of facts, experience and proof, yet unless we dismiss most of the truly great Thinkers of the past as vain dreamers merely because they adopted a thought-pattern different from ours, we must surely lend some credence to their teachings, especially when it is extremely unlikely that written evidence from remote times will ever be found.

The historian today finds it difficult to understand our own troubled century; he is rightly sceptical of the wisdom of mystics outside his rational discipline, yet he should bethink that in ages to come our modern world may become as little known as lost Atlantis, a possibility frightfully real. If a nuclear war or cosmic cataclysm ravaged our Earth today, fires, floods and earthquakes might destroy all written records, topple our proud buildings to dust, and stun the minds of men in a trauma obliterating all memories of catastrophe; the few survivors would sink to barbarism in frantic struggle for survival amid a shattered world, too shocked to brood on the horrors of the past. When at last generations later scholars turned to study our twentieth century, of our proud culture nothing might remain. Troy vanished from history; classical Professors swore the City of Priam was Homer's dream until untutored Schliemann unearthed Helen's jewelled diadem; Pompeii and Herculaneum buried by ashes from Vesuvius, which suffocated that erudite Admiral Pliny in AD 79, for eighteen hundred years became legends. Who knows in ages to come our great metropolises today may be a myth? In ten thousand years archaeologists in the absence of artifacts may deny we existed; the only memory of our tempestuous times may lie in the wisdom of Adepts. It is wrong to ridicule the old traditions; surely science should consider them.

The Secret Wisdom teaches that tens of thousands of years ago, Lemurians, humanity's Third Root Race, migrated from their drowned continent across India to form settlements on the Upper Nile; chronology becomes confusing. Berossus claimed that a King ruled Babylon 432,000 years before the Flood; if so, a contemporary monarch must have reigned in Egypt; a claim we may accept or reject.

The next great cycle of humanity evolved in Atlantis, an island continent in the Atlantic Ocean more than 200,000 years ago. Few subjects arouse such passion as Atlantis—unless it be Flying Saucers!—about two thousand books have been written proving its existence and almost as many refuting it; advancing knowledge in geology and climatology suggests that sooner or later science will accept the truth of lost Atlantis as it will of the UFOS haunting us today.

Under beneficent guidance of Initiates in the Solar Wisdom from Venus, the Atlanteans attained a wonderful civilisation at its zenith about 90,000 years ago, based on a psychic science controlling etheric forces; Adepts developed supernormal mental powers conjuring aid from elementals in other dimensions. From their Space Teachers the Atlanteans learned Sun worship, adoration of the Solar Logos for whom the visible Sun is only a symbol; they believed in life after death, reincarnation of the soul in the flesh through the Chain of Worlds to attain perfection in at-one-ment with God dreaming the living universe. Scientists mastered a power called Vril causing levitation, they wielded a titanic sidereal force producing those annihilating blasts so vividly described millennia later in the 'Mahabharata'. The first rulers, divine Kings from Space, brought intercourse between the planets; there was possibly communication with Wondrous Beings on Sirius, which had such mystical fascination for peoples of the ancient world. Earth might have been an outpost of the Galactic Federation, as the recondite knowledge of some Initiates might suggest.

Astronomers are often astounded when their recent discoveries appear to have been anticipated by ancient primitive peoples without our modern telescopes; they cannot attribute such knowledge to direct observation so tend to dismiss the fact as unscientific, especially if there appears to be no obvious explanation. Jean Servier, Professor of Ethnology at Montpelier, draws attention to the Dogon on the cliffs at Bondiagara in Mali, south of Egypt, who have long been aware that Sirius has two satellites, the periodicity of each was known; they say that the star's close companion is composed of a metal called Sogolu more lustrous than iron, one grain of this substance is 'as heavy as four hundred and eighty donkey loads'. Such a belief may be ridiculed at first as superstition, then astronomers recall that in 1862 Alvan G. Clark using an eighteen-inch refractor discovered a companion to Sirius with an apparent density fifty thousand times as heavy as water, a box of matches of this matter would weigh a ton; this wonder is explained by nuclear physicists as implying that its atoms are stripped of electrons, nuclei being closely packed together, a plausible explanation not proved. Our astronomers now agree to a second satellite of Sirius but unlike the Dogon have not determined its orbit. Initiates in the

Sudan venerate Sirius as the progenitor of our own solar system confirming most ancient occult wisdom. The Shilluk tribe in South Africa have always called Uranus[152] 'Three Stars', a planet with two moons, yet until its rediscovery by Herschel on 13th March 1781 Uranus remained unknown to modern astronomy. The Tuaregs in the Sahara Desert share a world-wide series of legends concerning Orion and the Pleiades. Such deep knowledge of the stars handed down by generations of primitive peoples for thousands of years can surely have been obtained only from astronomers in some long-vanished civilisation like Atlantis or from Spacemen?

The Atlanteans rebelled against the Space Overlords, who returned to the stars; possibly the titanic war between the Gods and the Giants revealed in the Greek legends and the 'Ramayana'! For thousands of years volcanic activity rent the continent into islands, which subsided into the sea; foreseeing eventual destruction many Atlanteans emigrated eastwards to the Nile Valley or westwards to America building colonies like their Motherland; the cultural similarities particularly in architecture, metallurgy and religious beliefs between the Egyptians and the Aztecs suggest common origin in Atlantis. Later in vain attempts to avert their doom the priests perverted their psychic wisdom to black magic, the Kings launched maritime invasion of the Mediterranean countries and North Africa to meet final defeat by heroic Athens. About 11,000 BC the last great island of Poseidon was destroyed by volcanic eruption; proud Atlantis sank in the ocean, soon to be a vague memory still cherished by many believers but derided by official science, which cannot find proofs. There are occult traditions that Spaceships from Venus winged down to save Chosen Initiates from destruction; this salvation seems perpetuated in the Christian teachings of the 'Angels of the Lord', who will descend from Heaven to rescue the righteous on Doomsday; which the Scriptures graphically describe like the flames and floods destroying evil Atlantis.[153]

Little evidence of this lost continent remained for posterity. Atlantis was mentioned in the 'Book of Dzyan' written originally in Senzar, later translated into Chinese, Tibetan and Sanskrit. The most valuable record of Atlantis, preserved by Plato in *Timaeus* states that his famous ancestor, Solon, visited Egypt about 590 BC and discussing Antiquity with Priests of Sais in the Nile Delta was told by a priest of very great age, that in ancient days

> '. . . the Atlantic was navigable from an island situated to the west of the straits which you call the Pillars of Hercules; the island was larger than Libya and Asia put together. . . . Now, the island was called Atlantis and was the heart of a great and wonderful empire, which had rule over parts of the continent: and beside these, they subjected parts of Libya as far as Egypt, and of Europe as far as Tyrrhenia.'

The Priest described how the vast power of the Atlanteans tried to subdue Egypt and Greece but the Athenians and their allies defeated the invaders and liberated the conquered peoples.

> 'But afterwards there occurred violent earthquakes and floods, and in a single day and night of rain all your warlike men in a body sank into the earth and the island of Atlantis in like manner disappeared beneath the sea.'

Solon wrote 'Atlantikos', an unfinished poem, probably based on Egyptian writings about Atlantis, which he mentioned, unfortunately both were lost; yet who knows what records may be unearthed from the sands of the Nile? Initiates believe that the Atlanteans deposited time-capsules detailing their history, when our world is ready, these secrets will be disclosed. Such an idea seems science-fiction; so many cosmic truths have been revealed to Man this century; the proof of Atlantis may be found in Egypt.[154]

Civilisation in fantastic Antiquity is scorned by Egyptologists, who establish chronology by dead-reckoning of dynastic lists of Kings found in inscriptions from some known date fixed in contemporary Babylonian history or from the Sothic cycle, a period of 1,460 years, the coincidence of the rising of Sirius and the first day in the civil calendar. Dating of organic objects such as wood or bone is effected by measuring their content of radio-carbon 14, the age of pottery by thermo-luminescence method determining the output of light emitted by the clay when heated, which has relevance to its age. Even the great experts differ. Petrie[155] dated the First Dynasty of Menes as commencing in 4777 BC, Breasted as 3400 BC, some authorities suggest 2850 BC, Egyptologists do recognise predynastic Stone Age cultures established from pottery and flints found in ancient graves varying in sophistication from the superior Gerzean to the primitive Tasian periods,[156] the earliest Neolithic times are vaguely estimated as 5 or 6000 BC, which seems just yesterday compared with the 20,000,000 BC alleged by Dr L. S. B. Leakey[157] for the fossilised jaw fragments of Kenya Pithecus Africanus found in January 1967 in Kenya.

It is unlikely that Egyptologists will extend their knowledge very much further back in time, radiocarbon dating can go back only to about 30,000 BC; the deep sands make dating by geologic methods practically impossible. While we honour the devoted Egyptologists for their brilliant discoveries, we must recognise the limitations of archaeology in establishing remote Antiquity and consider the slender resources left to us in literature and legends.

The oldest and most fascinating description of Ancient Egypt was preserved by Herodotus,[158] born to a noble family in Halicarnassus in 484 BC. To escape the city-tyrant, he went into exile and in 443 BC sailed from the Piraeus on his epic travels to the Scythians in the Black Sea, Syria, Babylon and spent some time in Egypt, exploring the Nile as far south as the first cataracts near Elephantine. His main purpose was to immortalise the conflict between Greece and Persia but with journalistic insight he discourses entrancingly on the nations of Antiquity giving a captivating, colourful, picturesque account as fresh today as when it was written twenty-four centuries ago. Herodotus, the 'Father of History', related such wonders that doubting scholars dubbed him the 'Father of Lies'; modern archaeology and research increasingly prove him a painstaking reporter of truth. This wonderful travelogue teeming with personal anecdotes, tit-bits and gems from the Intelligentsia in the countries he visited, was written with such wit and sparkling narrative that when Herodotus read his work to the assembled Greeks at Olympia, the young Thucydides was moved to tears and inspired to write his own great *History*.

Herodotus's shrewd observation and his witty style delight us today. Writing of the Egyptians, Book Two, Chapter 35:

> 'The men carry burdens upon their heads; but the women carry them on their shoulders. And the women piss standing upright, but the men sitting. They seek easement in their houses, but eat without in the ways, saying that what things are shameful but necessary should be done in secret, but what things are not shameful, in public. . . . They knead dough with their feet but clay with their hands. Other nations leave their privy members as they were at birth, except so many as have learnt from the Egyptians; but the Egyptians circumcise themselves. Each man weareth two garments, but each woman one only.'

In Book Two, Chapter 2, Herodotus states:

> 'Now until Psammetichus reigned over them, the Egyptians believed that they were the eldest of all men.'

Later in Book Two, Chapter 43:

> 'But Heracles is a very ancient god of the Egyptians; as they themselves say, it was seventeen thousand years to the time when Amasis began to reign since the twelve gods, whereof they hold Heracles to be one, were born from the eight.'

Herodotus was clearly awed by the antiquity of the Egyptians for he pursued his enquiries closely, writing in Book Two, Chapter 142:

> 'Thus far the Egyptians and their priests told the story. And they shewed that there had been three hundred and forty-one generations of men from the first king unto this last, the priest of Hephaestus. And in these generations there were even so many (high priests and) kings. Now three hundred generations of men are equal to ten thousand years; for three generations of men are an hundred years. And in the forty-one generations which yet remain in addition to the three hundred, there are one thousand and three hundred and forty years. Thus in eleven thousand and three hundred and forty years they said that no god in the form of a man had been king; neither spake they of any such thing either before or in after time among those that were kings of Egypt later. (Now in all this time they said that the sun had removed from his proper course four times; and had risen where he now setteth, and set where he now riseth; but nothing in Egypt was altered thereby, neither as touching the river nor as touching

the fruits of the earth, nor concerning sicknesses or deaths.'

In the eleven thousand years prior to Herodotus, the axis of our Earth became considerably displaced four times, the sun twice appearing to rise in the west, such movement in the Earth's crust, confirming ancient traditions of the Hindus, must have caused world-wide catastrophes. Probably only national pride made the Egyptian priests swear their country was not affected; destruction and chaos caused by the catastrophes surely account for the lack of records of civilisations in the remote past.

Herodotus mentioned that a few years earlier the priests at Thebes showed another Greek traveller, Hecateus, the historian, three hundred and forty-five colossal wooden statues, which Herodotus saw with his own eyes; all were high priests, father and son in unbroken descent. These Piromis were 'noble and good but far removed from gods but they said that in the time before these men the rulers of Egypt were gods, who dwelt among mankind! And the last of them that reigned over Egypt was Orus, the son of Osiris, who the Greeks name Apollo, who reigned over Egypt after putting down Typhon'.

Realising that the immense periods of time he quotes may be questioned, Herodotus believes the Egyptian Priests adding:

> 'Now Osiris is Dionysus in the Greek tongue. . . . Even Dionysus, the younger of them, is reckoned to have been fifteen thousand years old in the time of King Amasis. These things the Egyptians say they know certainly because they have always counted the years and kept records.'

The extreme antiquity of the Egyptian God-Kings is confirmed by Manetho born about 300 BC at Sebennytus on the west bank of the Damietta section of the Nile. He rose to be High Priest in the temple of Heliopolis. Herodotus in Book Two, Chapter 3 writes: 'For the men of Heliopolis are said to be the most learned of the Egyptians'. All the ancient world recognised Heliopolis as a great seat of learning and the University of Egypt; in the famous temple Manetho must have had at his disposal records of all kinds, papyri, hieroglyphic tablets, wall-sculptures and innumerable inscriptions, and above all perhaps the advice of his learned colleagues trained in the millennia-old traditions. Manetho, familiar also with the new philosophies and scientific teachings of the Greeks, was uniquely endowed to write a 'History', with such abundant material and erudite critics at his disposal. He wrote this history in the Greek for the enlightenment of scholars during the reign of the first Ptolemy, Philadelphus; it contained an account of the different dynasties of the Kings of Egypt compiled from genuine documents; with such intelligentsia supporting him Manetho must surely have written with the utmost accuracy. Unfortunately for posterity the work is lost with all its sources and probably perished in the flames when Julius Caesar accidentally burned the great library at Alexandria, destroyed by megalomaniac Roman Emperors or burned by fanatical Christians and by the Arabs in AD 642, of this valuable history only a few extracts are preserved in works by Julius Africanus and Eusebius.

The extant fragments of Manetho's *Aegytica* state:

> 'The first man (or God) in Egypt is Hephaestus, who is also renowned among the Egyptians as the discoverer of fire. His Son, Helios (the Sun) was succeeded by Sosis, then follow in turn Cronos, Osiris, Typhon, brother of Osiris and lastly Orus, son of Osiris and Isis. They were the first to hold sway in Egypt. Thereafter the kingship passed from one to another in an unbroken succession down to Bydis through 13,900 years. After the Gods, Demi-Gods reigned for 1,255 years and again another line of Kings held sway for 1,817 years then came thirty more Kings of Memphis reigning for 1,790 years, and then again ten Kings of this reigning for 350 years. Then followed the rule of "Spirits of the Dead" for 5,813 years.'

Perhaps 'Spacemen' were regarded as 'Spirits of the Dead'?[159]

At Thebes, city of Amon, proud capital of Pharaoh's Egypt, the Nile still dreams of ancient glory sighing for those dawns when white-robed Priests chanted hymns to Ra, the Sun-God, gilding the Earth with light. On the east bank rise forlorn the shattered colonnades of Rameses II, mute symbols of the past, seven miles to the west lies the

Valley of Kings, site of the royal tombs, their treasures rifled long ago, with the solitary exception of Tutankamun's, whose golden splendour revealed the wonders of old Egypt. Amid the many ruins along the palm-fringed river stands the well-preserved temple of Hathor, Goddess of Love, at Denderah, a sanctuary of the Osirian Mysteries taught by Adepts from dim Antiquity; this Secret Wisdom inspired most of the great philosophers and broods behind our materialistic civilisation today.

On the ceiling of the Denderah temple was carved a Zodiac, or Celestial Day, so remarkable that the original ceiling was removed and re-erected in Paris and a copy substituted.[160] The Signs of the Zodiac portray a configuration of the stars about 90,000 BC for the astrological symbols according to the Precession of the Equinoxes denote the passage of three-and-a-half Great Years, each 25,800 years, so that ninety thousand years have elapsed since this 'Star Clock' was recorded. The original temple long since crumbled to dust but the unique Zodiac was copied by Initiates eager to preserve this witness from the past. Such antiquity staggers our modern minds, conditioned to limit civilisation to a few millennia, yet similar zodiacs on temples in Northern India and on clay tablets found in Chaldea confirm this symbol of Atlantean times, the Children of the Sun colonising old Egypt.

Simplicius in the sixth century AD wrote that he had heard that the Egyptians had kept astronomical observations for the last 630,000 years, even if he meant months this would mean 52,500 years; Diogenes Laertius dated astronomical calculations by the Egyptians to 48,863 years before Alexander the Great, and Martianus Capella stated that the Egyptians had secretly studied the stars for 40,000 years before revealing their knowledge to the world.

Pre-dynastic rulers are apparently confirmed by the Turin Papyrus and the Palermo Stone.

Panodorus, an Egyptian monk about AD 400 wrote:

> 'From the creation of Adam, indeed down to Enoch and to the general Cosmic Year 1,282, the number of days was known in neither month nor year but the Egregori ("Watchers" or "Angels") descended to Earth in the general Cosmic Year 1,000, held converse with men and taught

them that the orbits of the two luminaries being marked by the twelve Signs of the Zodiac are composed of 360 parts.'

Berossus about 330 BC gives details of six dynasties or six gods, confirmed also by the *Chronicle* of Mabolas, who claimed support from the wise Sotates and Palaephotus, in the third and fourth centuries BC.[66] The same source declared that in the 24th Dynasty during the reign of Bocchoris, 721-715 BC a 'lamb' speaking with human voice prophesied the conquest and enslavement of Egypt by Assyria and the removal of her Gods to Nineveh; about sixty years later the terrible Ashurbanipal and his hordes sacked Thebes. Bocchoris was spared this disaster for Manetho adds, tersely: 'Sabacan, having taken Bocchoris captive, burnt him alive'.

This remarkable 'lamb' was said to have on its head a royal 'winged' serpent, four cubits in length. The 'winged serpents' of the Aztecs are now believed to have been spaceships. Traditions state that in the early eighth century BC the Roman King, Numa Pompilius, practised magic arts and held converse with the Gods. Was the 'talking lamb' who warned ill-fated Bocchoris the 'God' who spoke with Numa and Elijah? Was he a Spaceman?

Syncellus wrote:

> 'Among the Egyptians there is a certain tablet called the *Old Chronicle* containing thirty dynasties in 113 descents, during the long period of 36,525 years. The first series of Princes was that of the Auritae, the second was that of the Mestroens, the third of the Egyptians. The *Chronicle* runs as follows:
>
> ' "To Hephaestus is assigned no time, as he is apparent both night and day. Helios, the Son of Hephaestus, reigned three myriads of years. Then Cronus and the other twelve Divinities, reigned 3,984 years; next in order are the Demi-Gods number eight, who reigned 217 years".'[162]

The ancient Phoenician writer, Sanchoniathon, composed a history in the Phoenician language hundreds of years before Christ. The work was translated into Greek by Philo Byblus about AD 80; the history is lost, only fragments are preserved by Eusebius in the first book of his *Praeparatio Evangelica*. Sanchoniathon wrote:

© Lorillard 1973
Micronite filter.
Mild, smooth taste.
America's quality
cigarette.
Kent.
KENT
KING SIZE
King Size or Deluxe 100's.
Kings: 17 mg. "tar,"
1.1 mg. nicotine;
100's: 19 mg. "tar,"
1.3 mg. nicotine;
Menthol: 18 mg. "tar,"
1.2 mg. nicotine
av. per cigarette,
FTC Report Feb. '73.

KENT
MENTHOL
WITH
THE FAMOUS MICRONITE FILTER
DELUXE LENGTH
KENT MENTHOL
Try the crisp, clean taste
of Kent Menthol.
The only Menthol with the famous Micronite filter.

'Contemporary with these (Taautus-Thor-Thoth-Hermes) was one Elianu, which imports Hypsistus ("The Most High") and his wife called Beruth, and they dwelt about Byblus of whom was begotten Epigenus or Autichton, whom they afterwards called Ouranos (Heaven). . . .'

Then follows a description of war between Ouranos and his son, Cronus. Aided by the magic of Hermes, Cronus conquered Ouranos and also his own brother, Atlas, a remarkable parallel with the well-known Greek legends.[163]

The reference to Hyspsistus ('The Most High') equates with the Elohim and suggest Spacemen.

Herodotus, Manetho, Berossus, Panodorus, Syncellus, Sanchoniathon, and who knows how many hoary scribes, whose writings perished in flames long ago, confirm those wondrous tales of other lands across the world. We recall the 'Ramayana' of India, the *Shoo King* of China, the *Nihongi* of Japan, poets in all these countries marvelled in glowing pictures of glorious Immortals warring and wenching in earth and sky, their divine dynasties ruling mankind in a Golden Age. Thousands of miles away the sands of the Nile disgorge their stones, papyri and parchments telling of dynasties of God-Kings who governed Old Egypt. Because the spade unearths no Space Kings dare any archaeologist deny their existence? Our palaeontologists play with bones, can they measure wisdom from half a skull and two back teeth? The historians of Egypt like the Chroniclers of other countries agree that their first Kings were wondrous Beings from the stars.

Pharaoh was worshipped as the Son of Horus, descended from Ra, the Sun-God; Egyptian religion taught that Pharaoh was God; all the land and all the people belonged to him because he was the Giver of fertility, the Preserver of all.

An inscription of the Twelfth Dynasty states:

'Adore the King! Enthrone him in your hearts!
He makes Egypt green more than a great Nile. He is Life.
He is the One, Who creates all which is, the Begetter,
Who causes mankind to exist.'[164]

The people believed the Pharaoh to be divinely born on a loftier plane and descending to Earth to rule their lowly selves.[165] Ibn Aharon with remarkable insight reveals that Court ritual obliged Pharaoh in his personal habits to act like a God and to take nourishment and perform his natural functions in secret as though his glorious person lived in perfection.

Who were those God-Kings of Ancient Egypt? Surely they were Spacemen?

CHAPTER TEN

Space Gods of Ancient Egypt

The Ancient Egyptians believed in the 'First Time', an age when the Gods actually lived on Earth in a Golden Age of universal love and justice. Pharaoh himself was known to be a God, for thousands of years the country flourished as a theocracy; its politics, arts, science and medicine, completely dominated by the Priests. The average Egyptian, conditioned by religion, felt his whole existence in earthly life and after death controlled by scores of Gods in divine judgement, each ruling some aspect of Man's cosmic pilgrimage. Such a confusing pantheon of deities appears to have accumulated comparatively late in Egyptian culture, often being local Gods attaining national prominence or personalities in legends assuming reality like the characters in our own television serials today. The Egyptian mind, incapable of abstract thought, felt obliged to worship animal forms as representing different qualities of the Gods, who were themselves manifestations of the One Supreme God beyond Man's understanding.[166] Plutarch in *De Iside et Osiride* reveals that the famous Egyptian Mysteries enshrined the Truth behind the fables and the myths of popular worship, and by degrees in their secret rites led Initiates to Cosmic Light.

The earliest religion of Egypt appears to have been the worship of Earth-Father and Sky-Mother, a curious reversal of the Earth-Mother, Sky-Father, basis with its suggestion of Space Kings common to most religions of the early ancient world; later the Universal Mother brought forth the Sun God, Ra, who became regarded by the Egyptians as the Creator and Ruler of the world. This symbolism of Mother and Son is worshipped to this very day in the Divinities of the Virgin Mary and Jesus Christ. In its purest esoteric form Christianity perpetuates the Atlantean and Egyptian religion of the Sun.

Many thousand years ago when our whole Earth was ruled by Space Kings, vassals to a planetary Overlord, possibly from Venus, the Extra-terrestrials no doubt worshipped the Great Spirits residing on our Sun; the Illumined would realise that even those Wondrous Beings were subordinate to the Transcendent Soul dominating the Galaxy, Who was Himself dwarfed by the Ineffable Splendour of still greater Emanations of the Absolute. The ordinary Egyptian like common men everywhere unversed in the Cosmic Mystery would worship the physical Sun as the source of heat and light and venerate the Space Kings as divine; after the Extra-terrestrials departed from Earth later generations with confused race-memories coalesced the Sun and the Space Kings as Horus immortalised in legends, whose fantasy summarises half-forgotten history. Mythologists with brilliant insight have resolved the Egyptian myths into religious systems propounded by theologians of genius into subtle doctrines, which do such honour to the human intellect but since all these great and learned men were conditioned to believe life existed only on Earth their interpretation of ancient religion brought only glimmerings of light. Our new knowledge of the inhabited universe and Spacemen visiting our planet in ages gone now revitalises the old legends with pregnant wonder and synthesises the ancient beliefs in shining Illumination miraculously linking the glorious Past with our dazzling Future.

That great Egyptologist, Sir Wallis Budge, in his commentary on *The Book of the Dead*[167] states:

> 'From a number of passages drawn from texts of all periods, it is clear that the form in which God made Himself manifest to Man upon Earth was the Sun, which the Egyptians called Ra, and that all other Gods and Goddesses were forms of him.'

It is surprising that only fragments of the life, suffering, death and resurrection of Osiris are found in Egyptian texts; the only coherent story is given in Plutarch's *De Iside et Osiride*. Plutarch states that the Goddess Nut was beloved by Geb, from their union issued Osiris. Nut was identified by the Greeks with Rhea, daughter of Uranus; Geb was the Greek Cronos (Roman-Saturn.) Symbolism of the Greek legends and Hesiod's *Theogony* suggest that Uranus and Cronos represent successive dynasties of Space Kings; Uranus was dethroned by Cronus, who was later defeated by Zeus (Jupiter) and imprisoned in Britain. Osiris, being 'grandson' to Uranus and 'son' to Cronos was probably a Spaceman; it is said that in the ancient Egyptian language OS-IRIDE meant 'mouth of the iris'[168] or 'the voice of the light', which could probably be associated with a transcendent Being from a spaceship; there is an intriguing resemblance to Ahura-Mazda of the Persians, who may be considered as a Sky God or a Spaceman.

Osiris appeared as a culture-hero, who taught the Egyptians civilisation, then journeyed through many lands to civilise other peoples suggesting a world-wide culture in far ancient times with communication between Earth and other planets.[169] In his absence, his wife, Isis (Greek-Selene), Moon Goddess, or Hera, (Juno) wife of Zeus (Jupiter) ruled Egypt in great prosperity. When Osiris returned his jealous brother Set (Greek-Typhon) tricked him into lying down in a chest and being thrown into the Nile floating eventually to Byblus in Syria. Isis, mourning her husband, found the chest and returned it to Egypt, then set out to search for their missing son, Horus; meanwhile Set discovered the body and rent the corpse of Osiris in fourteen pieces, which he buried in various parts of Egypt. Isis greatly distressed gathered these fragments and over each spot built a temple. Osiris conquered death and became King of the Spirit world. This resurrection of Osiris was the inspiration of the Egyptian belief in life after death proclaimed in their funeral rituals and texts. The symbolism of the Dying King became associated with the magic of the growth of seed and plant life and became connected with the cult of Tammuz, Adonis and Jesus Christ.

Horus, identified with the Greek, Apollo, originally a totally distinct figure from Horus, Son of Osiris, was a Solar God, whose emblem from the very earliest times was the hawk or falcon. 'Hor' in Ancient Egyptian sounded like a word meaning 'Sky', the hieroglyphic symbol for God resembled a falcon on its perch.[170] This symbolism suggests a Space Visitant whose spaceship to the naïve Egyptians would resemble a falcon. In the Pyramid Texts, Har Wer, or Horus the Elder, fought endless battles with Set, later inscriptions ascribed the conflict as between Horus, Avenging Son of Osiris, and the malevolent Set.

Legend avers that when Ra-Harakhte ruled in Upper Egypt, he ordered his son, Horus, to vanquish the enemies assailing him. Horus in the form of a winged disk flew in the sky and routed the evil forces of Set. Horus-Behutet, the great celestial God, was generally represented as a winged sun-disk, battle scenes sculptured in the temple of Edfu show Horus like a huge falcon leading the army of Ra-Harakhte campaigning against the hordes of Set. In his battles Horus received aid from the ibis-headed Thoth, possibly a symbolism for a Spaceman, who devised magic weapons. The conflict between Horus and Set appears reminiscent of the celestial war in Hindu Mythology with Rama defeating the wicked Ravan wielding devastating bombs. At Shais, Horus appeared as a great shining disk with wings or radiant plumage accompanied by the Goddesses Nekhbet and Uazet in the form of crowned snakes, symbolism suggestive of spaceships.

Some Seekers for Truth have made a most profound study of the papyri rolls placed in Egyptian tombs between the knees of the dead and have found a remarkable comparison between Egyptian beliefs and the teachings attributed to Christianity thousands of years later. Huhi, the Father in Heaven, a title of Atum-Ra appears to be the Christian Ihuh or Jehovah; Ra, the Holy Spirit is God, the Holy Ghost. Iu or Horus, the manifesting Son of God, is Jesus the manifesting Son of God. The ever-coming Messu or Child as Egyptian became the Hebrew Messianic Child. Isis was the Virgin Mother of Iu or Horus, Mary, the Virgin Mother of Jesus. Osiris, whom Horus loved, equates with Lazarus, whom Jesus loved. Osiris prayed that he be buried speedily, Jesus begs that his death be effected quickly. Anup, the Precursor of Horus, Anup the Baptizer, became John, the forerunner of Jesus the Christ, John, the Baptist. Horus was known as the Gracious Child, the Fisher, the Lamb, the Lily, the Word made Flesh, the Krst, the Word made Truth, he came to fulfil the Law, Horus was the Link. Jesus was the Child Full of Grace, the Fisher, the Lamb, He was typified by the Lily, Jesus was the Word made Flesh, Jesus, the Christ, the Doer of the Word, Jesus came to fulfill the Law, Jesus was the Bond of Union.[171] Such comparison between Horus and Jesus requires close, dispassionate study; there is so much in the New Testament, indeed in the whole Bible, which is open to question. The Dead Sea Scrolls throw doubt on much we have been taught; perhaps the origins of the Christ Mystery are to be found in the Book of the Dead, which was probably inspired by ancient Hindu teachings originally derived from the Sun Worship of Atlantis and Lemuria.

Sculptures at Karnak and Thebes depict sun disks surrounded by serpents or 'spirits', winged disks made of wood covered with shining gold were placed over the doors of temples as potent symbols. A similar disk with wings among the Assyrians and in Iran represented the great Ahura-Mazda; the Cherubim which expelled Adam and Eve from the Garden of Eden were probably flying-disks not Angels. On the other side of the world the emblem of the Inca was a great golden disk, symbol of world-wide sun-worship.

An intriguing symbol of the Egyptian legends was the Divine Eye. Atum, the Creator, sent his Eye to rescue his son, Shu, God of the Air, and Tefnut, his sister-wife; when mankind plotted against Ra he hurled his Divine Eye against his enemies; on one occasion the Eye wandered away and Ra was obliged to send his magician, Thoth, to bring it back; another legend describes how the Eye fled from Egypt to Nubia and was brought back by Anhur meaning 'sky-bearer'. The Goddess, Hathor, sometimes identified with the star, Sept, Sothis or Sirius, but more often associated with Venus-Aphrodite, at the command of Ra took the form of the Divine Eye and waged war upon mankind; she slew so many men that Ra feared all humanity would perish, so he poured seven thousand jars of beer upon the fields; Hathor paused to admire her beautiful reflection in the beer then quenched her thirst, became drunk and abandoned the slaughter. The Eye of Horus caused immense devastation among the forces of Set, who at one time gained possession of it, but Horus soon regained the Eye again. The Eye became identified with the

Uraeus, viper symbol of the divine serpent, the talisman on the forehead of Kings.[172]

Egyptologists find themselves still puzzled by the significance of the Divine Eye; some identify the Eye of Ra as the Sun and the Eye of Horus as the morning-star, Venus, others argue the Eyes refer to the Moon. Students of UFOS at once recognise the Eye as a Flying Saucer, a Spaceship which would surely appear to the unsophisticated Egyptians like the Eye of a God in the sky. Hindu, Japanese, Greek and Celtic mythologies all tell of celestial battles waged by Divine Beings in solar disks or 'Eyes', which associate with the Egyptian legends describing the War in Heaven. The 'Uraeus' or 'divine serpent' recalls the 'fiery serpents' of Israel, the 'feathered serpents' of Mexico and the 'fire-breathing dragons' of China, possibly symbolism for Spaceships.

The most fascinating God of Old Egypt was surely Thoth,[173] who despite his bird's head to our scientific twentieth-century must seem the most human. Thoth, identified with Hermes, Messenger of the Gods (called by the Greeks 'Hermes Trismegistus'—'three times very great' and identified with the planet Mercury) said to be the son of Ra, was believed to be the Divine Intelligence, who created the Universe by the sound of his voice alone. This profound conception coincides with the Hindu tradition of Brahma uttering the sacred sound AUM, and with the Jewish teachings of God pronouncing the Word; this most ancient thought summarises our own ultra-modern science, which asserts that the whole universe and its myriad dimensions of matter is a manifestation of infinite vibrations. Thoth was the God of earth, sea and sky, inventor of all the arts and sciences, Lord of magic, patron of literature, scribe of the Gods, inventor of hieroglyphics, Author of Magical Books, founder of geometry, astronomy, medicine, music and mathematics, Master of occult Mysteries, recorder of history, Clerk to the Judges of the dead. Occult traditions teach that Thoth was an Atlantean, who aided in the building of the Great Pyramid in which he secreted tablets of wisdom and magical weapons. He is said to have fashioned and serviced the 'Eye of Horus'; he was Lord of the Moon. Was he an Extra-terrestrial who had landed there?

Sanchoniathon, the Phoenician historian, wrote:[174]

> 'The God, Taautus, (Thoth) contrived also for Cronus, the ensign of his royal power having four eyes in the parts before and in the parts behind, two of them closing as in sleep and upon the shoulder four wings, two in the act of flying and two reposing as at rest. And this symbol was that Cronus, whilst he slept, was watching and reposed while he was awake. And in like manner with respect to his wings, that while he rested, he was flying yet rested while he flew! But to the other Gods there were two wings only to each upon his shoulders to intimate that they flew under the control of Cronus, he had also two wings upon his head; the one for the most governing part the mind, and one for the sense.'

This confusion seems like the bewildered impression an ignorant shepherd would get of a spaceship with spacemen flying to and from Earth, perhaps with rocket or anti-gravity motors on their shoulders. Sanchoniathon probably repeating some garbled tale from the past found himself writing science-fiction knowing no science and little fiction. His weird account compares with similar descriptions given by Ezekiel and in native legends all over the world.

Throughout human history Thoth[175] has been highly venerated by Students of the Secret Arts, Magicians, Alchemists, Freemasons and all practitioners of occult wisdom as the Supreme Architect of the Universe transcending mortal man. Today in our scientific age we dispel the aura of wonder and see Thoth through friendly eyes as a Super-Scientist; we hope that in thousands of years' time some Man may have mutated into a Supreme Intelligence with mastery of immense knowledge; meanwhile we are tempted to believe that in our own Galaxy there may now exist Wondrous Beings of great Wisdom evolved after millennia of civilisation on some advanced planet; such a Visitant may have landed on Earth with the Space Kings and taught mankind. In recent decades GI Joe became a generic term for American soldiers who cheerfully lavished the wonders of the West on Europe, Japan and now Vietnam. Was Thoth, descending from the skies to bring mankind knowledge, a collective name for Spacemen? We love this Superman of Ancient Egypt; in our secret dreams we too aspire to become Thoth, God of Wisdom.

Amon, often identified with Zeus, was a local tribal deity of Thebes long after the Golden Age of the Space Kings, of little importance until about 2100 BC when appear the first records of a shrine dedicated to him. Under the Hyksos alien rule, Amon was eclipsed, but when the Princes of Thebes rallied Egypt to expel the invaders, their city rose to political and religious dominance, which the Priests sought to preserve by imposing the worship of their God on the whole country, erecting magnificent temples in his name along the Nile. First symbolised as a goose, Amon became humanised as a Man wearing on his head two plumes; he became patron of powerful Pharaohs, who took his name, then the Priests identified him with Ra, the old Sun-God, and gradually he became King of all the Gods. His name 'Amon' means 'hidden', he was associated with the air, then as the universal God; like the Jews fundamentally the Egyptians were monotheists believing in only one God, all lesser deities as in Japan were really aspects of the Supreme Spirit. Akhnaton objected to the association of Amon with Ra, and purified the religion by returning to the ideal of Aton, the Sun disk, the high spiritual concept esteemed by the old Space Kings; when this heresy was crushed Amon's power waxed and waned with the fortunes of imperial Egypt. It seems impossible to regard Amon, the universal God, as an actual Space King, his development did not occur until historical times, however his original conception as a bird thousands of years earlier may perhaps denote some association with space. Amon's power was theological and political, popular religion preferred the old Gods.

The Egyptians regarded the spaceships as boats of the Sun sailing across the sky, a symbolism of world-wide significance since carvings of solar marks are found in Ireland, Brittany, Sweden and other prehistoric sites. The boat of Ra emerged in the east and journeyed daily across the heavens to the west, representations on temple walls show ships of the sun against constellations of stars suggesting spacecraft from specific origin, often the murals depict a crew of Gods captained by Horus himself. Egyptologists have always assumed that the sun-ship referred to the sun itself but the orb of the sun often appears above the ship which sails beneath like a spaceship. Ancient traditions assert that the builders of the Great Pyramid buried a solar boat, a spaceship, near the edifice. The Israelites believed the Spacemen were 'Angels', Messengers from God in a wondrous land in the skies called Heaven, the peoples of Christian Europe called them 'Spirits' or 'Demons' and the Emperor Charlemagne passed severe laws against citizens having commerce with Enchanters from the skies. To the simple Egyptians these glorious Visitants probably appeared to be Immortals from Realms of Wonder, perhaps the re-embodied Souls of the Dead. When Pharaoh died, it was hoped that he would sail to the Other World for resurrection among this Celestial Company in the Land of the Sun, so the royal tombs contained paintings of solar barks manned by the Gods conveying Pharaoh himself.[176] The theologians and moralists intruded the Judgement of the Dead, when the deceased's soul was weighed by Anubis in the presence of Thoth and depicted scenes of paradise and purgatory; the soul or 'Ka' appeared as a living man, indeed like a shining Spaceman. This interpretation may be hotly contested, yet our knowledge of Spacemen in ancient times in many countries makes this supposition as valid as the conclusion of Egyptologists unaware of spaceships.

The oldest religious texts in the world comprise the ancient Egyptian *Teu-Nu-Pert-Em-Hru* or *Chapters-of-Coming-Forth-By-Day* known as *The Book of the Dead*. This collection of hymns, litanies, spells and words of magical power describe the journey of the newly-arrived Spirit in the Underworld through infernal regions of torment to the Hall of Judgement where his heart is weighed on a great balance by Anubis with Thoth as scribe in the presence of the forty-two Judges of the Dead. *The Book of the Dead* was not The Book in the same sense as The Bible and was not regarded by the Egyptians with the same literal veneration as the Jews esteemed their Bible as divinely written or inspired.

No single copy of *The Book of the Dead* contained the whole work, dating of the original is therefore impossible. The oldest copies consisted of one or more of the separate papyri of Ani, Hunefer, Kerasher, Netchamet and Nu, dating from the Eighteenth Dynasty about 1500 BC, though some sections were inscribed on coffin lids and monuments of earlier dynasties other chapters appeared later. The Egyptian *The Book of the Dead* bears fascinating comparison with the *Bardo Thödol*, the Tibetan *The Book of the Dead* of immense antiquity. Both works have much in common and reveal transcendent beliefs of a spirit world alien to our own material age, and were probably inspired by Beings of Sublime wisdom many millennia ago.

The distinguished translator, Sir Wallis Budge, stated that the home, origin and early history of this collection of ancient religious texts are unknown to us; Maspero, the great French Egyptologist declared that the religion and the texts were far older than the First Dynasty of Menes about 5000 BC, the German scholar, Erman, marvelled that this ancient literature beyond the slightest doubt is far older than the oldest monument and belongs to the most remote prehistory. The chants and prayers were handed down orally for many thousand years; some texts in the hieratic script were inscribed on coffins in the early dynasties and later various papyri written in beautiful and fascinating hieroglyphics were secreted among the linen cloths enwrapping mummies as 'guide-books' for the deceased in the Underworld.[177]

Adepts teach that hieroglyphics possess esoteric and exoteric meanings, a secret significance for Initiates and a conventional association for the uninstructed, just as today common words and phrases may have special import for Members of Masonic Brotherhoods. Egyptians who were not priests and foreigners even at the zenith of the Empire found translation of hieroglyphics difficult, indeed we ourselves can scarcely comprehend the sayings of our own priests and scientists, least of all perhaps, our politicians. It is said that by about AD 400 the art of reading hieroglyphics was completely lost. For nearly fifteen hundred years these fascinating picture-symbols remained a tantalising mystery like the script of the Etruscans; had it not been for Napoleon's invasion of Egypt they might baffle us still and the glorious history of the Pharaohs remain a closed book. French soldiers found the Rosetta Stone with inscriptions of identical text in hieroglyphics, demotic and Greek. In 1822 Jean Francois Champollion[178] deciphered the hieroglyphics and from old Coptic Egyptologists eventually evaluated the language of the Egyptians, a feat of philological fantasy. We today, who scarcely make sense of the English of Chaucer and find ourselves completely baffled by Anglo-Saxon, realise the startling mutations in language. Cicero could hardly have read the Latin of the Middle Ages, and his terse logical mind would have boggled at the loquacious Latin discoursed at our turgid Vatican Councils today. Egyptian inscriptions spanned five millennia. Could Cleopatra have understood the speech of much-married Ramses II or of Cheops, the alleged builder of the Great Pyramid? It is admitted that in ancient times Egyptians from the Delta could not understand the speech of Egyptians from Elephantine. Egyptologists number men of genius, whom the world honours, but surely their greatest linguist conditioned by our twentieth century can hardly attune to the alien thought-pattern of several thousand years ago. There seems evidence that even scribes of the Middle Dynasties copying the scripts could not fathom the precise interpretation of texts already ancient to them. Modern translators can only approximate the literal sense of a papyrus, unversed in the Egyptian Mysteries they cannot divine their inner meaning. In considering *The Book of the Dead,* we must therefore read between the lines and speculate on what those age-old symbols of that lost world possibly meant.

Certain chapters of *The Book of the Dead* are attributed to Thoth, whom the Greeks called Hermes, they are generally classed as Hermetic literature. *The Book of the Dead* propounded the Resurrection, later taught by Jesus, and it was usual for a copy to be placed in the coffin or swathed between the legs of the mummy. The Turin Papyrus from the Twenty-sixth Dynasty states that the earliest chapter was found by Herutatef, son of Cheops (Khufu) about 5000 BC during an inspection of the temples. Prince Herutatef was said to have been a very learned man, whose speech was difficult to understand.

A great Adept worked wonders in Egypt seven thousand years ago. According to the Westcar Papyrus:

> 'Herutatef informed his father Khufu of the existence of a man 110 years old, who lived in the town of Tettet-

Seneferu; he was able to join to its body again a head that had been cut off, and possessed influence over the lion and was acquainted with the Mysteries of Thoth. By Khufu's command Herutatef brought the Sage to him by boat, and on his arrival the King ordered the head to be struck off from a prisoner that Tetteta might fasten it on again. Having excused himself from performing this act upon a man, a goose was brought and its head was cut off and laid on one side of the room and the body was placed on the other. The Sage spoke certain words of power, whereupon the goose stood up and began to waddle and the head also began to move towards it; when the head had joined itself again to the body, the bird stood up and cackled' (See Erman *Die Märchen des Papyrus Westcar.*[179])

Even the Priests in their duel of magic with Moses never attempted this feat. If the tale be true, and the Egyptians believed it, such wondrous powers would be worthy of any Spaceman.

To the Ancient Egyptians ignorant of aerial technology a gleaming Spaceship in the blue sky looked down like the Eye of Horus or Ra, the Sun-God. The Papyrus of Ani, royal scribe at Thebes about 1450 BC, part of *The Book of the Dead*, was copied (rather miscopied for the text appears to have many serious errors) from ancient records, themselves probably inaccurate versions of most antique sources couched in archaic imagery, whose real meaning was long since lost. Translators last century, men of undoubted genius, unfamiliar with aeronautics, were obviously puzzled by many passages, the translations they offered must be quite different from the meaning of the original story in remote antiquity, especially as these learned pedants were totally ignorant of the possibility of visitations by Extra-terrestrials intervening in Ancient Egypt. It is obviously hardly possible for anyone today, even with our modern affinity with the Spacemen of prehistory, to divine the precise meaning of these exasperating hieroglyphics but occasionally we may see through the symbolism and recognise fascinating similarities with sacred texts all over the world telling of the War in the skies.

The *Papyrus of Ani*, translated by Sir Wallis Budge, Chapter 18 describes 'The Combat of the Two Fighters', Horus and Set. Amsu, the oldest Solar-God says(71):

> 'It is the Right Eye of Ra which raged against (Set) when (72) he sent it forth, Thoth raiseth up the hair-cloud and bringeth the Eye (73) alive and whole and sound, and without defect to its Lord.'

In lines (86) to (99) Ani refers to the 'Seven Shining Ones' and to 'Holy Ones, who stand behind Osiris . . . are they who are behind the Thigh in the Northern Sky.' Brugsch in *Astronomische und Astrologische Inschriften*, p. 123, states the 'Thigh was the Egyptian name for the Constellation of the Great Bear.' The ancient Egyptian scribe thus plainly states that the Celestials descended from a specific source in the sky, the Constellation of Ursa Major. Today, observers sometimes allege that UFOS often originate from the direction of the North Star, entering the vents in the Van Allen Belts over the North Pole. Some of the 'Shining Ones' are referred to by ancient Egyptian names interpreted as 'He doth not give his flame', 'He goeth in at his house', 'He that hath two red eyes', 'Blazing face coming forth, going back' and 'The One, who seeth by night and leadeth by day'. These terms coincide with most descriptions by peoples, ancient and modern, telling of the Spaceships traversing the skies.

> 'The Kings of Light have departed in wrath. The sins of men have become so black that Earth quivers in her great agony. . . . The azure seats remain empty. Who of the Brown, who of the Red, or yet among the Black (races), can sit in the Seats of the Blessed, the Seats of Knowledge and Mercy?'

This quotation from *Tongshatchi Sangye Songye* or the *Records of the Thirty-five Buddhas of Confession* comments on Stanza 12 from the *Secret Book of Dzyan* written in Senzar, the sacerdotal language known in remote Antiquity to Initiates all over the world and dedicated to the Sons of Light by Divine Beings ages ago. Madame H. P. Blavatsky in *The Secret Doctrine* states that 'The Kings of Light' is the name given in all old records to the Divine Dynasties. The 'azure seats' are translated 'celestial thrones' in certain documents. We today may consider 'The Kings of Light' to be Advanced Beings from other planets and the 'celestial thrones' to be Spaceships.

The Atlanteans taught aeronautics, Vimana Vidya (the

knowledge of flying in air vehicles) and their most valuable science of the hidden virtues of precious and other stones, of chemistry, or rather alchemy, of mineralogy, geology, physics and astronomy to the proto-Egyptians in the Nile valley. Madame Blavatsky wondered whether the story of the Exodus of the Israelites and the Hosts of Pharaoh drowned in the Red Sea was actually a version of the Atlantean traditions mentioned in the Dzyan Commentary.

> '. . . And the "great King of the dazzling Face", the Chief of all the Yellow-faced, was sad, seeing the sins of the Black-faced. . . . He sent his air-vehicles (Vimanas) to all his brother-chiefs with pious men within, saying "Prepare! Arise, ye men of the good law, and cross the land while (yet) dry".'

This remarkable Commentary refers to 'Lords of the Fires' with magic fire-weapons, 'Lords of the Dark Eye' versed in magical knowledge, Elementals, mechanical monsters which spoke and warned of every approaching danger, presumably Robots equipped with radar and sonar. The Solar Gods destroyed the Evil Magicians in tremendous floods, the Sons of Men led by the Sons of Wisdom escaped; many brought their wondrous civilisation to the Land of the Nile.

A tantalizing reference to the War in Heaven and Earth, analogous perhaps to similar descriptions in the Indian, Chinese and Greek legends is given in the *Papyrus of Ani,* Chapter 17, Section 112; this suggests the intervention of a Spaceship during a battle at Annu, later known as On or Heliopolis about five miles from modern Cairo, the great religious college in On taught the worship of Horus and Ra, the Sun-God.

> (112) 'As to the fight(?) by the Persae tree hard by in Annu, it concerneth the Children of impotent revolt, when justice is wrought on them for what they have done. As to (the words) "that night of the battle", they concern the inroad (of the Children of impotent revolt) into the eastern part of heaven, whereupon there arose a battle in heaven and in all the earth.
>
> 'O Thou, who art in the Egg (i.e. Ra) who shinest from thy disk and riseth in thy horizon and dost shine like gold above the sky, like unto whom there is none among

the Gods, who sailest over the Pillars of Shu (the ether) who givest blasts of fire from the mouth (who makest the two lands bright with thy radiance deliver) the faithful worshippers from the God whose forms are hidden, whose eyebrows are like unto the two arms of the balance on the night of the reckoning of destruction.'

Hieroglyphics in Ani's Papyrus represent Ra and Horus as human-headed birds which may be interpreted as meaning Spacemen.

This description of a Celestial in a shining spacecraft speeding through the skies, blasting armies with fire, recalls those flaming 'shields' mentioned in the *Annales Laurissenses* which in the year AD 776 routed the Saxons besieging the Franks at Sigiburg.[180]

The same Chapter XVII continues:

'(112) . . . I know the being, Matchet, (the Oppressor) who is among them in the House of Osiris shooting rays of light from (his) Eye, but he himself is unseen. He goeth round about heaven robed in the flames of his mouth, commanding Hapi (lands of the Nile) but remaining himself unseen. . . . I fly as a hawk. I cackle as a goose. I ever slay, even as the Serpent Goddess, Nehebka. . . .'

'(140) . . . Thou livest according to thy will, thou art Uatchit, the Lady of the Flame, (141) Evil cometh among those who set themselves up against thee . . . (145) Uatchit, the Lady of the Flames, is the Eye of Ra. . . .'

The ancient Stanzas of Dzyan honour the 'Lords of the Flame', Sanskrit Vedas mention 'Lords of Light', the Egyptian *The Book of the Dead* praises the 'Lady of the Flame'. Surely this suggests Extra-terrestrials with laser light weapons dominating our Earth in far Antiquity?

Several references in *The Book of the Dead* are made to the 'Shining Ones' possibly Wondrous Beings from the stars; the Bible would call them 'Angels of the Lord'.

'Behold, O ye Shining Ones, ye Men and Gods . . . Osiris. Ani is victorious over his foes in the heavens above and (on the earth) beneath in the presence of the god-like Rulers of all the Gods and Goddesses' (Chapter 134, 15/17).

'I speak with the Followers of the Gods. I speak with the Disk. I speak with the Shining Ones' (Chapter 124, 17).

> 'I am One of those Shining Ones who live in rays of light' (Chapter 78, 14).
>
> 'The holy Rulers of the Pylons are in the form of Shining Ones' (Chapter 125, 5).

The Book of the Dead vividly chronicles Celestial Visitants in the four quarters of the sky, which recall the colourful accounts by the Cosmic Brotherhood Association of Yokohama describing those extraordinary sightings over Japan today.

> 'Hail, thou beautiful Power, thou beautiful Rudder of the Northern Heaven! Hail, thou who goest about Heaven, thou Pilot of the World, thou beautiful Rudder of the Western Heaven! Hail, thou Shining One, who livest in the Temple, wherein are the Gods in visible forms, thou beautiful Rudder of the Eastern Heaven! Hail, thou who dwellest in the Temple of the bright-faced Ones, thou beautiful Rudder of the Southern Heaven' (Chapter 148, 1/6).

This lyrical description shows that those gleaming Spaceships in the skies apparently frequented Egypt often to make such an impression on people's minds. Those simple souls by the Nile gazed at the wonderful craft glowing in the blue heavens with rejoicing, their cheerful greetings showed they welcomed the Celestials as friends; long experience taught them that the Heavenly Strangers brought them benevolence. When misfortune or need befell the Egyptians, it was natural that they would implore aid from heaven and would invoke these Gods with many earnest and flattering prayers to come to their aid; which is just what we do today. Do we not gaze at the sky and supplicate 'Our Father Which art in Heaven' to grant our prayers?

We contrast this rapturous evocation by the Egyptians for the Spacemen with the savage laws enacted by Charlemagne[181] against the 'Demons' and all who contacted them. Yet who are we to comment? If Extra-terrestrials in their wonderful ships landed in our mad, materialist world today, would not our politicians, our priests, our scientists, try to steal their secrets then shoot them?

But the skies above the Nile were not always serene. Flaming verses from *The Book of the Dead* recall the 'War in the Heavens' as described in Chinese Classics with

Sun Disks flashing beams of light at fiery dragons, battles in the air, on land and under the sea.

> 'Stretched forth on the flank of the mountain sleeps the great Serpent, one hundred and eighty feet long and fifty feet broad; its belly adorned with scintillating flints and stones. Now I know the Name of the Serpent of the mountain. Behold it is "He who dwells in the flames". After navigating in silence Ra darts a glance at the Serpent, suddenly his navigation stops, as though He who is hidden in his bark waits in ambush. . . . Behold he dives in the water and is seen submerged forty feet deep. He assails Set, launching at him his javelin of steel' (Chapter 108).[182]

This simple description seems an eye-witness account by some Egyptian peasant of a duel between two spaceships or between a spaceship and some monstrous tank waged with laser-beams and guided missiles between rival invaders from other planets, perhaps the conflict between Saturn and Jupiter sung by the Classical Poets. We are reminded of the Celestial Wars described in the 'Mahabharata' and of Hesiod's *Theogony*; in naïve words such as these some simple coolie may describe the American bombers attacking Communist tanks in Vietnam today.

Throughout the many papyri comprising *The Book of the Dead* are scattered intriguing phrases such as 'The Ancient of Days', 'Spirits of Light', 'Sons of Darkness', 'Legions in the Sky', 'Hidden Gods', 'Deities in the Divine Eye', 'Winged Disks', 'I, Horus, am Yesterday'. 'I am Tomorrow', 'I course through Space and Time'.

It seems difficult to believe that these key-words are purely philosophical concepts without any factual basis, even our so-called educated, sophisticated minds today brain-washed by television and advertising could hardly visualise such esoteric symbols if the prototypes did not exist. To convince the whole nation of simple Egyptian peasants that such mythical 'Spirits' held complete domination over their lives, past, present and future, would appear impossible had the Celestials no reality. The 'Spirits of Light', the 'Sons of Darkness', the 'Winged Disks' were surely real and represented those Wondrous Beings descending to Earth to teach mankind then warring among themselves in that conflict in the Heavens mentioned in the world's Classics. In such homely words would a simple, unsophisticated people describe Visitants from an advanced planet with a technology utterly beyond our Earth's experience.

References to transcending time as well as space are pregnant with meaning for us today. Einstein's Theory of Relativity with its Time-Dilation paradox make stellar travel across many light-years possible in theory if not yet in fact; occultists and students of multi-dimensional physics now believe that Super-Intelligences could devise techniques for travelling through time as easily as through space.

The Gods of Ancient Egypt pose questions more fascinating for us than for those white-robed Priests beside the Nile. We with our modern insight recognise the Deities in those Winged Disks as Spacemen. Like the Egyptians of old we watch the heavens and we wonder.

CHAPTER ELEVEN

Pyramid and Sphinx

The Great Pyramid, Symbol of Ancient Egypt, stands exactly in the centre of the world land map, its edges diverge from the four cardinal points by only a few minutes. The site of this huge edifice may be more significant than its astounding construction. To fix this focal position, its builders must have surveyed our Earth from Space, made a global map, projected flat, then drawing a meridian through the precise middle of our planet's land surface they found it exactly divided the Nile Delta. Such cartography quite beyond the geographical knowledge of men in ancient times confined to Earth, evokes comparison with the remarkable Piri Reis map,[183] apparently dating from Pre-Columbian times, which clearly showed the contours of the Americas and an Antarctica in correct relation to Europe and Africa proving the existence of maps possibly drawn by people from Space. The Pyramid was probably built by Spacemen or by Initiates mastering extra-terrestrial science.

The Egyptologists, whom we justly honour for their brilliant resurrection of that ancient, eccentric Land of Khem, accept that the Great Pyramid was built by Khufu (Cheops) about 3000 BC. Herodotus stated that this tyrannical Pharaoh forced a hundred thousand men to toil constantly for ten years to prepare the causeway and underground chambers and a further twenty years to build the Pyramid itself, originally the height was 480 feet, each triangular side slanted 756 feet and it covered an area of 571,536 square feet. Originally smooth polished casing stones covered the slopes pointing to a pyramidal cone of crystalline copper with esoteric significance associated with Venus.[184] The rays of the sun and moon must have blazoned the shining stones as a beacon beckoning the Spaceships.[185]

Two and a half million blocks, each averaging two and a half tons, according to Herodotus none of the stones was less than thirty feet long, were dragged by gangs of slaves from Arabian quarries and the Libyan hills, cut, polished and fitted precisely into place, their joints hardly perceptible, as thin as paper. Bunsen believed the Pyramid to have been built about 20,000 BC and calculated its vast mass as 82,111,000 cubic feet, which would weigh 6,316,000 tons.[186] Could even the most docile man-power with primitive tools be actually deployed to fashion such a mammoth structure? Scholars and cranks linking the Pyramid with the Bible and Solomon's Temple have laboured to fathom some hidden message secreted in stone for posterity. Most men contrive to find what they are looking for, so it is hardly surprising that visionaries discover in this mound of stone support for their delusions, yet some of the measurements found appear to possess significance transcending chance coincidence. The height of the Pyramid is one thousand millionth of the distance from Earth to the Sun, measurements embodied in the building are said to reveal the radius and weight of the Earth, the length of the Solar Year, the Precession of the Equinoxes, the value of 'pi', that is the relation between the circumference of a circle and its diameter. Pyramidologists, Bible in one hand, measuring-tape in the other, prophesied the Second Coming of Christ and the Day of Judgement for 1874, 1914, 1920, 1936 and 1953.[187] It is difficult to believe that the Ancient Egyptians, kind and considerate though they may have been, would have gone to such toil, tears, blood and sweat, and heaped up so much stone just to warn our cynical century five thousand years later that some day the world would end. We ourselves brandishing our hydrogen-bombs do not seem to worry much, why should the Egyptians have bothered about us? So far those Master-builders have guessed wrongly. Perhaps the Pyramid was built for some other reason?

The general belief that the Ancient Egyptians had a profound knowledge of mathematics, geometry and astronomy is fantastically wrong. Sir Leonard Woolley and

Jacquetta Hawkes in their fascinating *Prehistory and the Beginnings of Civilisation,*[188] Vol. 2. p. 669 state:

> 'The Babylonians possessed a scientific knowledge of algebra, geometry and arithmetic. The Egyptians, on the contrary, had in these subjects no real science at all. . . . By dint of considerable ingenuity and infinite patience the Egyptian was able to meet all his practical needs by the use of a means childishly imperfect; the sources available to us suggest nothing in the nature of advanced science, and we may well believe that in that respect he was incurious as well as ignorant.'

The Rhind Papyrus of the Twelfth Dynasty, 2000 BC describes the Egyptian decimal system of numeration; they could do simple multiplication and division and could manipulate simple fractions but complex mathematics was beyond them; unlike the Babylonians they were apparently unable to prognosticate lunar eclipses.

Sir Leonard Woolley adds:

> 'This empirical method, however, cannot explain how the Egyptian was able to calculate correctly the volume of the frustrum of a square-based pyramid, given the height and the measurements of lower and upper base, the formula for which operation is found in a Moscow Papyrus; the problem, unique in Egyptian mathematics as known to us, can scarcely have been solved on the purely arithmetical base elsewhere invariable, and may indicate a borrowing from Babylonian algebra.'

Egyptian astronomy lacking advanced mathematics was based on observation rather than prediction; since the Priests were unable to calculate with any exactitude the orbits of planets. Oddly enough the Egyptians believed that Mercury and Venus rotated around the Sun but the Sun dragged them with itself around the Earth. Observation of the heliacal rising of the bright star, Sothis or Sirius, just before the Nile flood was due, led to the Sothic Cycle, i.e. when the rising of Sirius coincided with the first day of the Calendar Year; this Sothic Cycle comprised 1460 years and was apparently recorded for AD 139 and 1321 BC, possibly for 2781 BC and 4241 BC.

The building of the Great Pyramid obviously demanded great mathematical and astronomical knowledge; in view of their elementary science could the Egyptians in Cheops's day have possibly built it?

Commenting on Cheops, Herodotus who could not resist enlivening his *History* with spicy gossip, in Book Two, Chapter 126, reports irreverently:

'And Cheops came to such wickedness that when he lacked money, he set his daughter in a brothel and enjoined her to charge thus and thus much; but they told me not how much. And she demanded the sum enjoined by her father, and also resolved to leave a memorial of her own. And she besought each man that went in unto her to give her a present of one stone. And from the stones, they said, was made the Pyramid that standeth in the midst of the three in front of the Great Pyramid and each face thereof is one plethrum and an half long.'

Herodotus somewhat unconvincingly explains how the Pyramid was built on a series of stairs, he alleges:

'Howsoever, the topmost parts of the Pyramid were finished first, and then the next, and lastly the parts at the bottom near the ground. And it is recorded in Egyptian writing on the Pyramid how much was spent on radish and onion and garlick for the labourers. And if I well remember what the interpreter told me reading the writing, a thousand and six hundred talents of silver were expended.'

For a Historian 'who never told a lie', Herodotus seems at times to have behaved like a gullible tourist; what the native Guides did not know, they evidently made up, just as their unwashed descendants do today. Herodotus cheerfully accepts that they started at the point of the Pyramid and built downwards, then on the smooth outside casing the publicity-boys wrote glowing advertisements in hieroglyphics for radishes and garlick; really this is tantamount to accusing Sir Christopher Wren of writing, on the dome of St Paul's, adverts, for Nell Gwynn's oranges! The outer casing was adorned with hieroglyphics until as late as fourteenth century AD but no man alive could read them. It is likely that Herodotus was told an equally unreliable tale regarding the actual operation of building; the Arabs believed the Great Pyramid was built by 'Djinns' or 'Spirits'; oddly enough they were probably right. The 'Spirits' came from Space!

Our cynical modern-minds find it difficult to believe that even a megalomaniac Pharaoh with complete dictatorship would really spend thirty long years and squander his country's resources building his own tomb, when the world offered more tempting delights. It is still more doubtful whether the powerful priesthood would have supported this gloomy project, when for a fraction of such vast masonry they could have lined both banks of the Nile with temples. Even a docile people going home to their mud huts would revolt at such mad extravagance. Mighty edifices of stone were erected in prehistoric times in Brittany, Greece, Mexico, all over the world, but usually with some religious purpose never to gratify the whim of one man. No body was found in the Pyramid, a seal of Khufu happened to have been left there, this cannot prove he built it; no funereal inscriptions decorated the walls, Pharaohs were usually buried in the Valley of Kings. Occultists swear the various chambers and passages prove it to have been a Temple of Initiation presumably dating from Atlantean times.[189]

Some astronomers have dated the Pyramid by the long dark entrance passage, which pointed to Alpha Draconis, the then Pole Star in 2170 BC; astrologers claim that allowing for the precession of the equinoxes, it could have been a sidereal year, 25,868 years earlier, about 28,000 BC; occultists mindful of the Dendera Zodiac suggest three sidereal years earlier, or 79,000 BC during the Golden Age of the Divine Dynasty, the Space Kings. One of the Books of Hermes describes certain pyramids as standing on the sea shore dashed by the waves, sea shells at its base suggest a great flood hinting at the belief that the Pyramid was built before the submergence of Atlantis.[190]

In *The Secret Doctrine,* p. 750, Madame Blavatsky states in comment on the antiquity of the Egyptians:

> 'And yet there are records which show Egyptian priests —Initiates—journeying in a North-Westerly direction, by land, via, what became later the Straits of Gibraltar; turning North and travelling through the future Phoenician settlements of Southern Gaul; then still further North until reaching Carnac (Morbihan) they turned to the West again and arrived, still travelling by land, on the North-Western promontory of the New Continent.'

A pity if they had to walk all the way! It is a wonder they were not translated to the West in a Spaceship like Enoch!

In remote times the British Isles were still joined to the

Continent; the peoples of Antiquity venerated Britain as the Home of the Gods, a remnant of lost Atlantis. Students of prehistoric Britain have commented on the surprising links between Britain and Ancient Egypt; old Welsh is said to have had affinities with the language of the Egyptians, Brinsley le Poer Trench[191] in his fascinating *Men Among Mankind* stresses esoteric Egyptian influence on the religion and temples of Ancient Britain, particularly associating Arthur, the 'Dragon King' and the Somerset Zodiac with Egypt and India. Comyns Beaumont[192] actually believed that early Egyptian and Jewish history really took place in Britain and not the Middle East advancing arguments more plausible than appear possible.

Sensitives today claim that the Great Pyramid still radiates magnetic force and that the immense blocks of stone were levitated by Extra-terrestrials utilising anti-gravity or sonic vibrations,[193] perhaps the same power motivating the Spaceships, one of which is alleged to have been buried nearby. Traditions suggest that Thoth, the Great Teacher of Ancient Egypt, possibly a Spaceman, secreted occult records in a hidden chamber, so one day wisdom from other worlds may come to light within the Great Pyramid.

In the sands beside the Pyramids at Gizeh near Cairo crouches the Sphinx, majestic yet remote, like an alien intruder on our planet, symbol of some Super Race from the stars. The significance of this great monument is lost to us, we, who now land spaceships on the moon, still stand in awe and marvel at the stone monster and fathom in vain the motives of those strange folk who built it there. A vast human head in royal headdress rears thirty feet above its lion's body two hundred and forty feet long carved from solid rock; its haughty features scorn the mutilations of men and gaze with enigmatic smile across the Nile beyond the rising sun transcending space and time to the fathomless infinitudes of the universe. That serene countenance shines with cosmic power radiating an aura to still the minds of men evoking echoes of a bygone protean age, of a wondrous, glorious civilisation ruled by the Gods. Such grand nobility dominating the transient passions of humanity recalls those colossal heads of prehistory hewn on the peaks of the Andes and the cliffs of New

Mexico; their mute lips telling in wordless message of those golden[194] days when Earth was young and all men basked in the beneficence of the Space Kings, Teachers from the skies.

The Sphinx in lonely silence watched the Atlanteans bring to this Land of Khem the culture from their drowned continent, its hollow eyes, which see our sputniks, witnessed the War in the Heavens between the Gods and the Giants, then the Flood engulfed its huge form in ocean until another cosmic cataclysm drained the waters away to leave it stranded in the desert. For long centuries this stony beast saw primitive man start civilisation again, then the shifting sands swallowed it from sight and human memory. Six thousand years ago in the Fourth Dynasty King Khafra unearthed the monster and secured for himself immortality by inscribing his royal cartouche on the Sphinx's side but still the sands threatened to bury it again. About 1450 BC Thutmosis IV as a young Prince tired from hunting slept between the great paws, when the Sun God appeared to him in a dream and urged him to clear away the sands which covered it.[195] In AD 162 Emperor Marcus Aurelius gazed with understanding eyes and resurrected the Sphinx for men to marvel at, but in Christian times only its blanched face battered by Turkish musketfire peered above the sand until last century Egyptologists brought most of it to light,[196] yet even now some great storm could bury it for ever.

The Atlanteans are believed to have worshipped the Sun purely as a physical representation of the Solar Logos, when their Adepts emigrated to the Nile they established the religion of the Sun and built the Great Pyramid and the Sphinx. This human head on the lion's body is said by Initiates to symbolise the evolution of Man from animal, the triumph of the human spirit over the beast. Beneath the monster should be a temple communicating to the Great Pyramid where ages ago white-robed Neophytes sought initiation into the Mysteries of the Secret Wisdom.[197] Millennia later Egyptian priests associated the Sphinx with Harmachis, an aspect of Ra, the Sun God.

Astrologers may argue that the Sphinx with its human head on a lion's body represents Man on Earth during the Age of Leo, when the precession of the equinoxes impelled our Earth through the Constellation of Leo about 10,000 BC though it could have been during the Leo of some previous Great Round about 85,000 BC. While ridiculed by Egyptologists, who really have no relevant data for criticism, such vast antiquity consorts with occult traditions of Lemuria and Atlantis glorying in a world-wide golden Empire of the Sun. Spacemen from other planets possibly visited Earth hundreds of thousands of years ago, the Sphinx may signify their presence by symbolism beyond understanding today.

Old India associated the Sphinx with Garuda, half-man and half-bird, the celestial chariot of the Gods; the ancient Persians identified the Sphinx with the Simorgh, a monstrous bird, sometimes standing on Earth, sometimes walking the ocean, while its head propped up the sky. The Magi of Babylon linked the Simorgh with the Phoenix, the fabulous Egyptian bird, which kindling a flame was self-consumed, then reborn from the flames, possibly symbolism for the renewal of the human race after world-destructions. The peoples of the Caucasus believed that the winged Simorgh or twelve-legged horse of Huschenk, legendary Teacher said to have built Babylon and Ispahan, flew northwards across the Arctic to a wonderful Continent. A learned Chaldean told Cosmos Indicapleustes in the sixth century AD:

> 'The lands we live in are surrounded by the ocean, but beyond that ocean there is another land, which touches the wall of the sky; and it is in this land that Man was created and lived in paradise. During the Deluge Noah was carried in his Ark into the land his posterity now inhabits.'[198]

Supporters of the Hollow Earth theory will doubtless construe this fertile land beyond the ice as the flourishing continent they postulate inside the Earth itself; UFO Students note that the Spaceships appear to approach and depart via the North Pole, presumably through the polar gaps in the Van Allen radiation-belts and may argue that this fabulous country to the North, whither the Simorgh and the twelve-legged horse flew, was really another planet.

The Simorgh became the Eagle of Jupiter[199] borne on the standards of the Roman legions across the Ancient world, a symbol of divine power, it was adopted by

Byzantium and became a heraldic device of the Holy Roman Empire, as the two-headed Eagle it was flaunted by the Hapsburgs of Austria and still finds place of honour in coats-of-arms of the few Monarchies left today. Sphinx, Simorgh. Eagle. Spaceship? We wonder?

The Sphinx itself conjures a mystery more baffling yet perhaps more pregnant for humanity than we realise. Some Egyptian paintings show the Sphinx as having wings and a human face, the likeness of Kings or Queens; we think of the famous winged bulls of Nineveh and speculate on possible symbolism for Spacemen. The Egyptian Priests of Sais told Solon of the great war between the Atlanteans and Athens and spoke of the association between Egypt and Greece; we find ourselves further intrigued to discover both countries linked by the Sphinx.

Greek mythology represents the Sphinx as a she-monster, the daughter of Typhon and Chimaera, both fire-breathing monsters who lay waste Asia Minor until slain by Zeus and Bellerophon in aerial battles suggestive of conflict between Spaceships. She terrorised Thebes in Boeotia, the most celebrated city in the mythical age of Greece, reputed birth-place of the Gods Dionysus and Hercules.[200] This Greek Sphinx had the winged body of a lion, the breast and face of a woman. Pisander declared the Sphinx came to Greece from Ethiopia, probably meaning Egypt. The Theban Sphinx molested travellers, posing a riddle then devouring all who could not answer it. A young stranger named Oedipus,[201] meaning 'swollen feet', told by the Delphic Oracle that he was destined to murder his Father and commit incest with his Mother, on the road to Thebes brawled with and killed King Laius, not knowing he was his Father. Oedipus challenged the Sphinx, who demanded 'What creature goes on four feet in the morning, on two at noonday, on three in the evening?' 'Man!' answered Oedipus with smart retort. 'In childhood he creeps on hands and feet, in manhood he walks erect and in old age helps himself with a staff.' The Sphinx mortified by this correct answer, hurled herself from a rock and was killed. The Thebans in delight made Oedipus King, he married the late King's widow, Jocasta, and fathered four children; the Gods sent a plague and Oedipus learned he had murdered his Father and married his own

Mother. Jocasta hung herself; Oedipus put out his eyes and wandered blinded, accompanied by his daughter, Antigone, until the Eumenides, avenging Goddesses, removed him from Earth. Aeschylus, Sophocles and Euripedes wrote classic plays on this tragedy; our psycho-analysts conjure up this Oedipus-complex, Man's tyranny by his Mother, alleged to be the cause of psychoses today. This strange tale confounds belief, can we possibly connect it with Ancient Egypt and Spacemen?

That profound scholar, Immanuel Velikovsky, with masterly erudition identifies Oedipus with the heretic Pharaoh Akhnaton about 1375 BC.[202]

Who was Akhnaton, this strange mystic, philosopher-King, who three thousand years ago established for a brief moment on our Earth a realm of universal peace, love and beauty, worship of the divine Sun, Spirit of Creation, the cosmic religion of the Spacemen for which mankind is still not ready?

Eighteenth Dynasty Egypt about 1500 BC flourished at the zenith of imperial power, Mistress of the civilised world; treasures and tribute from Babylon, Assyria, Palestine, Crete and Ethiopia in wondrous abundance enriched the valley of the Nile. Hatshepsut, chronicled in the Bible as the Queen of Sheba, paid a State visit to Jerusalem to meet Solomon in all his glory; she returned enchanted by more than wisdom, their son, Menelik, is said to be ancestor of Hailie Selassie, the present Emperor of Abyssinia. The Queen's nephew, Thutmosis III, the great conqueror of Antiquity, fought brilliant campaigns in Palestine, Syria and Nubia to extend a beneficent Pax Aegyptica over the fertile crescent of the Middle East, triumphs continued by Thutmosis IV and Amenhotep III. Sophistication and prosperity inevitably brought decadence, the two thousand year old religion of Amon had lost its inspiration, swamped by materialism. Egypt needed a Reformation.

The young King ascending the ancient throne of the Pharaohs in 1375 BC at the age of fifteen showed the genius and cosmic comprehension of an Avatar from Venus rather than the immaturity of youth; he lived in a spiritual sublimity transcending the worldly morals of Earth making the fatal misjudgement of expecting his subjects to be saints instead of sinners. Amenhotep (Amun-rests) IV was deformed, his skull long, features ascetic and delicate, with the eyes of a prophet; his abdomen large and lower limbs swollen; he may have suffered from epilepsy due to psychic forces charging his restless soul. He promptly displaced the old polytheistic degenerate religion of Amen to the simple and light-giving worship of Aton, the One God, symbolised by the Disk of the Sun; his New Age disciples welcomed the change but such iconoclastic reformation at once provoked the fanatical priests and upset the populace, who preferred the fleshpots of this life to fantasies of the life-to-come. Amenhotep changed his name to Akhnaton (Aton is satisfied) and moved the imperial capital from No-Amon (The City of Amen-Thebes) to a new dream city called Akhetaton,[203] which he was having built in idealism and beauty further down the Nile at our modern Tell-el-Amarna. Akhnaton with his lovely wife Nefertiti, whose sculptured features make her the most striking woman in all Antiquity, and their seven daughters, lived in this City of the Sun renouncing the dead traditions of religion, philosophy and art, and ushered in a golden age of cosmic brotherhood, compassion, naturalism and glorification of universal life, the unfulfilled dream of that later philosopher-Emperor Marcus Aurelius, the hope of visionaries today, the wondrous civilisation of the Spacemen.

Akhnaton's ideas were millennia ahead of his time; the people were not ready for the Kingdom of Heaven on Earth. Will they ever be? Divine frustration meets all Reformers; we today are heirs to history, all the inspired Prophets of the past have preached their glorious Message, yet behold our world menaced by the hydrogen-bomb! Akhnaton's great 'Hymn to the Sun' hailed Ra-Harakhte as an idealistic, universal Spirit sustaining all men everywhere, a resurrection of the solar religion of the Atlanteans and the early Egyptians, which was later supplanted by the local then nationalist worship of Amon as God of Egypt; the young visionary sought to unite all humanity in one cosmic wisdom-religion embracing Angel to insect, star to atom, with a way of life expanding Man's awareness of the glorious, living universe. But human nature was the same then as it is today. The clay tablets unearthed at El Amarna in 1887 written in cuneiform in the diplomatic language of Akkadian grimly reveal that the Hittites and other subject peoples scorned Akhnaton's pacifism as weakness; Egyptian Governors frantically implored aid which never came, crumbling of the Empire fostered discontent in Egypt. The frustrated Army was encouraged by the dispossessed Priests of Amon to depose the King and to return the Capital to Thebes. Akhnaton, left in isolation, became estranged from Nefertiti, his wife, his unfinished city fell to ruins, he spent his days in religious mysticism, communing with Aton, soon accumulations of disasters at home and abroad ravaged his precarious health; he died, possibly poisoned, in 1358 BC, the seventeenth year of his reign, only thirty-two years old, defeated in mind and body yet triumphant in soul. Like some Teacher from another planet Akhnaton had brought cosmic religion to Man only to meet sorry rejection, now three millennia later our strife-torn world is slowly realising beyond the failure of conflicting creeds the practical idealism of the young Pharaoh's philosophy, the common kinship of all men, the worship of the One God in the living universe, the glorious Brotherhood of all creatures on the countless stars in Space. Akhnaton was succeeded by his son-in-law, Smenkhkara, followed by the boy-King, Tutankhamun, whose tomb with its golden treasures dazzled our century in 1922. The revengeful Priests of Amon erased all reference to Aton yet today in our Space Age the teachings of Akhnaton shine with new meaning.

What possible relation could there be between this saintly Pharaoh, Akhnaton, who sought to reform the world, and that tragic King Oedipus, husband to his own Mother? Could these extraordinary characters at different times in different countries have really been the same person? Behind the image of Akhnaton is there deeper mystery?

Velikovsky with impressive arguments states that sculptures show Akhnaton had swollen limbs, 'Oedipus' in Greek means 'swollen legs'; inscriptions suggest that Akhnaton took Tiy, his Mother, as Consort, and fathered her child, even as Oedipus unknowingly married his Mother, Jocasta, and begot two sons and two daughters. Abhorrent though incest is to our twentieth century, in Ancient Egypt the Pharaohs considered themselves a divine dynasty, so for reasons of State to secure the throne brother married sister to produce a successor, although there were doubtless exceptions to this practice. Even the Egyptians abominated marriage between Mother and son, if tolerating unions between Father and daughter, enjoyed by Ramses II. The Mitannians and Ancient Persians, worshippers of Indo-Iranian Gods, believed union between Mother and son had sacred significance, most holy merit. Close political relations between Egypt and Mitanni possibly brought Zarathustrian influence over the Egyptian Court and offers a plausible explanation why Akhnaton and Tiy, both dominant individuals, may have married each other; no doubt explaining why his lawful wife, the lovely Nefertiti, left him. Akhnaton's body was never found. Tiy's shabby tomb suggests her suicide, Jocasta hung herself. Somewhat tortuous evidence implies that Akhnaton after being deposed suffered blindness and wandered with his daughter, Meritaten, who suffered ignominious death like the tragic Antigone, daughter of Oedipus, buried alive. Akhnaton vanished, Oedipus was finally removed by the Eumenides, avenging Goddesses, from the Earth.

Like Shakespeare, who rarely invented his plots but transmuted old tales with the magic of genius, so Aeschylus about 500 BC borrowed old stories for his own great tragedies. For centuries the tale of the blind, incestuous Egyptian King must have been sung by bards through many lands; Aeschylus gave the drama local colour by transferring the scene with Greek characters to Thebes in Boeatia, a city which by some strange coincidence bore the same name which the Greeks gave to the great Capital of No-Ammon on the Nile. In popular imagination Egypt was symbolised by the Sphinx, so Aeschylus surely seized this opportunity for 'good theatre' to make the Sphinx introduce the Prologue to his noble trilogy, 'Oedipus the King', 'Oedipus at Colonus' and the 'Antigone'. An astonishing explanation, but as every playwright well knows, quite possible.

Apart from its dubious inspiration to the Freudian psychiatrists, what possible connection can this story of Akhnaton or Oedipus have with our present thesis of Spacemen?

What if the tale conceals far greater mystery than imagined?

The Greeks regarded the winged Sphinx as daughter of Typhon and Chimaera. Greek mythology described Typhon as a destructive hurricane, a fire-breathing monster, who struggled against Gods and Men until subdued by Zeus with a thunderbolt; he begot the Harpies described by Hesiod as fair, winged maidens, who swooped down on men, though other writers called them disgusting birds with women's heads, who fouled things beneath. The Chimaera too was a fire-breathing monster, part-lion, part-dragon, which lay waste Lydia in Asia Minor until slain by the hero, Bellerophon, on his flying horse, Pegasus. These legends seem fantastic until we consider them as garbled race-memories of the War in the Heavens, when Typhon, Chimaera and the Sphinx resolve into Spaceships. Oedipus (Akhnaton?) was borne to the skies by the Eumenides. The Greeks held the Eumenides, also called Erinyes, in awe even terror; they were dreaded by the Romans as the Furiae or Dirae, the Avenging Deities. Poets represented them as fearful winged maidens with serpents twined in their hair and blood dripping from their mouths, feared by the Gods and Men, they punished disobedience both in this world and after death. Such fanciful descriptions seem poetic imagery yet in general terms are reminiscent of tales now told by peasants in South America alleging terror by Spacemen. Could Oedipus (Akhnaton?) have been translated to another world in a Spaceship?

In his remarkable book *Ages in Chaos* Velikovsky[204] reconstructs ancient history from the Exodus to Akhnaton starting at physical catastrophes chronicled in the Book of Exodus and the Papyrus of Ipuwer, he suggests the startling theory that about six hundred years have been duplicated by the Egyptologists making Hatshepsut contemporaneous with Solomon about 950 BC and Akhnaton contemporaneous with Elijah about 850 BC not 1375 BC as conventionally believed. Correlation of ancient chronologies appears extremely difficult, so impressive are Velikovsky's researches that his sensational findings are difficult to reject.

In the early ninth century BC Elijah frequently confounded the Prophets of Baal by calling down fire from heaven; he conversed with 'Angels' (Spacemen) and in the presence of Elisha was translated to the skies apparently in a luminous spaceship. According to the Second Book of Kings, Chapter 2, verse 11,

> 'And it came to pass, as they still went on, and talked, that behold there appeared a chariot of fire, and horses of fire, and parted them both asunder; and Elijah went up by a whirlwind into heaven.'

A century later Romulus was said to have been whirled to the skies while giving judgement on the Palatine Hill; the Book of Enoch states that centuries earlier Enoch was taken to heaven by a whirlwind.

If 'Angels' or 'Spacemen' visited Israel, surely they must have appeared in Egypt? Considering that the conventional history of Egypt lasted four thousand years extremely scanty records remain, almost all those eulogise the Pharaohs or dutifully praise the Gods; our modern interpretation of hieroglyphics obviously expresses our own connotation of the symbols used and can hardly mean precisely what the scribes intended. The history of the Schism between Akhnaton and the Priests of Amon, analogous to the contemporary strife between Elijah and the Priests of Baal, is deduced from a few papyri and murals supported by the El Amarna tablets; there remain so many pregnant questions awaiting answer. Like our own Reformation reaction against the old established religion had been accumulating for centuries, but what prompted this young 'Luther' to cast down the idols of Amon and to restore the cosmic worship of the Sun, even to building a dream city worthy of a Golden Age? Whence did this royal genius obtain his ideas? His mature conception of the universe and Man's relation with his Creator, his revolutionary views on diet, social philosophy, soul-harmony, town-planning, international pacifism, seem millennia in advance of our own culture today. Could a mere youth unaided transform the centuries-fixed thought-pattern of Egypt? 'God' guided Moses, 'Angels' spoke with Elijah, was Akhnaton inspired by Spacemen?

CHAPTER TWELVE

Exodus

Alone at the Palace window the old King watched the glittering stars fade in the east, the last streaks of lightning split the heavens as thunder rolled on to the western hills. After storm beyond the memory of Man, Earth stirred in uneasy sleep awaiting the dawn. Ominous tension charged the air, the King's haughty features twitched, emotion strained his tired face, his lustrous eyes flashed with anger ill-suppressed; this peaceful scene of his country below should have filled him with calm, instead his heart quaked at the new calamity the morrow might bring. Could fresh affliction curse the land? Water turned to blood, frogs, lice, cow-pox, boils, hails, locusts and three days' darkness, had plagued the country blighting Man and beast. What worse could befall?

The King scowled at that encampment to the north; already overseers were prodding the slaves to build fortifications against their fellow-barbarians from the east. His superstitious subjects blamed these grievous calamities on those arrogant foreigners, who in a few centuries had multiplied to menace the whole country, now the rabble were boasting that their mighty God would descend and deliver them from bondage. Their Leader's warning still thundered in his ears. Let my people go! The King sighed. Could he expel the slaves he needed, to swell the armies of his enemies? Insult his own Priests in surrender to some foreign God? He, the Divine King of a proud country, defeated by an outcast? The King gazed at yon broad river ruffled by the dawn breeze; the years rolled back from his brow, memory relived that golden youth when he and his foster-brother, a foundling from the rushes on that stream had played and laughed in this same Palace, hunted royal lion in the desert and campaigned against the Black

Dwarfs of the South? Since that mad day when his head-strong brother murdered an overseer for beating a slave and fled the country to the desert, the two had never met until this last fateful month. While the Gods had made himself King of the greatest country in the world, his brother had become a fine General, an Adept in the magic arts, a holy Mystic, now rumour gave him the favours of a wondrous God from the skies clothed in light. Gods! The land was haunted by thousands of Gods; even he, the King, was imprisoned by Priests. Did the Gods still visit Earth? That record in the Temple told of the fire-circles, solar-boats, seen by his great Ancestor, over this very Palace two hundred years ago. A God had saved his life? The Eastern campaign! He smiled grimly. In the assault on that city the army was routed, with only his bodyguard he was ambushed by the enemy. When all seemed lost a God appeared, his glorious wonder turned defeat to victory. The Gods did manifest to men. His brother had baffled his greatest scientists. These plagues? Calamities? Coincidence? There had been plagues before. His brother evoked supernatural powers, with the aid of this jealous God he could destroy the whole land. Must innocent people suffer? He would let the foreign slaves go back to their country. But had they a land of their own? He frowned. He was the King. Should he surrender to. . . ?

A star fell from the sky and hovered overhead; its weird glow lit the ground. A dazzling beam blinded the King, sweeping every building below. When he opened his sore eyes, the shining ray flashed from sight. Nameless horror chilled his soul. Something had happened. The universe breathed tragedy. In the Palace a woman screamed.

From every house wailed shrieks of anguish, the sun rose on agony. The King quaked, crushed by calamity. What new horror had. . . ? Cries of servants. Shouts from soldiers. Oaths from the royal stables below. Impassioned sobbing. He turned and beheld his young Queen, face distraught, hugging to her breast the Crown Prince. Fear stabbed his heart. Their son lay still. Sorrow echoed on the morning air. All families mourned. The first-born were dead.

A curse grew into a cry, to a tumult rending the skies. The unknown God! Let the foreigners go lest all the people perish. Before the silent body of his son, the King bowed to the will of his people, the voice of God. In grief he gave his royal sign.

The slave-camp rang with revelry; the foreigners rejoiced. Drunk with freedom, the mob plundered the stricken city, then singing wild hymns, men, women and children marched behind their Leader towards the East.

In the Palace the King hearkened to his Counsellors; the Priests swore blasphemy, the soldiers vengeance. With foreboding the King led his cavalry in swift pursuit. Trapped by the inland sea the slaves stood helpless. As in a dream the King saw their Leader, once his beloved brother, raise his staff. The waters parted forming walls glistening white and blue in the sun. With shouts of joy the rabble rushed across. The painted chariots thundered in triumph. Suddenly the Leader dropped his arm. The giant walls dissolved to waves, swirling torrents sweeping man and horse down to the deep. The King watched in mute horror. God had saved a new nation, while his army drowned.

Such a story should be science-fiction, a fable to moralise the follies of Man. In our familiar Book of Exodus this tale is better told.

Egypt had suffered national disaster, not a home in the land but mourned its dead, slain by God Himself. Her Priests dishonoured, her army disgraced, her slaves freed, the fertile lands of the Nile polluted by plagues, this must surely be the blackest calamity any nation had ever suffered. The records of a civilised people must leave a solemn requiem, a grim recital to warn generations unborn of the penance of the past for their blasphemy against the Lord. The scribes are dumb. Those painted hieroglyphics praise the might of Kings, the prayers of Priests, the solemn splendour of the Gods, yet of the most shocking catastrophe in seven thousand years' history Egypt is silent. As if the Exodus never happened!

The Children of Israel left many countries; on frequent occasions they must have entered Egypt only to leave in hostility; the account of the Exodus seems not to be real history but magic and myth transmitted in Hebrew liturgy to glorify Yahweh and to inspire the Jewish people. Madame H. P. Blavatsky likens the Exodus to legends told of

Atlantis; that profound scholar, Cyrus H. Gordon in *Before the Bible* sees in the Exodus epic affinities with the Homeric literature of Greece and the heroic poetry of Ugarit, all three composed about the same time. Egyptologists, Assyriologists, archaeologists of renown, men of science, who should know the facts, find no evidence whatever of the Exodus; for many centuries in the Second Millennium Semites had been coming and going from Egypt; no Egyptian text refers to the miraculous deliverance mentioned in the Bible.[205]

The professional opinion of Egyptologists is cogently summarised by Dr Barbara Metz, herself an Egyptologist of distinction in her fascinating book *Temples, Tombs, and Hieroglyphics,* P. 151,

> 'The connection of the Hebrews with Egypt has been the subject of long and wearisome discussion among historians; few Egyptian records even mention Israel, and none of them are particularly informative about that nation or the people who founded it. There is no Egyptian reference to Moses, nor to Joseph; no text contains even a faint echo of the long captivity, which began with the enslavement of the Hebrews by a Pharaoh who knew not Joseph and ended with the miracles of the Exodus. It is no wonder that the theories about the Hebrews in Egypt vary considerably. One school of thought would place the Exodus in the fifteenth century BC; another in the thirteenth, a third version contends that there was no single large exodus of enslaved peoples but a series of small exodi, so to speak, which were coalesced by Jewish traditions and historians into a single event.'

If that garrulous gossip, Herodotus, who knew everything about everybody, had heard of the miraculous deliverance of the Jews from Egypt, he would surely have discoursed with wondrous delight.

A papyrus by the Egyptian prophet, Ipuwer, complained of universal catastrophe, the river Nile being like blood; Nefer-rohu declared that the sun was veiled, men could not see; Velikovsky associates these portents with astronomical, historical and geological evidence to suggest a collision between Mars and Venus producing cataclysm on Earth, enabling the Israelites in Egypt to take timely advantage and escape. Some scientists believe that three thousand years ago Earth might have been brushed by a comet, whose tail of noxious gases could have caused many of the so-called Plagues; atmospheric turbulence might even have parted shallow waters for the Israelites to cross. The Faithful still scorning science see the Hand of God.[206]

Egyptologists, like the scientists, know only what they know; most of these distinguished men admit that their knowledge is limited by the facts before them; the development of archaeology like science shows that the scholars are always ready to jettison old ideas for new theories as soon as fresh evidence appears, an attitude few theologians follow. The discovery of the El Amarna tablets flooded light on the times of Akhnaton. Who knows some day a peasant digging in his field may unearth a hieroglyphic stele, the Private Diary of Ramses II, complaining how his forty-ninth honeymoon was spoiled by Israelites, or some Bedouin shepherd near Sinai may find some filthy skins daubed with curious characters relating the 'Life and Loves of Moses' by his secretary, Miriam. Nonsense? Who knows? Has not the fantastic find of the Dead Sea Scrolls revolutionised our conception of Christianity? If real evidence does come to light confirming 'Exodus', no one will be more excited than the Egyptologists; meanwhile though their learned opinions must be respected, these need not be accepted as final facts; just one new find and tomorrow all could be changed. Since, surprising though it seems, the sole account of the Exodus is found in Hebrew literature, we have no alternative but to study the story in the Bible in the light of ancient and modern knowledge and dispassionately scrutinise the tantalising and confusing facts, which for so many centuries the world accepts as Holy Truth.

Exodus describes the epic duel between Moses, inspired by God, and a tyrannical Pharaoh for liberation of the enslaved Israelites from Egypt three thousand years ago. What was the scene of this Drama? Who were the characters, whose contention thrills us even today?

The Book of Exodus is not a factual, critical record of events, history as we write it today; the Jewish chroniclers made no claim to write exact 'history' at all, they were primarily concerned to show God's Revelation to Man through His Chosen People, the Children of Israel. Tradition states that the Pentateuch, the first Five Books of the Bible, was written by Moses, although Philo and Josephus do concede that chapters after his death were finished by Joshua. With all due respect to the learned Moses, this hotch-potch of religious narrative in such turgid style does his great mind ill-justice; it is doubtful whether its literary merit would attract any publisher today. Scholars generally agree that Exodus was derived from several sources comprising four main groups, the present Biblical text being composed possibly centuries after the alleged events. If we can project ourselves to two or three hundred years time and imagine a group of theologians drafting the story of (say) Dunkirk from a miscellany of folk-tales and ancestral memories, all contemporary records having been destroyed perhaps in nuclear war, no doubt we would find the apparent 'miracle' explained by a defiant Montgomery conscripting God and plaguing the obdurate Hitler to let our BEF go. When Hitler repented and launched the Luftwaffe God struck it from the skies. Fantasy, even blasphemy? Who knows? If our civilisation is soon destroyed, such future conjecture of Dunkirk as our own Exodus could really happen.

By 1300 BC the virile Pharaohs of the Nineteenth Dynasty strove to reconquer much of the Egyptian Empire lost by Akhnaton's pacifism, but found their armies confronted by growing aggression from the Hittites expanding southwards through Syria and Palestine. Hordes of Semites, prisoners of war and refugees poured into Egypt settling in the fertile lands of the Delta called Goshen. These aliens, tolerated by the easy-going Egyptians, soon aroused resentment by their domineering arrogance until some Pharaoh felt obliged to subdue the foreign menace ruining the country. Harsh laws conscripted the Asiatics to build fortifications; some of the slaves were Israelites.[207]

Who was the God, Who commanded Moses? The Lord, Who spoke to Moses from the 'burning bush' (Exodus 4, 6) said: 'I am the God of thy father, the God of Abraham, the God of Isaac, and the God of Jacob.' Genesis, 18, describes how on the Plains of Mamra, Abraham 'sat in the tent door in the heat of the day. And he lifted up his eyes and looked, and lo', three men stood by him.' One of the 'men' Abraham recognised as 'Lord'. He had met the 'Lord' on several occasions, notably when the Lord established an 'everlasting covenant' with Abraham and his descendants promising them the land of Canaan. At Isaac's entreaty the Lord remedied his wife's infertility (Genesis, 25) and swore that their seed should 'multiply as the stars of heaven', which they did in Goshen much to the alarm of the Egyptians, who saw their State threatened. Manifestations of the 'Lord', alone or accompanied by 'Angels' in His 'power and glory' had dominated Hebrew life and religion; Moses knew at once that the Apparition was Yahweh, Jehova, the God of Israel. The Hebrew 'El Shaddai', (God Almighty) is reminiscent of the Syrian God, Addu, (Hadad) mentioned frequently in the El Amarna Tablets, but is probably more cogently related to the Assyrian 'Shaddu' meaning 'mountain', especially as the 'Lord' usually appeared on mountains whither He would summon His prophets. Ugaritic texts refer to Yawe as a younger God, the son of El; the Sumerians equated Him with Enlil, the Babylonians with Marduk. The Covenant between God and Abraham was paralled by similar divine protection between Athena and Odysseus, Aphrodite and Anchises, Ishtar and Hattusili, so the special relationship claimed by the Israelites was not unique, most ancient countries and too many modern lands believe themselves to be God's 'Chosen People.'[208]

The word 'God' obviously must have at least two distinct meanings. Today we realise that God, the Absolute, is dreaming into existence countless finite, ever-recurring universes in many parallel dimensions, worlds co-exist spatially in different frequencies of matter, all mirrored by complementary universes of anti-matter; there may possibly be other manifestations of Creation beyond our cognisance. Surely it is no longer maintained that God, the Creator, somehow entered His Cosmic Dream and descended to an insignificant speck of dust in His vast universe to meddle in the affairs of an ignorant nomadic people, to murder their enemies whom He created, for a purpose which is still not clear! The Israelites, knowing nothing whatever of worlds elsewhere, saw God as a Wondrous Being, Who descended from the skies a cloud or fiery wheel (Cherubim);

exactly as the Ancient Indians, Chinese, Japanese and Egyptians beheld their own Gods wing down in chariots of fire. Today we realise that the God of Moses was an Extra-terrestrial landing on Earth in a Spaceship.

Who was 'the new king over Egypt, which knew not Joseph?' (Exodus, 1-8)? Egyptian texts reveal no reference whatever to Joseph. Many Semites were sold into slavery in Egypt; one may have attained high office possibly during the Hyksos domination, but there is no Egyptian confirmation of the Biblical romance. There must have been several incursions of Semites through the centuries into Egypt and probably as many cases of exodus. Since no Egyptian inscription ever mentions Joseph, Moses or the long captivity, it is obviously difficult to date precisely the events of Exodus; murals depict Semites building the 'treasure' cities Pithom and Raamses, (Exodus, 1-11) so it is conventionally assumed the Pharaoh of the Oppression was Ramses II (1292 BC—1225 BC) his son, Merneptah, may have been the Pharaoh of the Liberation, though Egyptologists without any supporting facts naturally disagree. The real truth is that no-one knows the date of the Exodus, the Pharaoh concerned, or whether the events chronicled in the Bible actually happened. The remarkable paradox is that while the *History* of Geoffrey of Monmouth describing the early Kings of Britain is dismissed as legend, similar Hebrew tales concerning the same period are not only accepted as literally true to the last full-stop but for three thousand years have been made the foundation of the Jewish and Christian religions becoming the basis of our Western culture.

The Hyksos invasion and centuries-long conquest of Egypt by Asiatics a few hundred years earlier reminded Ramses of the growing 'fifth-column' of foreigners, so preparing for war with all-conquering Hittites, he interned the Israelites and set them to toil building those mighty monuments making him probably the best-publicised monarch in history. In arresting potential enemy-agents Ramses took the same security precautions of every country in wartime, the Israelites naturally resented this tyranny and demanded release. If all the Germans and Italians interned in Britain during the war demanded freedom and repatriation to join the enemy forces, we can well imagine our

Government's forceful answer! Ramses was probably quite impressed by Moses's God, Jehovah. Did he not owe his very life to the intervention of a God? In 1287 BC Ramses struck north to Kadesh, the great fortress of the Hittites on the Orontes in Lebanon. Poor intelligence and crafty enemy strategy led to the route of the Egyptian army, Ramses with only his bodyguard found himself surrounded by thousands of Hittites facing annihilation. In desperation he prayed to Amon and as his inscriptions recorded later 'At the cry of my despair, swiftly came the God to me, took my hand and gave me strength till my might was as the might of a hundred thousand men'. Ramses counter-attacked, by lucky coincidence a fresh Egyptian division turned up at the crucial moment, like Blücher at Waterloo, and Ramses gained a glorious victory, the Hittites in records from their royal archives of Boghazkoi swear Ramses suffered smashing defeat; which proves that war communiqués in those days had as much double-talk as today. It was fashionable for the peoples of Antiquity to boast of the divine intervention of a God, which makes us wonder whether perhaps it did actually happen? Cicero in *Of the Nature of the Gods,* Book One, Chapter 2, describes how in 498 BC Castor and Pollux intervened to aid the Romans in the Battle of Lake Regillus; Herodotus, Book Four, Chapter 118, and Plutarch in *Theseus* state that in 490 BC at the Battle of Marathon a superhuman figure was seen by a great number of the Athenians fighting on their side against the Persians; the *Annales Laurissenses* describe Flying Fiery Shields from the skies routing the Saxons besieging Sigiburg in AD 776. Could Ramses have been saved by an actual Spaceman?

After the war, Ramses settled down to raise a family, even in our own age of staggering birthrate we marvel at his fabulous virility. Ramses's victories in bed surpassed those in battle. Egyptologists bewonder in awe and envy that Ramses fathered about a hundred sons and fifty-nine daughters, many of whom he married begetting his own grandchildren. In our own days of Child Allowances such exhilarating enterprise would have proved more profitable than football-pools. Such a Man among Men was not to be browbeaten by Moses even with God on his side.

Ramses despite—or perhaps because of—sexual exercise, reigned sixty-seven years, longer that Queen Victoria, and was succeeded by his middle-aged son, Merneptah, (Beloved by Ptah), who soon found himself confronted by Libyan invasion from the South. Like his redoubtable father, Merneptah in his dire distress sought advice from the Gods. The night before the battle Merneptah saw a vision of the God Ptah offering him a sword and telling him to banish fear. With God on his side Merneptah won the expected victory.[209] It is not certain that this vision was a Spaceman, although about this time only a few hundred miles away the Greeks were laying siege to Troy. Homer lyricises the aid each side received from the Gods, who may have been Extra-terrestrials. Would it be too surprising if one of the Spacemen left the beautiful Helen for half an hour and flew over to Egypt to help hard-pressed Merneptah? Tradition states that Helen herself having indirectly burned those topless towers of Ilium was mysteriously wafted from Troy to the lands of the Nile, although some Greeks swear it was another beauty with the same name, the same figure and the same face, who by odd coincidence had also left her kingly husband to elope with a dashing young Prince. What a pity the Greeks had no Sunday newspapers, Aeschylus would have lost his laurels to Athenian columnists! If indeed Merneptah was the Pharaoh in those final negotiations with Moses, he too had first hand knowledge of the Gods.

The great patriarchal world-figure of Moses is veiled in myth and mystery, apart from Hebrew traditions no reference to Moses is found in contemporary records, although his life and works bear close resemblance to other culture-heroes in Greek and Ugaritic mythology. The birth and future destiny of Moses were said to have been prophesied to Pharaoh, who then ordered the murder of all Hebrew boys, so state the Talmud and the historian, Josephus (*Antiquities,* II—ix), an intriguing parallel to Herod's slaughter of the Children, (St Matthew, 11-16). To save her baby's life, his Mother, Yochabed, a daughter of Levi, placed him in an ark of bullrushes in the brink of the river, where he was found by Bathia, Pharaoh's daughter; she adopted him and brought him up as Prince Ahmose at the Egyptian Court. Similar stories were told of many heroes of Antiquity; notably Cyrus (Herodotus, 1-110) and Romulus (Livy, 1-4); Sargon, the first Semitic King of Babylon, was born to a poor woman, who placed him in a basket of reeds to float down the Euphrates until he was found and adopted by a gardener of the royal palace. The name 'Moses' may originate from the Egyptian 'mosi' meaning 'born' or from 'mashah' 'drawn' (from the waters) but some scholars claim it to be Ugaritic. Dr George Hunt Williamson in his remarkable *Secret Places of the Lion*[210] professes to know that in other incarnations Moses was the Ruling Prince of Lemuria, Hammurabi, Law-Giver of Babylon, Joseph, King David, Daniel, Joseph, Father of Jesus, Merlin, Montezuma and Joseph Smith, Founder of the Mormon Church. Unfortunately Dr Williamson does not divulge the sources of this exhilarating revelation nor of the secret understanding alleged between Moses and his 'dear friend' Ramses II, whose great soul apparently incarnated as Amunhotep III (Father of Akhnaton), Jonathan, Plato, Philip, an Apostle, King Arthur of the Round Table and Swedenborg. It might be fascinating if fruitless to speculate what world-figures embody Moses and Ramses today?

Occultists believe that Moses became a most inspired Adept in the Egyptian Mysteries, initiated in the Secret Wisdom preserved from Atlantis and Lemuria befitting him for his future role as Leader of Israel. The Talmud[211] states that when only three, Moses took the royal Crown from Pharaoh's head and placed it on his own, as a test two plates were set before him, one containing fire the other gold. An unseen 'Angel' directed his hand to the fiery coal, which he put in his mouth and was thereafter slow of speech. Had he grasped the gold, he would have been killed. Moses grew up a handsome Prince, trained in Court manners and in war; he dressed royally and was beloved by the people. When he was eighteen he visited his father and mother in Goshen, seeing an Egyptian overseer striking a Hebrew, he slew the Egyptian and fled to join Kikanus, King of Ethiopia, for whom he won great and glorious victories. The Talmud asserts that the Ethiopians crowned Moses as their King and gave him the widow of Kikanus as wife; Adonith however not unnaturally objected to being a wife 'in name only', so she strove to arouse the people against Moses, whom they greatly loved. Moses voluntarily abdicated, but fearful of returning to Egypt travelled on to Midian. Resting by a well he met the seven daughters of Jethro, a shepherd, with whom he lived for some years, marrying Ziporah, a daughter of his host, a curious analogy to the marriage between that other Wanderer about the samc time, Odysseus, who married Nausicaa in roughly similar circumstances.[212]

Two years later Moses led his flock to Horeb, the Mountain of God.

> 'And the angel of the Lord appeared unto him in a flame of fire out of the midst of a bush: and he looked, and the bush burned with fire, and the bush was not consumed' (Exodus, 4-2).

From the 'burning bush' the voice of 'God' warned Moses not to approach closer, then informed him that the 'Lord' had heard the cry of His people in affliction in Egypt and He commanded Moses to go to Pharaoh and demand their deliverance. 'God' would lead the Children of Israel into a land flowing with milk and honey. Throughout the centuries learned Commentators have made little sense of this appearance of 'God' within a burning bush which was not consumed; any conventional explanation appeared most improbable. Our new experience of Flying Saucer phenomena at once presents wondrous and thrilling illumination, interpreted by the landings of Spaceships reported today. A glowing UFO viewed through the branches of a tree would be described by most unscientific minds as a 'burning bush': it would be dangerous to approach too near the forcefield of the Spaceship.[213] According to the Talmud Moses noticed a staff in the Midianite garden and took it as a walking-stick; by the strangest of coincidences this chanced to be that very staff which was carried by Adam out of Eden, and passed down to Abraham, Noah, Isaac, Joseph and now to Moses; it had been suggested that this was actually a vril rod with wondrous powers used by Initiates in Atlantean times; admittedly a somewhat fanciful explanation, such a rod might really have produced the apparent miracles which Moses worked.

Moses, his wife and sons, returned to Egypt. It is astounding to read in Exodus, 4-24, that when they stopped at an inn, the 'Lord' met Moses and tried to kill him! This inexplicable incident demonstrates the somewhat irrational account of Exodus reported in the Bible, and admittedly tends to weaken the plausibility of all the other fantastic events. With his elder brother, Aaron, Moses confronted Pharaoh, who remained unmoved despite the wonders wrought by Moses and the nine plagues sent by the 'Lord'. The tenth plague causing the deaths of the first-born made Pharaoh relent, the Israelites laden with treasures of the Egyptians, fled east. Avoiding the short route along the coast, possibly to miss the frontier fortresses, they turned south and crossed the shallow waters of the Red Sea near Suez. Fresh winds are conventionally believed to have caused a temporary parting of the waters making a ford for the Israelites to cross; a sudden storm possibly whipped up the waves and swamped the Egyptian chariots struggling in mud. A curious legend alleges that Pharaoh found himself transported to Nineveh, evoking visions of a Spaceship; presumably he walked back home?

Even the 'Lord', a powerful Spaceman, who for some reason still obscure, adopted the Israelites, was obviously faced with practical difficulties in effecting their deliverance. He could hardly blast Goshen with nuclear-bombs like Sodom and Gomorrah killing Egyptians and Israelites too; yet Pharaoh would yield only to irresistible force. The plagues suggest the 'Lord' tried some form of chemical and germ warfare, as employed in those Celestial Wars over China, then finally He decided on the selective execution of some Egyptians. The Israelites were ordered to paint their doorposts with blood and to eat only certain foods, then the 'Angel of the Lord' would 'pass them over'. What possible connection could there have been between 'food' and being 'passed over' by the Avenging Angel? The London *Daily Express*, Saturday, April 16th 1966, reported that an anti-radiation vaccine is being tested by scientists at Cornell University, New York, who may be on the verge of a sensational break-through. The vaccine made from the oriental jackbean plant has already proved successful on mice and could protect whole populations against radio-active fall-out from nuclear-attack. Perhaps the restrictions of diet to certain foods might have given the Israelites immunisation against some lethal radiation used by the 'Lord' to kill Egyptians; evidence of the chemical-biological techniques available to the Spacemen. Fantastic though this theory seems, it is not impossible. Next century our cosmonauts landing on another planet may adopt a friendly tribe, later they may be obliged to rescue it from captivity with weapons like the 'Lord' used to free the Israelites in Egypt.

> 'And the Lord went before them by day in a pillar of a cloud to lead them the way, and by night in a pillar of fire to give them light to go by day and night' (Exodus, 13-21).

Many observers today, particularly Associates of the Cosmic Brotherhood, Yokohama, who during the last decade claim to have seen several Motherships in Japanese skies, all agree that the huge, opalescent skyships closely resemble clouds, numerous testimonies confirm that at night the Spacecraft look like pillars of fire. The 'Lord' was apparently making a lengthy visit to Earth, though hardly the forty years alleged for crossing the 'Wilderness' between Egypt and Palestine. His headquarters would probably be the Mothership, a great aerial 'aircraft-carrier' from which He would descend to Earth in a 'Saucer' or 'Scoutship'. He commanded the Israelites to 'make me a sanctuary that I may dwell among them'. In Exodus 25, the 'Lord' fully described the shape, construction, wood, hangings and ornamentations of gold, silver and brass, of this tabernacle where He might reside in secret screened from the people. The tabernacle contained the Ark of the Covenant constructed to precise specifications, being an oblong chest of dry wood, overlaid with gold, which to our scientific minds actually appears to have been an insulated box charged with electrostatic energy of high voltage powerful enough to kill any person who touched it; hence the injunction for worshippers to keep at a respectful distance, since the place whereon it stood was 'holy ground'. In ancient times Initiates appear to have been versed in psycho-electrical science, possibly inherited from the Spacemen. In Britain the Druids used electrical forces such as Dis Lanach, (Lightning of the Gods) and Druis Lanach (Lightning of the Druids) with which they shrivelled their enemies; Numa Pompilius, an early King of Rome, wielded magic weapons. In old Baghdad were found 'ritual objects' which on examination proved to be voltaic batteries.[214] Primitive peoples had superstitious veneration for lightning; it is likely that the Priests of Israel like witchdoctors all over the world used electro-static electricity, perhaps in ways not followed today.

The Priests in the ancient world developed a psycho-electrical wisdom different from our own science and possessed knowledge which our researchers today are just discovering. The 'Lord' in Exodus 28 gave detailed instructions on the making of the garments and insignia worn by Aaron and other Priests, enumerating the various jewels and chains of pure gold ornamenting the 'breastplate of judgement' containing the Urim and Thurrim, these two intriguing devices apparently enabled the Priests to speak to the 'Lord' wherever He might be in the heavens.[215] To the Ancients, jewels had profound astrological significance, which our scientists scoffed until they discovered the fantastic properties of semi-conductors, transistors and lasers transforming electronics; it now seems that the crystals of jewels possess strange powers. Today micro-electronic instruments eavesdrop in Embassies, telemeter from satellites, rubies focus laser-beams with incredible potency and precision; the Urim and Thurrim were probably miniature radios like the tiny discs said to be used by Spacemen today. Mythology and folk-lore abound with intriguing references to jewels with fatal influence on their unlucky owners. This transcendent science was probably imparted to Initiates on Earth by the 'Lord' or other Teachers from Space.

> 'And it came to pass on the third day in the morning that there were thunders and lightnings and a thick cloud upon the mount and the voice of the trumpet exceeding loud, so that all the people that were in the camp trembled.
>
> 'And Moses brought forth the people out of the camp to meet with God; and they stood at the nether part of the mount.
>
> 'And Mount Sinai was altogether on a smoke because the Lord descended upon it in fire and the smoke thereof

ascended as the smoke of a furnace and the whole mount quaked greatly' (Exodus 19, 16-18).

God had previously warned Moses forbidding the people to go up into the Mount as they would surely be put to death. The phenomena described apparently picture the landing of the Mothership on the summit of Mount Sinai watched by the awed, uncomprehending Israelites.[216]

The delivery of the Ten Commandments to Moses by the 'Lord' on Mount Sinai is hallowed by Jews and Christians as a divine Revelation unique in human history, proving that the Israelites must be God's 'Chosen People'. Believers in the Scriptures should know that Minos, the Founder of Knossos, received the Cretan law from a God on a sacred mountain, quoted by Dionysius of Halicarnassus in *Roman Antiquities*, 2-61; a stele unearthed at Babylon depicts Hammurabi, the great Law-giver, accepting his famous laws on tablets of stone from the God, Shamash, also on a mountain.[217] Most countries venerate some holy mountain associated with their Gods. The Revelation to Moses receiving the Ten Commandments written on stone slabs on Mount Sinai could be merely a conventional representation to inspire Israelite patriotism; if the Event actually did occur, it would apparently suggest enlightenment by some Spaceman.

After leading the Israelites through the Wilderness to the borders of Canaan, Moses ascended Mount Nebo, from whose lofty summit the 'Lord' showed Moses the Promised Land, which he could not enter; at that blessed sight the Patriarch died. Moses was a hundred and twenty years old, 'his eye was not dim nor his natural force abated'. Mount Nebo was sacred to Mercury, identified with Thoth and Hermes; its slopes were frequented by Initiates of an ancient cult, who were said to worship the planet Mercury, suggesting that the mountain might have been a landing-place for Spacemen from that occult world.

The 'Midrash' states that Moses was 'half-God, half-man', actual King of Israel. Whether the Liberation detailed in Exodus really happened is open to question; the traditions of Moses so firmly rooted in Jewish consciousness for more than thirty centuries have inspired not only

Hebrews but all humanity. This heroic Leader strove to convert the Israelites from their tribal Gods to monotheism, the worship of the One God. Jehovah Himself was probably a Spaceman, but the esoteric teachings of Judaism acknowledge the Supreme Essence of God, the Creator; thus Moses through his epic inspiration fulfilled the dream of Akhnaton.

It is a fascinating, challenging paradox that the reality of Moses seems proved to us not by the Bible but by the phenomena of our own Space Age. Those meetings of Moses with God evoke Adamski's encounters with Orthon from Venus; the 'power and the glory' dazzling the Israelites resemble the shining spaceships astounding men today. Those wondrous times of the Old Testament are come again. All over the world devoted men and women eagerly await the landings of Extra-terrestrials from the stars; perhaps already Spacemen are inspiring some new Moses to liberate humanity from the bondage of our tragic twentieth century.

Did Spacemen visit Ancient Egypt? Can the supernatural events of Exodus be paralleled by Extra-terrestrial intervention in the Lands of the Nile?

A badly decayed papyrus among the papers of the deceased Professor Alberto Tulli, Director of the Egyptian Museum of the Vatican, translated by Prince Boris de Rachewiltz was identified as part of the Annals of Thutmosis III about 1500 BC (Velikovsky 900 BC).

> '. . . In the year 22, of the 3rd month of winter, sixth hour of the day, the scribes of the House of Life found that there was a circle of fire coming from the sky . . . it had no head. From its mouth came a breath that stank. One rod long was its body and a rod wide, and it was noiseless. And the hearts of the scribes became terrified and confused, and they laid themselves flat on their bellies. . . . They reported to the Pharaoh. His Majesty ordered . . . has been examined . . . or he was meditating on what had happened and which is recorded in papyri of the House of Life. Now after some days had gone by, behold these things became more numerous in the skies than ever. They shone more than the brightness of the sun, and extended to the limits of the four supports of the heavens. Dominating in the sky was the station of these fire circles. The army of Pharaoh looked on with him in their midst. It was after supper. Thereupon these fire circles ascended

> higher in the sky towards the south. Fishes and winged animals or birds fell down from the sky. A marvel never before known since the foundation of this land! And Pharaoh caused incense to be brought to make peace on earth. . . . And what happened was ordered by the Pharaoh to be written in the annals of the House of Life . . . so that it be remembered for ever.'[218]

Thutmosis IV, grandfather of Akhnaton, sleeping under the stars between the paws of the Sphinx 'dreamed' that a 'God' commanded him to clear away the sand and reveal the Sphinx in its true grandeur. Was the Pharaoh's 'vision' a Spaceman?

Herodotus in Book Two, Chapter 91, vividly describes the Temple of Perseus, the son of Danae and Zeus, in the city of Chemmis near Thebes, adding:

> 'The people of this Chemmis say that this Perseus often appeareth up and down their country and often also within the temple; and a sandal two cubits long which he hath worn is found, and whensoever this appeareth all Egypt flourished. . . . And they say that when he came to Egypt for the same cause as the Greeks say, to wit, to fetch the Gorgon's head from Libya, then he came to them also and recognized all his kinsmen.'

Perseus, the slayer of Medusa, whose face petrified all men to stone, flew through the air with winged sandals evoking memories of Spacemen.

About 670 BC the growing might of Assyria threatened the Middle East; in campaigns of ferocious cruelty Sennacherib burned the cities of Israel and advanced on Egypt. Hezekiah united with Pharaoh Tiharkah (Herodotus says 'Sethos') to oppose the common enemy. Herodotus (Book Two, Chapter 141) describes how when Sennacherib, King of the Arabians and Assyrians, marched his vast army into Egypt none of the Egyptian army would come to Pharaoh's aid; the monarch greatly distressed entered the inner sanctuary and before the image of the God bewailed his impending fate. He fell asleep. The God appeared and told him to be of good cheer as he himself would send those who should help him. The Pharaoh rallied an army of traders, artisans and market-people and marched to Pelusium on the Egyptian border.

> 'Then when the adversaries came thither, fieldmice poured forth over them by night and consumed their quivers and consumed their bows and the handles of their shields, so that on the morrow they fled away unarmed and many were slain' (Herodotus, Book Two, Chapter 141).

We are reminded of a famous cartoon of World War One by Bruce Bairnsfather. 'Old Bill' surveying the shattered trenches and smashed dug-outs observes to another 'Tommy' that the damage must have been caused by mice. German Intelligence Officers studying this cartoon in bewilderment complained indignantly 'British propaganda! The attack was carried out by mortar-fire. The High Command does not conscript mice'.

Herodotus surprisingly impressed concluded:

> 'And now this King standeth in stone in the temple of Hephaestus with a mouse in his hand and writing saying thus "Look on me and be pious".'

This curious reference by Herodotus to multitudes of fieldmice gnawing the quivers and bowstrings of the Assyrians recalls the war between Nimrod, King of Babylon, and Abraham, who called down an immense sun-darkening clouds of gnats, which devoured Nimrod's soldiers to the very bones. Shades of Hiroshima and Nagasaki! To the blissfully ignorant, death from radio-active bombs might appear like the gnawing of countless mice or being eaten alive by gnats.

The Book of Isaiah 37 suggests that this deliverance occurred not at Pelusium but Jerusalem itself. Hezekiah, alarmed at the Assyrian invasion, sought urgent aid from the prophet, Isaiah, who said the Lord promised to 'send a blast' unto Sennacherib. On receiving petitions for assistance from the harrassed Egyptian King, Tirhakah, Hezekiah himself prayed help from the Lord. Who delivered His answer through Isaiah.

> 'For I will defend this city to save it for mine own sake, and for my servant, David's sake.
>
> 'Then the angel of the Lord went forth and smote in the camp of the Assyrians, a hundred and four score and five thousand; and when they arose early in the morning, behold, they were all dead corpses' (Isaiah 37, 35/6).

This blast from heaven recalls the destruction by the Angels of the Lord of Sodom and Gomorrah; recent examination of this area suggests nuclear bombing by Spacemen. Nennius in his *History of Britain* recalls that St Germanus prayed to the Lord for three days and nights, on the third night at the third hour fire fell from heaven and totally burned the castle of Vortigern killing him and all his wives. Nennius also mentioned 'St Patrick resembled Moses as an Angel spoke to him in a burning bush, he too lived one hundred and twenty years and no one knows his sepulchre'. An interesting supplement to the events alleged in Exodus!

The greatest personage ever to tread those historic sands of the Nile was surely Apollonius, the 'miracle-worker' of Tyana, whom some people believe to have been Jesus. Before Apollonius was born in 4 BC, an Apparition materialised to his Mother and revealed that he was Proteus, the God of Egypt, the child she was to bear would be himself. Apollonius accompanied by his faithful Damis visited India and most of the lands of the Mediterranean; the picturesque biography by Flavius Philostratus rivals the work by Herodotus as the most fascinating travelogue in Antiquity.[219] This wondrous benign figure spent much time among the Gymnosophists, the naked philosophers of the Upper Nile; his inspired Teachings were possibly received from Spacebeings, for when he vanished at the age of one hundred the Cretans swore he ascended to heaven. For centuries after his 'death', Apollonius was worshipped as a God.[220]

Tangible evidence of Spacemen in Ancient Egypt is difficult to find, especially as our Egyptologists, unsympathetic to extra-terrestrial activity, might not recognise it. In five thousand years time what trace will remain to show that our own Royal Air Force once dominated Egyptian skies? In Libya patches of desert are found to be littered with intriguing glass-like pebbles called tektites, which contain the radio-active isotopes alluminium 26 and beryllium 10. The Armenian physicist. M. Agrest, in his brilliant article in the *Literaturnaya Gazeta* of Moscow, explains that they must be less than one million years old; since the tektites are not of volcanic or cosmic origin, they were probably formed by intense heat and radio-activity; he suggests they were fused in the sands by Spaceships suddenly braking to a stop or perhaps by blast-off; other Soviet scientists postulate an inter-stellar-ship probing the surface of the Earth beneath with special 'sondes' causing tektites. M. Agrest[221] also draws attention to the cyclopean terrace at Baalbek amid the mountains of Lebanon, which mystified the globe-trotting Mark Twain; some of the huge blocks of stone weighing more than a thousand tons would take 40,000 men to budge them by man-power. We are reminded of giant structures in South America and speculate again over the Pyramids. Lebanon is not far from Egypt and the Libyan Desert. Who cut these blocks? Why? Was Baalbek a launching-site for Spaceships?

On the sandstone plateau of Tassili in the middle of the Sahara Desert are rocks lavishly covered with hundreds of fascinating brightly coloured paintings depicting giraffes, elephants, antelopes, hunters with bows and arrows chasing gazelles, scenes on tropical plains millennia ago. Dr Henri Lhote[222] discovered the giant fresco of a human figure eighteen feet in height, which he called 'The Great Martian' since like many smaller portraits it had a remarkable round head suggestive of a space-helmet. These intriguing drawings evoke Oannes, the fish-like creature, who, according to Berossus, taught the early Babylonians. Similar figurines in clay found in Japan called 'Dogu' are believed to represent Spacemen in pressure-suits. The Tassili frescoes may depict the 'Gods', Teachers from the skies, who visited Libya and Ancient Egypt.

Those golden sands of the Nile still shroud the secrets of this mysterious and magic land of Egypt; her shattered columns and scanty inscriptions reveal only a tantalising glimpse of her great and glorious past. If we view those mute remains of countless millennia and compare the tattered papyri with the Bible and the wondrous epics of other peoples in Antiquity, we must surely agree that the wisdom of old Egypt was inspired by her Gods, the Spacemen.

CHAPTER THIRTEEN

Space Kings of Babylon

Babylon! This magic name evokes a land of wonder, veiled by mists of time in dim antiquity, a realm of enchantment, where God Himself descended from the skies in memorable, meaningful revelation, still ruling Men's lives today. From that womb between the Tigris and the Euphrates issued the religion of our Bible, the civilisation of our West, the very hope of our world. The soul of Man ever yearns for this spiritual home, where myth becomes reality; here long ago supernatural happenings enhallowed common Earth illuming the empty lives of men with wondrous meaning. On yon horizon like a mirage glowed the Garden of Eden, above this flooded ground floated Noah and his Ark, here toppled the Tower of Babel whence men dared challenge the Gods, there the 'Lord' stood with Abraham at his tent door, by those sad, grey waters wept the exiled Jews. From the massive walls of Babylon came mighty Kings to conquer the Middle East, in the famous hanging gardens seductive Queens flaunted their beauty, in those lofty towers austere Priests studied the stars. But stern centuries of Empire degenerated to profligacy and vice until this vast metropolis, the 'scarlet woman' cursed by the Prophets, met destined destruction, ravaged by virile soldiery, looted, debauched, deserted, buried beneath the mud, a mound of bricks forlorn and forgotten. For nearly two thousand years Babylon was the centre of civilisation, her language, her laws, her learning, enlightened the world; her wondrous religion inspired men's souls, on her sun-baked soil was staged the cosmic drama still dominating mankind. Proud Babylon is fallen; her mute stones spell a warning for our wanton cities today.

The ancestors of the mysterious Akkadians are said to have been the Chandra or Indovansas, the Lunar Kings, who ruled India ages ago, then brought Indian religion and science to Chaldea. These Celestials were probably Spacemen from other planets, who first landed on our Moon then descended to Earth, as suggested in legends all over the world.

The Babylonians claimed immense antiquity. Berossus, a priest of Bel at Babylon, about 250 BC, lived some time at Athens and wrote in Greek 'Babyloniaca', which he dedicated to Antiochus I, a history of Babylon based on Chaldean records of the temple. He stated these written accounts preserved with the greatest care comprehended fifteen myriads of years containing a history of the heavens and the earth and the sea, of the birth of mankind and of the great rulers of the past. The Babylonian priests were renowned for their learning and it seems certain they would treasure every record of their ancient past. Berossus paid high regard to truth, and it is tragic that his learned work was unfortunately destroyed, all that remains are fragments quoted by Apollodorus, Alexander Polyhistor, Syncellus, Josephus and some alleged forgeries by Eusebius.[223] This erudite priest from Abydenus believed that ten Kings (Divine Dynasties) reigned 432,000 years then the God Cronus (Spaceman?) foretold the Flood to Sisithrus, who built an Ark, sent out three birds and landed in the mountains of Armenia. Cronus also advised Sisithrus to write a history from the Beginning and to bury the account securely in the City of the Sun at Sippara. Nabonasir (730 BC) is said to have collected all the mementoes of earlier Kings prior to himself and destroyed them, so that the enumeration of the Chaldean Kings might commence with him; destruction repeated by megalomaniac Emperors from China to Rome causing almost total absence of all records from the remote past.

The Sumerians like the Ancient Indians, Japanese, Egyptians and Greeks, believed in a Golden Age when Earth was ruled by the Gods, then heroes and superhuman Kings. The Sumerian King-List mentions five cities as existing before the Flood; Eridu, Bad-tibira, Larak, Sippar and Shuruppak.[224]

> 'When kingship was lowered from heaven, the kingship was in Eridu. In Eridu Abulim became King and reigned

28,800 years. Alalgar reigned 36,000 years. Two Kings reigned 64,800 years. . . . Five cities were they. Eight Kings reigned 241,000 years. The Flood swept thereover.'

These astonishing reigns probably refer to dynasties; they parallel the Indian traditions of Rama ruling for 18,-000 years and the incredible ages reached by Methusaleh and Patriarchs of the Bible.

Mention of the post-diluvian descent of Spacemen and subsequent intercourse between Earth and heaven is quoted in the Sumerian King-List. In *Ancient Near Eastern Texts relating to the Old Testament* edited by J. B. Pritchard (Princeton University Press) on p. 114 translations are given of the popular legend of Etana, who apparently consorted with Spacemen. The introductory Note states:

'After the Flood Kingship was lowered again from heaven. In Kish (Ur) Etana, a shepherd, he who ascended to heaven and consolidated all countries, became King and ruled 1,560 years. Balik, Son of Etana, ruled 400 years. Cylinder seals of the Old Akkadian period depict a figure by the name of Etana—a mortal in all respects, except that his name be written with the determinative for "God," a usage applied also to Kings of the Old Akkadian and some of the succeeding dynasties—is the subject of an elaborate legend. The subject is thus clearly one of great antiquity. Its popularity, moreover, is attested by the fact that the legend has come down to us in fragments of three recessions. The Old Babylonian (A), the Middle Assyrian (B) and the Neo-Assyrian from the library of Ashurbanipal (C). With the aid of these three versions, of which the latest is by far the best preserved, the outlines of the story may be reconstructed as follows:

'Etana had been designated to bring to mankind the security that Kingship affords. But his life was blighted so long as he remained childless. The one known remedy appeared to be the plant of birth, which Etana must bring down in person from heaven. The difficult problem of the flight to heaven was eventually solved by Etana's enlisting the aid of an eagle. The eagle had betrayed his friend the serpent, and was languishing in a pit as a result of his perfidy. Etana rescues the bird and as a reward is carried by the eagle on a spectacular and fitful flight. The text fails us at the critical juncture. But the fact that the king-list records the name of Etana's son and heir, and the further fact that myths depicted on seals do not normally commemorate disaster, permit the conclusion that the ending was a happy one after all.'

The Babylonian eagle or Simorgh was well-known to be associated with the Gods; it is not clear as to the significance of the serpent, except that it was often a symbol for a wise man; perhaps the legend conceals an historical incident wherein a King ascended in a spaceship to another planet.

'God' cured Sarah, Abraham's wife, of her barrenness.

A startling version is given by Alberto Fenoglio in [225] *Clypeus,* Anno III, N.2, presumably quoting from *Ur, Assur und Babylon* by H. Schmoekel, translated as follows:

> 'In excavations in Nineveh there was discovered in the Library of King Assurbanipal clay cylinders on which is described a voyage to the sky. It narrates how King Etan, who lived about five thousand years ago, called "The Good King," was taken as an honoured guest on a flying ship in the form of a shield, which landed in a square behind the royal palace, rotating surrounded by a vortex of flames. From the flying ship alighted tall, blond men with dark complexions dressed in white, handsome as Gods, who invited King Etan, somewhat dissuaded by his own advisers, to go for a trip in the flying ship; in the middle of a whirlwind of flames and smoke he went so high that the Earth with its seas, islands, continents, appeared to him like "a loaf in a basket" then disappeared from sight.
>
> 'King Etan in the flying ship reached the Moon, Mars, Venus, and after two weeks absence, when they were already preparing a new succession to the throne, believing that the Gods had carried him off with them, the flying ship glided over the city and touched down surrounded by a ring of fire. The fire abated, King Etan descended with some of the blond men who stayed as his guest for some days.'

This remarkable text not known to our British Museum evokes the experiences of Enoch, Ezekiel and Adamski; we hope it may be true.

Proclus in *Timaeus,* Book One, quotes Iamblichus as saying:

> 'The Assyrians have not only preserved the memorials of seven and twenty myriads of years (270,000 years) as

Hipparchus says they have, but likewise of the whole apocasteses and periods of the seven rulers of the world.'

The ancient Persians, who subsequently conquered the Babylonians, believed that before Adam Earth was ruled for 7000 years by wicked Atlantean Giants and for 2000 years by the beneficent Peris, Sons of Wisdom, possibly Spacemen. Gian, King of the Peris, had a magic shield proof against the Devs' wizardry but impotent against Iblis (Satan). The Persians counted ten antidiluvian Kings, agreeing with Berossus; they also claimed a most ancient race of Kings whose statues were said to stand in a gallery within the Kaf mountains; all seventy-two wise Kings were called Suliman; three reigned each a thousand years. The great King, Huschenk, who restored civilisation, fought the Giants on a flying horse; his famous grandson, Tahmurath, on his winged steed liberated Peris imprisoned by the Giants; his successor, Giamschi, sung by Omar Khayyam, built Esikar, or the ancient Persepolis.[226]

Extra-terrestrials may function in a time-consciousness vastly different from our own. Some advanced planets may bask in civilisations lasting millions of years, where their people attain physical, mental and spiritual powers surpassing our imagination. The Vedas, *The Book of the Dead,* our own Scriptures, tell of Gods beyond Space and Time; to us they appear eternal, just as Man might seem immortal to a transient butterfly. Observers from Space may have surveilled our Earth for millions of years and watched many civilisations rise and fall when our lands were oceans and our mountains mere rocks on the seashore. The Spacemen may return to Earth every thousand years, to us a rare isolated occasion without significance, to Extra-terrestrials sweeping our Galaxy even others beyond, a survey each millennium may be systematic control. Space Visitors whose minds and perceptions operate on planes beyond our cognisance must obviously find communication with Earthlings somewhat difficult, just as we would have difficulty communicating with pygmies in the African bush. Jehovah talked down to Abraham and Moses almost like our Victorian missionaries patronising the Hottentots; communication between alien civilisations without mutual experience is most difficult; the Aztecs, a great and intelligent people, welcomed the Spaniards with more wonder than we would accord to men from Mars.

Abraham, Moses, Berossus and all the Priests of Israel and Babylon would be lost, almost insane, in our nuclear age, and would need to be brain-washed to condition them to our present thought-patterns; similarly our own archaeologists of genius translated to Babylon might scarcely comprehend the Spirit of three millennia ago;[227] their own evaluation of that age assessed by twentieth-century minds might prove quite wrong; it is certain that three thousand years hence scientists will make sorry guesses about our own tortured times. The Patriarchs, philosophers and historians in Antiquity were profound thinkers with fewer distractions than ourselves, they were heirs to valued traditions from a remote past, they were practical men too, faced with all the problems of daily life; they knew what really happened, their eyes saw, their ears heard, they recorded their experiences, events so startling, that despite mistranslations and misunderstandings they have inspired the centuries to our own days. Much as we respect our own brilliant historians and devoted archaeologists, should we not suspend our criticisms of those ancient chroniclers and consider their cultural background? Who were the Babylonians and what did they think about their own country, which they surely knew better than we do?

Babylon and Assyria covered approximately the southern and northern areas of modern Iraq; although Palestine was not part of the Babylonian Empire it was clearly within the Babylonian sphere of influence with close religious, political, literary and cultural links associating the two peoples; many of the experiences which we believe unique to the Jews were actually shared by the Babylonians who shared similar traditions. Man has lived on Earth more than a million years, it is therefore impossible to designate the original inhabitants of any country. In early historical times the people of Mesopotamia were probably ancient Semites from Arabia or Iran, where climatic conditions were presumably much more beneficent than today. About 4000 BC Sumerians speaking an archaic, agglutinative language akin to Chinese, said to resemble the original tongue spoken in drowned Lemuria, migrated from India bringing with them the religion, science and traditions of the old Vedas; this migration may have occurred millennia earlier, especially as Sumerian culture is believed to echo the wonderful Sun Empire of Mu.[228] Excavations at Ur, presumed birthplace of Abraham, show that about 2500 BC the Sumerians had attained a brilliant civilisation, Sir Leonard Woolley's discoveries of magnificent gold vessels, beautiful jewellery, wondrous ornaments and weapons in the tomb of Queen Shubad fascinate us today and compare in splendour with similar finds from contemporary Egypt, evidence of remarkable craftsmanship and technology.[229] The Sumerians had considerable knowledge of mathematics; they divided the circle into 360 degrees and the hour into sixty minutes, each with sixty seconds. We accept this legacy from Ancient Sumer without full appreciation of the profound philosophical, astronomical and mathematical attainments required to conceive this division of time into hours, minutes and seconds, concepts which our own sophisticated science cannot surpass. Perhaps the Sumerians adopted this measurement of Time from their Teachers from Space?

The Sumerians developed a system of writing from pictographs into cuneiform wedges inscribed on tablets of clay baked in the sun. Sumerian, one of the great languages of history, during the third and fourth millennia was widely used for commerce, law and administration, immortalising the fascinating Gilgamesh Epic, our world's first literature. About 2500 BC fresh invaders settled in the south and intermingled with the Sumerians; the newcomers spoke Akkadian, a Semitic language containing many Indo-European words, roots of the future Greek, Latin, German and our modern English, suggesting that the migrants originated from Iran, even India. Akkadian in Sumerian script formed the diplomatic and ritual language of the Middle East, the Latin of the ancient Semitic world eclipsing Egyptian. The Amarna letters to ill-fated Akhnaton from his sorely-pressed Governors all over his besieged Empire were written in Akkadian.

In evaluating reports of Spacemen landing in Antiquity, consideration must be given to the intellectual background of the people whom they allegedly contact; more respect is generally accorded to educated men than to superstitious savages, although sometimes even today there may not be much difference. Civilisation lies primarily in ideas rather than objects. Pythagoras and Plato left no relics for our museums yet their table-talk made them the most civilised men in all Greece; our archaeologists excavating the hut of Homer might judge him a cave-man. Sumerian and Akkadian must have developed through very many millennia to coin words symbolising the sublime concepts and poetic imagery of Babylonian literature; such expressive languages indicate the immense antiquity and cultural attainments of these fascinating folk far better than objects found in the mud. In five thousand years time future archaeologists digging up London may find only Woolworth's, not quite so impressive as the British Museum but perhaps more typical of our own tawdry times.

After the Akkadians came Amorites settling in Babylon followed by more Semites, who occupied the Upper Tigris becoming the Assyrians. About 800 BC Chaldean tribes assumed dominance; generally however the Chaldeans are esteemed as a most ancient Sabaean Sect of star-worshippers possessing occult wisdom and learning; the famous astrologers of Antiquity.

The confused history presented by archaeology becomes more complicated by new discoveries. The central position of Mesopotamia between Europe and China, Russia and India, focus of the whole Eur-Asian land-mass, obviously made the country a magnet during the great migrations of prehistory; many turbulent races must have occupied this fertile land. Babylon's strategic site would attract special study from Spacemen, a suggestion supported by the Sumerian legends and the Old Testament.

Many tiles unearthed in Babylon depict flying dragons, the symbol of Spaceships used by the Chinese; the Babylonians believed that God existed in the 'Sea' of Space; the Jews prayed to their 'Father in Heaven'; all Antiquity worshipped the Supermen in the skies. Initiates of Babylonian Mystery Schools often styled themselves as 'Sons of the Dragon', meaning originally 'Disciples of the Spacemen'. Ugaritic poems referred to Baal, Son of Dagon, as 'Rider of the Clouds',[230] he was believed to have a wonderful palace on a lofty mountain in the North, similar to Solomon's Temple. Spacemen may be called 'Riders of the Clouds'; they, too, are said to approach from the North through vents in the Van Allen belts; they also originate from realms of wonder, a magic land, called by Agobard, Archbishop of Lyons in AD 840, 'Magonia'.[231]

According to Alexander Polyhistor:

> 'Berossus describes an animal endowed with reason, who was called Oannes; the whole body of the animal was like that of a fish, and had under a fish's head another head, and also feet below, similar to those of a man, subjoined to the fish's tail. His voice too and language was articulate and human, and a representation of him is preserved even to this day. This Being in the day-time used to converse with Man, but took no food at that season; and he gave them an insight into letters and sciences and every kind of art. He taught them to construct houses, to found temples, to compile laws, and explained to them the principles of geometrical knowledge. He made them distinguish the seeds of the earth and showed them how to collect fruits; in short, he instructed them in everything which could tend to soften manners and humanize mankind. From that time so universal were his instructions, nothing has been added material by way of improvement. When the sun set, it was the custom of this Being to plunge again into the sea and abide all night in the deep, for he was amphibious. After this there appeared other animals like Oannes.'[232]

Polyhistor continued:

> 'Berossus wrote concerning the generation of mankind, when there was nothing but darkness and an abyss of water. Men appeared with two wings, some with four and two faces, organs of male and female.'

Fragments from Abydenus stated:

> 'A semi-daemon called Annedotus very like to Oannes came up a second time from the sea . . . then Davs, the shepherd, governed for the space of ten sari (a sarus= 3,600 years); he was of Pentibiblon, in his time four double-shaped personages came out of the sea to land, whose names were Evadocus, Everigames, Ennebolus and Anementus.'

In esoteric language the 'sea' or the 'deep' often meant 'regions of Space'; a creature with a fish's head and another head underneath and human feet appears to have been a man wearing a spacesuit. The reference to androgynes with four wings and two faces seems vaguely suggestive of Ezekiel's famous sighting by the Chebar River and probably refers to Spaceships not to Spacemen themselves. Today, Spaceships are believed to descend to the ocean depths, so Oannes like Neptune could actually have emerged from the sea itself. Like Jehovah, who retired to the tabernacle, Oannes every night returned to the 'deep', presumably to his spacecraft.

Berossus was a learned Priest; his history must have been accepted by his erudite colleagues, whom he probably consulted. They believed that several Wondrous Beings had civilised the Babylonians. Who are we to disagree?

Babylon, rebuilt by Nimrod, 'a mighty hunter before the Lord', was more than a city, it was a civilisation dominating men's minds for thousands of years; to scholars it was the fount of wisdom, the centre of millennia-old magic;[233] to the populace those temples of pleasure promised tempting delights. Still glorying in our own vanished Empire, we British can scarcely comprehend that the time-scale from the great Sargon, King of Kings (2371 BC) to the conquest of Babylon by Alexander (323 BC) is longer than the history of Britain between Julius Caesar's frustrated invasion in 55 BC and the enterprise of Mr Harold Wilson today. For more than twenty centuries the manners and morals of Babylon impressed the peoples of Palestine and their neighbours. Without Babylon there could be no Bible; Hebrews and Babylonians, brother-Semites, shared the same legends, the same customs, the same Gods under different names but inherited from the same common source. The Psalmists lament the exiled Jews weeping and wailing by the waters of Babylon longing for Jerusalem; no doubt some did, but many captives allured by the bright lights fraternised with the frolicsome Babylonians and gladly settled there. A few years ago the Elders of Tristan da Cunha exiled in Britain sighed for their own shattered island, their children seduced by our civilised pleasures decided to stay; many who did return home were soon pining for Piccadilly and lost no time in returning; so must Babylon have attracted all its neighbours including the Jews. In its two thousand years, this great metropolis of Babylon surpassed in size and culture most of our capitals today.

Herodotus, who had seen most of the famous cities of Antiquity, marvelled at the grandeur of Babylon. He vividly describes the city as a square fortified by massive walls with a perimeter of fifty miles, eighty feet high and twenty feet thick, wide enough on top for a four-horse chariot to wheel around; set in these walls were 'an hundred gates all of brass' . . . 'Now this wall is the outer wall, but another wall runneth round within, not much weaker than the other. . . .'[234] The King's palace was a miniature city, an ancient Kremlin, adorned by those fabulous Hanging Gardens, one of the Seven Wonders of the world. Above the great golden Temple of Bel arose a lofty tower, where the renowned Chaldean astrologers predicted eclipses and plotted the influence of the planets on human destiny; a vast artificial lake provided water for the huge population, a tunnel ran under the river bed. Such immense constructions would strain our architects and builders today; they prove that the Babylonians had attained superb techniques and in some respects at least were highly civilised.

But it is when describing the customs of Babylon that Herodotus delights us most—and himself, too. In Book One, c. 197 he explains:

> 'They bring out their sick into the market-place (for they use not physicians) and any that hath himself suffered such a thing as the sick man suffereth, or hath seen another that suffered it, approacheth the sick one and counselleth him touching his malady. And it is not permitted to pass by in silence without asking what malady the sick man hath.'

Most sickness originates in the mind; our hospitals are full of the mentally sick. Confession is good for the body as well as the soul; instead of more confusion from psychiatrists, the sorely afflicted might find remedy from fellow-sufferers who have cured themselves. Public therapy as in Babylon might save our Health Service but where could we park sick beds in our streets?

The Babylonians were allergic to Doctors. Methuselah and his friends lived long enough without them. One of

Hammurabi's famous Laws about 1780 BC decreed:

> 'If a Surgeon has made a serious wound in a Gentleman with a bronze knife and has thereby caused the Gentleman to die . . . they shall cut off the Surgeon's hand.'[235]

Babylon had many one-handed Surgeons; today we might have more, if we adopted this poetic justice.

Our twentieth-century world finds itself obsessed by sex; sexual frustration, anti-conception pills, the fantastic birth-rate, pose more menace than the H-bomb. Two thousand years of human experience had taught the Babylonians to deal sanely with sex. The citizens of Babylon needed no 'kitchen-sink' drama, no pornographic novels, no erotic nudes, no sexy night-clubs to slake their passions; no divorce-lawyers earned fat fees, no willing young ladies flaunted French lessons, no call-girls, no 'bunnies', titillated customers. The wise old Babylonians offered a rational, satisfactory solution to all sex-problems without the hypocrisy mocking our modern world. That shrewd student of human nature, Herodotus, knowing the virtues and the vices of men and women comments dispassionately:

> 'Every woman of the land must needs once in her life go sit in the temple of Aphrodite and lie with a stranger. And many also that think not fit to mingle with the residue, but are haughty by reason of their wealth, ride to the temple in covered wagons and there wait; and a great train followeth behind them. But the more part do this: they sit in the precinct of Aphrodite with a crown of cord about their heads. And there are always many women there for some come, as others go. And thoroughfares marked with the line extend in every direction among the women, along which the strangers pass and make their choice. And whensoever a woman sitteth down there, she departeth not home before a stranger cast money in her lap and lie with her inside the temple. And as he casteth in the money, needs must he say thus much "I adjure thee by the Goddess Mylitta". (Now Mylitta is the name of the Assyrians for Aphrodite.) And the money is of any amount for a woman will never reject it, (for that is not allowed her, because the money is sacred) but she followeth him that first casteth money in her lap, despising no man. But when he hath lain with her, she hath performed her duty to the Goddess, and departeth home and thereafter thou canst not give her anything so great as will entice her. Now all

that have any beauty or stateliness depart quickly; but those that are ill-favoured wait a great while, not being able to fulfil the law; for sundry wait a space of even three years or four' (Book One, c. 199/200).

Women in Babylon enjoyed high social status and sexual freedom; a man had legally only one wife but could take concubines, a custom satisfying to the women themselves; sharing a husband better than left single. In Babylon there were no frustrated spinsters or lonely widows; if a woman wanted sexual satisfaction she could enjoy it without shame.

When the Space People wish to influence the course of mankind, a Celestial may descend to Earth and father a hero by some mortal wench like lusty Zeus in mythology, but sometimes Extra-terrestrials may leave a baby of their own to be adopted on Earth in chosen environment, so it might grow up and shape historical events, aided and inspired from Space. Many 'fruits of Venus' left on doorsteps might be babies from the planet Mars. Contemporary events in the Bible suggest that the Spacemen were taking special interest in the Middle East about 800 BC, particularly in the affairs of Babylon.

About 800 BC in Babylon ruled the greatest Queen in all Antiquity, Sammuramat, immortalised as Semiramis, whose wonder still enchants us today. Egyptologists extol Queen Hatshepsut, possibly the Sheba seduced by Solomon; Homer sings of beauteous Helen, 'the face that launched a thousand ships and burnt the topless towers of Ilium'; Virgil romanticises Dido, who mourning Aeneas died for love; yet none of these royal ladies evokes the magic and mystery of fabulous Semiramis, Queen of golden Babylon. Even the indolent Rossini, writing as usual in bed, composed a sparkling Opera in her honour, a compliment he denied to naughty Helen.

Semiramis was believed to be the daughter of the fish Goddess, Ataryatis, and Oannes, God of Wisdom, whom Berossus described as bringing civilisation to Babylon; Ataryatis wearing a spacesuit like her husband might look like a fish, too. Their baby-daughter, Semiramis, was said to have been miraculously fed by doves, symbolism perhaps for Spaceships, until she was found by Simmas, the royal shepherd. This adoption is a remarkable parallel to these other famous foundlings, Sargon, Moses and Cyrus; who proved to be men of destiny beloved by the Gods. Semiramis was brought up at the Babylonian Court among that highly sophisticated society, and possibly received instruction in the Secret Wisdom from the Magi. In 811 BC Babylon was conquered by Ninus, King of Assyria, founder of Nineveh, known to history as Shāmshi-Adad V, who in masterly campaigns devastated much of Asia; after subduing Media he launched a great assault on Bactria. Semiramis shrewdly married Menon, one of Ninus's Generals, and with him performed remarkable exploits during the Bactrian war which swiftly brought her to the notice of the King. Menon is said to have committed suicide at a suspiciously convenient moment for his ambitious wife; her notorious beauty and dazzling personality captivated Ninus, who promptly married her. The love-lorn Ninus lived only long enough to father a son, Ninyas then he too conveniently died leaving Semiramis, Empress of his huge dominions. Semiramis gave her husband a fabulous funeral and buried him under a huge mound allegedly a mile and a quarter high and the same dimension square, typical of the vast constructions which she raised in Babylonia. Even Shakespeare thousands of years later was impressed by this fantastic mausoleum. In *Midsummer Night's Dream* he made Bottom the Weaver and his cronies enact their farcical tragedy of Pyramus and Thisbe by 'old Ninny's tomb' in claptrap which must have made that Monarch turn in his grave.

Now Queen, Semiramis proceeded to rebuild Babylon with palaces, temples and dykes draining floods from the Euphrates, feats which earned praise from Herodotus,[236] some traditions associate her with erecting the famous Hanging Gardens, though other authorities suggest Nebuchadnezzar built them for a favourite wife pining for her verdant homeland. After reorganising her own country, Semiramis felt the urge to reorganise her neighbours. She invaded Egypt, Ethiopia and Libya; when there were no worlds left to conquer like Alexander five centuries later Semiramis turned to India. For this classic enterprise Semiramis is said to have marshalled armies comprising 3,000,000 foot, 500,000 horse and 100,000 chariots, with 2,000 ships prefabricated for transport overland and assembled for crossing rivers built by men from Cyprus and Phoenicia; even allowing for wild exaggeration, this was surely the most stupendous expeditionary force in all Antiquity; the planning, provisioning and logistics of such an expedition must have equalled the Allied assault on Hitler-held Europe on D-day. Semiramis routed Strabrobates of India in a great naval battle destroying a thousand of his ships, her engineers bridged the Indus and this martial Queen led her vast forces into the heart of India. She overcame her shortage of elephants by having mechanical elephants constructed from hides so lifelike that the real elephants were deceived, but not for long. Even in those distant days elephants never forgot; they may be short-sighted animals but soon know if they are making love to a mechanical mate. Strabrobates counterattacked, Semiramis was forced to retreat in hostile country and lost most of her army.[237]

On return to Babylon Semiramis made war against the Medes and the Persians, suddenly after a Regency of forty-one years she abdicated in favour of her son, Ninyas, and disappeared. People believed that she turned into a dove and flew to the skies, suggesting perhaps that like Elijah roughly the same century, she was translated in a Spaceship. Her disappearance parallels the translation to the skies of Apollonius or Tyana in AD 98, for centuries this wonderful man was worshipped as a God. Semiramis for many years was worshipped as a Goddess being identified by the adulating Babylonians as an embodiment of Ishtar, Goddess of Love, identified with the planet, Venus.

Her name 'Semiramis' or 'Sama-ramos' was said to signify the 'Divine Token', the 'Standard of the Most High', the Elohim, Celestial Lords, who were probably Space Beings. This emblem, the figure of a dove, surrounded by an Iris, recalls Os-Iris of Egypt, and is similar to the Egyptian 'Eye of Horus' apparently a Spaceship. In Semitic languages the word 'Sama' means 'Sun', Semiramis therefore appears to have had some close association with the Sun, which may infer that she was a Celestial; the Queen was accompanied by the Winged Sun Disk of

Assyria, which later symbolised the great Persian God, Ahura-Mazda.[238]

Notorious Queens are usually embellished by extravagant legends; it is often difficult to separate fancy from fact. Semiramis was held in awe by Assyrians, virile warriors hardly noted for their deference to women; it is remarkable that these fierce soldiers submitted to leadership of their Amazon Queen; they left a column to her greatness found in 1909 describing her as 'A Woman of the Four Quarters of the World'. Ctesias, Physician to Ataxerxes II, in 402 BC stated that the giant cliff carvings of Darius at Behistun a century earlier represented Semiramis surrounded by a hundred bodyguard. Herodotus and Diodorus Siculus paid tribute to her greatness; the Armenians called their country around Lake Van Shamiramgerd in honour of the Warrior Queen. In an age of masculine supremacy women were usually treated as inferiors especially among Semitic races, the fame of Semiramis surely suggests that her personality and power must have been phenomenal, even fantastic, to weld together millions of men in one fighting force conquering most of the Middle East then storming India. For centuries Semiramis symbolised golden Babylon. After her mysterious disappearance the men, who had known her in life, worshipped her as a Goddess, proof of her magic influence, which vibrates across three thousand years to thrill us today. We honour the great and noble women of our own twentieth century but can we think of any woman—or any man—whose fame will span the next thirty centuries? Most of our public figures are mercifully forgotten while they are still alive. If any earthly Queen originated from Space surely she was Semiramis!

The next time the Celestials inspired a woman to lead armies to victory was in AD 1425 when Joan of Arc liberated France.

It is a fascinating coincidence that if Velikovsky's time-sequence is correct, if six hundred years of Egyptian history were apparently duplicated, Akhnaton, the Heretic King, must have been contemporary with Semiramis, both being influenced by Space Beings.

The strategic position of Assyria in Northern Mesopotamia made her a buffer between north and south; her grim warriors for centuries shielded Babylon and the lands beyond from the hordes of Cimmerians massing behind the Caucasus and the Hittites advancing from Anatolia. In his epic poem 'The Destruction of Sennacherib', Byron with some justification wrote:

'The Assyrian came down like a wolf on the fold,
And his cohorts were gleaming in purple and gold.'[239]

Assyrians fought with a ruthless ferocity, terrifying their neighbours, yet their barbarities pale before the Nazi death-camps and H-bomb horrors shaming our own century. The urbane Babylonians fell an easy prey to the virile Assyrians but civilised their conquerors, their religions and cultures intermingled. Nineveh, capital of the all-conquering Assyrians and cross-roads of important trade-routes, rose to fame and power; her palaces and temples were distinguished by colonnades of human-headed lions with wings resembling the Sphinx and winged human-headed bulls, which may have been symbols for Spacemen and Spaceships.[240] To the agrarian peoples of Assyria ignorant of machines, Spacecraft might appear in memory like mighty bulls with wings; these winged lions and bulls usually have five legs; could the reason be to differentiate them from real animals, is it too fanciful to suppose five legs perhaps represent the landing-wheels of the Spaceships?

The God Ashur[241] resembled Jehovah and was specifically represented by the winged sun-disk, which we now associate with Spacemen, and significantly enough with insignia for national Air Forces today. About 630 BC Ashurbanipal collected at Nineveh thousands of tablets recording every facet of Assyrian culture forming one of the most magnificent libraries of Antiquity. At his death the Babylonians revolted, aided by Medes from Iran, they crushed Assyria and in 612 BC destroyed Nineveh. The new Babylonian Empire began by Nebuchadnezzar extended its sway to Israel; the Captivity of the Jews, grievous though it was to Prophets of the Bible, was only a minor incident to imperial Babylon, which in 539 BC fell to Cyrus of Persia; after two centuries of Achaemenid domination the city surrendered to Alexander the Great in 323

BC. Alexander had grandiose plans to make Babylon capital of a world-empire, but those whom the Gods love, die young; he was stricken with a fever, probably aggravated by a surfeit of wine at a banquet and died at the early age of thirty-two leaving the world and himself unconquered. Proud Babylon sank to ruins, centuries later its splendour, its pomp, its very site, were forgotten; the palace of Semiramis became buried in mud.[242]

The science of the Babylonians impressed the peoples of Antiquity as it does ourselves today. Herodotus marvelled at the Temple of Marduk, a towering eight-storied structure, crowned with two vast golden shrines; they were unmatched in beauty and occupied a square a quarter of a mile in perimeter; the statue of Marduk weighed twenty-six tons of pure gold; the Tower of Babel is said to have been built with fifty-eight million bricks, comparable with the Pyramids; the great walls of Babylon with their mighty gates of bronze and the wonderful temple of Bel were wonders of the Ancient World rivalled by Nineveh and Persepolis.[243] Necklaces, amulets, pottery and furnishings in the tomb of Queen Shubad of Ur, the golden treasures of the Achaemenids and the gold discs and pendants found in Scythian graves, all show an artistry, elegance and marvellous craftsmanship suggesting a highly cultured civilisation, despite the incessant wars, which were probably not as cruel as the conflicts in our own century. Metallurgists five thousand years ago attained remarkable technology in smelting ores at temperatures up to 1200° C and produced bronze from copper and tin, which craftsmen made into vases, axes and swords of considerable beauty and strength; chemists mixed wonderful dyes and drugs,[244] which we today are glad to copy; there is also reason to believe that the Priests could utilise static electricity. Although physicians had apparently no advanced knowledge of bodily functions, surgeons did perform delicate operations, even removing cataracts at great personal risk to themselves; if they blinded their patient the Law required that their own offending hand be cut off. Would our own Doctors show such devotion today?[245]

For centuries the Chaldeans were famed for their magic, which inspired the Greeks and the Arabs then the

Alchemists, forerunners of our modern science. Babylonian mathematicians used decimal and sexagesimal systems; they knew the value of 'pi', the so-called Pythagoras theorem, square and cube-roots, elementary geometry and algebra solving complicated quadratic equations. Considerable mathematical and engineering skill was required to construct the great walls and domed temples and dykes across the Euphrates; the famous Hanging Gardens, really a series of balconies, were watered by an ingenious pumping system of irrigation.

The Chaldeans were universally regarded as great astrologers; for two thousand years they studied the planets and the stars from their tall ziggurats and prophesied the influence of the stars on human destiny. If we assume that only a hundred Priests kept continuous surveillance of the heavens from the scores of lofty towers, then in two thousand years the Babylonian skies were observed for about 2,000,000,000 man-hours, probably longer than all the man-hours devoted by modern astronomers since Newton! For twenty centuries the Babylonians kept incessant vigil on the heavens comparable with our radar watch today. What prompted such close and continuous observation? We with our space-capsules and satellites in our Space Age still cannot comprehend the vital importance of the stars for the peoples of Antiquity; we irrationally attribute their interest to ignorance or dismiss it as paganism without pausing to wonder why the skies should exert such fascination to allegedly primitive minds, although the commercial, technical, diplomatic and military skill of the Babylonians, Assyrians and Persians in many respects almost equalled our own today.

The Chaldeans are said to have had little knowledge of theoretical astronomy, their conception of the universe differed greatly from ours; critics forget that in five thousand years time our own dubious theories may be ridiculed. It is alleged that the Chaldeans believed the planets to be Divinities; perhaps we misinterpret their scanty texts; they may have meant that the planets were inhabited by Gods, the Spacemen; if so, their knowledge of the planets probably surpassed the uncertainties of our own astronomers, who are currently trying to make up their minds about the inhabited universe. Cuneiform tablets record the heliacal risings and settings of Venus, ephemerides or positions of the sun, moon and planets, and of eclipses from 747 BC onwards; the Priests fixed the Calendar, and the length of the year; they knew of the nineteen year Cycle of Meton; the tables of Nahuriman quoted by Strabo are incredibly accurate. Kidinnu about 375 BC calculated the solar-year with an error of only 4 minutes and 32.65 seconds, a precision which mystifies our modern astronomers.

In AD 45 Apollonius of Tyana on his way to India paused at Babylon and met the Magi of whom he said, 'They are wise men but not in all respects', sentiments suiting our own scientists today. On the ceilings of Babylonian temples he saw images of the heavenly bodies, the Gods moving through the ether. From the roof hung four golden gyges, winged wheels like the celestial vehicles described by Ezekiel.[246] The Magi of Persia told Alexander the Great that wings carved over temples represented the Eagle dwelling near the Sun, whose Spirit or Simurg descended to man.[247]

The cold clear night air of Babylon was ideal for astronomical observations; though no telescopes have been found, the Chaldeans had glass and lenses of quartz and it is surely likely that even by accident some Priest must have chanced to look through two lenses at once and thus discovered the properties of the telescope like Lippe and Galileo; surely the magnifying qualities of glass must have been utilised for studying the stars. In two thousand years of observation the Priests probably noticed many strange sightings in the skies; they would probably glimpse the Spaceships of Jehovah and His 'Angels' descending to the Prophets of Israel and indeed to themselves. Winged statues abounded all over Assyria, Babylonia and Persia; any Stranger marvelling at the architecture and tall watchtowers would have sworn that Babylon symbolised the Space Age.

An appreciation of Babylon is essential to the understanding of the Bible; the Patriarchs were not ignorant shepherds; they were heirs to the wisdom and culture of an historic civilisation; like the Priests of Babylon they saw and spoke with Spacemen.

CHAPTER FOURTEEN

Space Gods of Babylon

For two thousand years Babylon vanished from history, remembered only by scholars mourning the past and preachers moralising on that wanton city and its warning to our sinful modern world. Until early last century Mesopotamia was a land of mystery, vague symbol of the mutability of Man, this mud wilderness was once the cradle of mankind, here blossomed the Garden of Eden, now only Bedouins wandered these dusty plains like the Patriarchs of old, heedless of the treasures and the black oil beneath.

For the solitary Europeans this flat, featureless landscape breathed a magic thrilling their souls; somewhere on this barren expanse the 'Lord' in all His Power and Glory appeared to Abraham, these bricks once built the Tower of Babel, perhaps yon hillock hid the palace of Belshazzar on whose wall wrote that ghostly hand the night great Babylon fell. Beneath this scanty soil lay buried a fabulous civilisation, the origins of our own Bible, the source of life itself.

Those brick mounds occasionally yielded tablets scratched with curious wedged marks; for forty years scholars had puzzled over this cuneiform script without success; no bilingual Rosetta Stone appeared to interpret these signs, unlike hieroglyphics the strange symbols defied solution.

In the early nineteenth century a young German teacher, Grotefend, applied himself with remarkable ingenuity to the decipherment of cuneiform tablets discovered at Persepolis and by brilliant logic spelled 'Darius, Great King, King of Kings, Son of Hystapes' and 'Xerxes, Great King of Kings, Son of Darius'. During the next thirty years the Frenchman, Burnouf, and the German,

Lassen, resolved more letters but without a linguistic key scholars remained baffled. The cuneiform texts captured the interest of a Major Henry Rawlinson, a servant of the East India Company, seconded to the Persian War Office; in 1837 he studied the famous inscription of Darius on a cliff face in the mountains of Behistun, where twenty-five centuries ago the Great King was sculptured in triumph over prostrate foes, described in fourteen columns of writing. With considerable risk, Rawlinson lowered down the cliff on a rope, copied the inscriptions which he found to be in three languages, Persian, Elamite and Babylonian; by 1846 the text was translated, though many difficulties remained. Meanwhile Botta had discovered Nineveh and Layard was excavating at Nimrud, more and more tablets were found, many proved to be syllabaries in Sumerian and Semitic, within a few years Assyriologists could read the cuneiform writing and in 1876 George Smith, another amateur, astounded the world by translating the Gilgamesh Epic, the Story of the Flood.[248]

During the recent decades thousands of tablets have been discovered, notably the great library of Assurbanipal in Nineveh, their decipherment has given archaeologists a vivid panorama of Babylonian life and culture. Yet difficulties remain. The same interpretive problems perplexing Egyptologists baffle Assyriologists too. Hebrew scholars question Biblical texts yet the Hebrew tongue has been jealously preserved continuously for thousands of years; immense problems must surely arise in interpreting the precise meaning of the ancient Egyptian and Babylonian languages, which for centuries were lost.

'Traduttore—Traditore.' 'Translator—Traitor.'

The gifted Italians brilliantly summarise the fundamental pitfall of all translations, the impossibility of perfectly interpreting each nuance, each exquisite expression, each precise meaning, from one language to another. Different languages develop in different environments, spoken by different races with different traditions and different experiences. Literary critics stress that translations of modern works are pale, distorted reflections of the original compositions; throughout the centuries translations of famous Greek and Latin Classics reveal significant modifications. It is a perennial complaint that our elders never comprehend the younger generation, how then can we pretend to understand a foreign people of five thousand years ago with whom we share no common traditions? During General Elections we seldom understand our rival politicians, we cannot comprehend why so many sects should squabble about the lucid, simple words of Christ; most people secretly admit they make little sense of much of Shakespeare, whom we British glorify provided we need not read him. Cohorts of lawyers are assiduously employed debating and disputing the solemn, measured words of Acts of Parliament. Yet we conventionally accept the translations of our Assyriologists as being exact, even though two independent translators seldom agree. Bernard Shaw jested that Britain and America were divided by a common language; if we cannot fully understand our transatlantic cousins, as recent history clearly shows, can we really understand those dim and distant Babylonians?

What actually did happen in Babylonia? What did people see? What did they hear? Judges, solicitors and police, all admit exasperation in trying to equate common eyewitness accounts of the simplest accident; famous Generals inflict us with wildly differing versions of the same battle; newspapers go to fantastic lengths in presenting controversial slants of identical news stories. The same eye-witness may dream up many conflicting versions of what he allegedly saw, finally he becomes less and less sure himself. When a man is quite certain of his facts, he often lacks the vocabulary, the phraseology, to convey his precise impression to others, especially if the latter are preconditioned to a different thought-pattern. The natives of the Ellis Islands in the South Pacific follow the 'Cargo Cult' and worship a white 'God' called John Thrum, who in 1941 flew down from the skies bringing them gifts, then five years later ascended to heaven. Our theologians laugh that the alleged 'God' was an American airman in the War against Japan, of course, we must agree. When they read some cuneiform text describing a white God flying down from the skies the same theologians solemnly swear that the Babylonians saw and spoke with God Himself, the Creator of the infinite Universe! What of the aeroplane or a Spaceship? Forgetting the Indian Vedas the Professors smile that flying-machines were not then invented, there were no men on the stars. Our Air Force experts may condescend that the Babylonians evidently did see something, it must have been the planet, Venus, unusually bright in the Mesopotamian skies, though for thousands of years the natives would surely have known Venus like the moon. The learned mythologists decide that the Babylonians saw nothing, they all imagined a personification of the North Wind; they saw imaginary cartoons as on a weatherman's chart. The Assyriologists, whose decipherment of cuneiform shines as one of the most brilliant conquests of the human intellect, interpret these baffling texts in the only words they know, in phrases from our archaic Bible or verses of literary elegance, heedless of Spacemen or Spaceships; they tell us not what the Babylonians really saw but what they themselves might have seen, had they been there.

The virile Gods and alluring Goddesses of Babylon live in a wonderful mythology, whose Semitic magic distils fascinating tales of the Creation, the dissension and passion of the Immortals in Heaven, the amorous exploits of Celestials on Earth, the epic adventures of heroes, proud Man's rebellion against Lords from the skies, the Flood with homeless humanity civilised again by Teachers from Space. As we thrill to the deeds of Merodach, the love-cult of Ishtar, the slaying of Tammuz, the wanderings of Gilgamesh, told in bewitching, colourful poetry transmuting those dull clay tablets into the earliest, greatest literature in the world, we suddenly realise we have read it all before, the same wondrous story springing from some deep mysterious source in lost Antiquity. Indra, Amaterasu, Osiris, Isis, El, Astarte, Jehovah, Lilith, Zeus, Aphrodite, Jupiter, Venus, Thor, Freya, and their celestial companions all seem to merge with Merodach, Shamash, Ishtar and those brilliant deities of Babylon. The Gilgamesh Epic echoes the adventures of Kret[249] of Ugarit anticipating the travels of Odysseus, until it dawns upon us that we must be reading the same ancient tales of love and war and fantasy; the personalities, the passions, the places, seem to soar beyond time and space in the same transcendent realms, only the names are different. India, Japan, Egypt, Syria, Judaea, Greece, Rome, Scandinavia, even the Americas, agree with Babylon; millions of people all over the world for thousands of years worshipped the same Gods and Goddesses, surely the same Celestials from Space.

Detailed study of the Gods of Assyria and Babylon seems superfluous, surely we know them all before we begin, a simple exercise in comparative theology affords an empirical assessment of the pantheon of Gods leaving those clay tablets to prove our theory correct. Those same Wondrous Beings from the skies, who inspired the ancient peoples of India, China, Japan and Egypt in the East and Greece, Scandinavia and the Americas in the West, must certainly have descended to the muddy plains of Mesopotamia to instruct men there like they did all over the Earth. The Babylonians must have seen the same War in the Skies, experienced the same catastrophes and cherished the same confused memories of their Space Kings. Before even considering Babylonian religion and myths, we can confidently expect to find a primeval God, Who created the Universe, Earth and Man from Chaos, Gods of the Sun, Moon and Planets, a fertility Goddess, who would descend to the Underworld, a God who would be slain to rise again, old Gods dethroned by virile young Gods, Celestials ruling Earth in a Golden Age, followed by war between Gods and Men, waged by aerial ships speeding like light with annihilating bombs, fights with Sky Dragons, cataclysms ravaging Earth, change of climate, collapse of civilisation, a Wagnerian Gottesdämmerung, a twilight of the Gods abandoning our planet to be worshipped by men at whose urgent prayers a God would land in secret to give aid or cosmic instruction to Initiates. We have heard all this before, over and over again, as yet we may not know the names, which hardly matter. Were cuneiform never deciphered, we could still predict with accuracy the Gods and myths of Babylon from the universality of the Spacemen.

The Father of the Sumerian Gods was Anu,[250] who

was believed to dwell in the Constellation of the Great Bear, like the 'Seven Shining Ones' in Egyptian Mythology, significantly the direction from which the Spaceships approach the Earth. Anu was dethroned by Enlil, who in turn was overcome by Merodach (Marduk) paralleled in Greek mythology by the succession of Uranus-Cronus (Saturn)-Zeus (Jupiter) suggesting three waves of Invaders from Space, who ruled Earth in the Golden, Silver and Iron Ages sung by the classical Poets. The name En-lil meant 'Chief Demon', he was a Sky God, 'Lord of the Storm' and probably represented by the great winged bull, especially in the City of Nippur, where his temple was called 'Mountain House'; since the God was believed to dwell on the top of a mountain, although there were no mountains in Mesopotamia. Under his more popular title 'Bel' Enlil destroyed a Dragon and was identified with the Pole Star of the Equator; we recognise the usual attributes of the Spacemen corresponding to similar descriptions by the Egyptians and Greeks. Merodach or Marduk, the patron God of Babylon, was often known as 'the Bull of Light', which may have signified a Spaceship; the 'Epic of Creation' described how 'He set the lightning in front of him, his body he filled with blazing fire', he rode the storm-chariot, irresistible, awe-inspiring, he fought and slew the monster, Tiamat,[251] in titantic conflict, signifying the war between the Spirits of Light and the Powers of Evil, paralleled in Egypt by the struggle between Horus and Set. In Assyria Merodach was identified with the all-conquering War God, Asshur, who was represented by a disc enclosed by two wings above which was the figure of a warrior with bent bow and arrow on string. Ea (Oannes), God of Wisdom, also dwelt near the North Pole, he was described as having a human head inside a fish's head, suggesting he was an Extra-terrestrial wearing a space-suit from some advanced planet descending to teach mankind. In Palestine Oannes under the name Dagon was greatly beloved and he was occasionally worshipped by the Hebrews, he was believed to have fathered the fabulous Semiramis.

Sin, the Moon God, worshipped at Ur, was symbolised by the Crescent Moon, which later became the emblem of

Islam just as the old sun-symbol of the Cross was adopted by Christianity; the Chaldeans associated the moon with the metal silver. Nergal, God of War, was identified with the planet Mars, his metal being iron. Nebu, like Thoth, guided the Gods, he invented writing and was associated with Mercury, a planet of occult mystery; his priests were famed as astrologers, his metal the rare platinum. Ninil, the Assyrian War God, represented Saturn, his metal lead. Jupiter was identified as Merodach, and the metal tin. Most fascinating of all was Ishtar or Inanna, the only great feminine deity of the Semitic world, associated with an eight-pointed star, the planet Venus; her metal was copper.[252] Zu, a storm God, appeared like a thunderbolt and many centuries later in the Arabian Nights was typified as a 'roc', which swooped on a ship and carried off Sinbad, just as UFOS are said to kidnap seamen, like perhaps the crew mysteriously missing from the ill-fated *Marie Celeste*. It is significant that the Babylonian ideograph for 'Star' was the same as for 'God', although for 'God' it was repeated three times stressing a close link between the Gods and the Stars.

The most popular deity in Babylon was Shamash, the beneficent Sun God, associated with the metal gold; the great Lord of Light, who on a mountain-top presented King Hammurabi with tablets of the famous Laws of Babylon about five hundred years before Jehovah gave the Ten Commandments to Moses on Mt Sinai. The Book of Exodus, attributed to Moses, was revised by Ezra during the Captivity in Babylon, it is therefore possible that the Prophet copied the earlier Babylonian tradition to inspire Jewish faith in Jehovah, although other well-known Leaders in Antiquity such as Minos of Crete are also believed to have received Laws or Guidance from Gods on mountains. In Assyria Shamash was sculptured with the winged-disk; in Babylon a cuneiform inscription of the first millennium BC, probably copied from a more ancient monument, shows Shamash, the Sun God, sitting in his shrine with a four-pointed star and rays suggesting a Spaceship. Inscriptions honour Shamash as the 'Illuminator of the Regions', 'Lord of Living Creatures', 'Judge of Good and Evil'. The God dwelled in the eastern mountains, opened the gate of the morning and lit up heaven and earth with beams of light. Such description suits the rising sun but it could possibly be the Babylonian impression of a resplendent Spaceship from the East, the 'Power and Glory of the Lord'. It is significant that Hammurabi, a wise and benevolent ruler, received instruction from Shamash about the same time that Abraham talked with Jehovah only a few miles away, a remarkable coincidence, suggesting that Shamash and Jehovah were possibly one and the same Spaceman, a Cosmic Master guiding Initiates on Earth.

Tiglath-Pileser I, a mighty warrior, who about 1120 BC conquered much of Palestine and Armenia, styled himself as Viceroy of Shamash on Earth; Assurnazirpal III and Shalmaneser II in the ninth century BC exalted the sun cult of Shamash, which had close affinity with the Egyptian worship of Ra. A bas-relief from the north-western palace at Nimrud shows Assurnazirpal attended by a winged human figure arrayed like the King; numerous reliefs picture other Assyrian monarchs accompanied by human counsellors with wings or winged humans with the head of a bird; stylised above these scenes hovers the winged Sun Disk. Only a generation after Shalmaneser II Assyria and Babylon were ruled by the fabulous Semiramis, whose fantastic career suggests she originated from Space. In 714 BC Sargon II extended his rule north to the Caspian Sea where he built a sanctuary to Shamash; his son, Sennacherib, campaigned against Hezekiah of Jerusalem, about 670 BC Sennacherib's forces invading Egypt were decimated at Pelusium by what now appears to have been a nuclear blast by Spacemen.

The Assyrians were tough soldiers and hard-working peasants, their priesthood were inspired by Chaldean Initiates, the builders of Nineveh's great temples were practical men of affairs, they were not vague dreamers ruled by insubstantial myths; they would not sculpt winged humans beside their all-powerful Kings, any more than we would paint golden Angels in public portraits of our own Queen, unless the winged humans actually were on Earth counselling their King. The humans themselves, of course, were not freaks or some fantastic mutation having wings, the winged figures were the Assyrian conception of men, who could fly, that is Spacemen. If, as many people now believe, Spacemen land on Earth in the closing decades of our present century, they will surely be depicted for posterity in the company of our own Queen; since Venusians are said to resemble Earthmen, it is likely that the Artist will portray the Extra-terrestrials as having wings to denote them as Spacemen. The Assyrians plainly show in their sculptures that their Kings were honoured by Space Beings; those murals exist now in our own museums for all to see. The proof stares us full in the face; our eyes see the Spacemen, should our minds not see them, too?

Ishtar or Inanna, Queen of Heaven, the Semitic Venus, was Goddess of sexual love and also of war, a fascinating though realistic duality; her real character in Sumer and Babylon was as the great Earth Mother, as Astarte, Ashtoreth and Aphrodite, she inspired the fertility cult of the Ancient World and probably the Christian conception of the Virgin Mary. In Assyria Ishtar appeared as a War Goddess, a Valkyrie, leading armies to battle; sometimes she was known as Belit, the patroness of certain American Sisterhoods of Lesbians practising today. Wonderful poems in Sumerian and Akkadian tell of Ishtar's love for Tammuz, the God of Spring, who like Osiris, Adonis and Attis, was slain to live again. This ancient fertility myth of the Dying God, the Resurrection, the triumph of life over death, may be the true source of the story of Jesus. Ishtar, like Persephone, descended to the Underworld to redeem her lover from Ereshtigal, Goddess of Death. This truly marvellous epic from ancient Sumer inspired the Greek myths and anticipated the inner meaning of Christianity; Man like Nature dies to live again; the secret tradition of the old Sun cult, which Initiates believe to be the cosmic religion of the Spacemen.

The Gilgamesh Epic written in Akkadian still ranks as one of the greatest works in world literature, and probably inspired Homer's 'Odyssey', the Heroic poem of Kret of Ugarit,[253] even incidents in the Old Testament; fragments of the Epic were found among the ruined library of the Hittites at Boghazkoi. Gilgamesh, part-divine and part-human, named in the Sumerian King List as the fifth

King of the first Dynasty of Erech after the Flood, ruled so tyrannously that the Gods created the hero, Enkidu, to punish the oppressor; after a trial of strength, the two vow eternal friendship, then set off on the perilous enterprise of slaying the fire-breathing[254] giant, Huwawa. After victory, Gilgamesh is tempted by Ishtar whom he rejects, so the outraged Goddess sends down a 'Bull' (Spaceship?) from Heaven to devastate Erech; the 'Bull' (?) is eventually slain by Gilgamesh. Enkidu dies and Gilgamesh fearing death sets out to seek immortality; he scorns the dissuasions of Shamash and goes forth to find Ut-napishtim, the Flood hero, who has won immortality. On the way Gilgamesh comes to a tavern run by the Goddess Siduri (in Babylon the inns were run by women) who in seductive appeal enjoins him to tarry and make merry with a wife, the true business of mankind; the hero declines and after adventures so reminiscent of Odysseus at last arrives at the dwelling of his ancestor, Ut-napishtim, from whom he begs the secret of immortality. Ut-napishtim then narrates the full story of the Flood in wonderful imagery; of how the Gods decided to destroy mankind, Ea (Oannes) advised him to build an Ark and load it with every kind of living creature; after violent storms, the Deluge finally ceased, the boat landed on a mountain, Ut-napishtim sent out three birds in turn, then disembarked and sacrificed to the Gods. This wonderful story obviously inspired the tale of Noah and his Ark, though its fascinating poetry far surpasses the account in Genesis. Ut-napishtim reminds Gilgamesh that no man can resist the final sleep of death; like Odysseus the weary hero wanders back home.[255]

The intervention of the Gods in human affairs, their guidance to heroes, their destruction of civilisation, the quarrels among the Deities themselves, evoke the Classics of India, China, Egypt and Greece, confirming the tales of war in the skies and cataclysm on Earth. Strangely enough, the Genesis story of the Tower of Babel when men attempted to 'reach unto heaven' is not mentioned in Babylonian literature, although the same tale is found in Mexico, Africa, Australia and even Mongolia. The vivid descriptions and real characterisation of the Gods of Babylon do suggest that they were not mythical representations of natural forces or merely fertility symbols, but confused, even exaggerated memories of Spacemen, who once ruled Mesopotamia and whose descendants in historical times occasionally landed and inspired Kings and Prophets.

The Chaldean temple-towers or 'Ziggurats' were composed of seven stories, each a different colour symbolising a star; the first white, the colour of Venus; the second black corresponding to Saturn; the third a shining red, the colour of Mars; the fourth blue for Mercury; fifth orange for Jupiter; sixth silver for the Moon; seventh gold, the colour of the Great Star, our Sun. These stages had a magical and astrological significance; the Priests chanted hymns to the stars and on solemn occasions held sacred ceremonies, later followed by festivals attended by the nobility, where young temple dancers would perform esoteric ballets full of meaning to the Initiates.[256]

The learned Chaldeans did not build these lofty towers for thousands of years just to plot horoscopes, but for some great purpose whose secret we have lost; perhaps from their summits in the skies the Priests could communicate by telepathy or other means with their Teachers in the skies.

The Chaldeans were revered by all the people of Antiquity as powerful wizards, who practised magic, foretold the future and summoned demons from infernal realms to work their will. Like the Egyptians, the Chaldeans had inherited from their ancient Space Teachers a psychic science mastering the elements and natural forces operating on subtle mental planes, remnants of this Ancient Wisdom persist among witch-doctors and weather-magicians, who confound our scientists today. The Babylonians like many races world-wide believed in benign and evil spirits, demons, ghosts, nymphs and elementals dwelling in streams and trees; they worshipped an animism, a living universe where everything from stone to star, insect to archangel, possessed some subtle life of its own influencing human beings. The records of Assyria and Babylon teem with magic spells to kill or cure, invocations to protective deities, propitiations to malevolent spirits, good and evil occultism, communication with the dead, white and black magic, degenerating to superstitions, psychic dangers averted by rituals, talismans worn by people even today. Many of the magic practices continued until the Middle Ages, some developed into mediaeval alchemy, which reason transmuted into our modern science.

Much of the phenomena now attributed to UFOS in Mediaeval times were considered to be manifestations of aerial demons. Agobard in AD 840[257] described wizards from the skies stoned to death in Lyons: Ariosto, the Renaissance poet about AD 1510 in 'Orlando Furioso', Canto 1, Stanza 8, wrote about 'proud demons sailing the heavens in great ships of glass', which we today regard as Spaceships. Demonology tortured the greatest minds of the Christian Church culminating in centuries of cruel persecution against alleged witchcraft. Paracelsus and Montfaucon de Villars in *Le Comte de Gabalis*[258] in the seventeenth century wrote learnedly of Sylphs, Salamanders, Gnomes and Nymphs appearing before men, stressing the enchantments of Babylon, supported by many ancient and mediaeval theologians quoting paranormal phenomena some of which we associate with Spacemen.

Like our Ancient Britons the Babylonians believed the demons were former Gods, Beings from Space. A Sumerian tablet from Ur about 2000 BC mentions Lilith described in the Talmud as a fascinating demoness with long wavy hair. Solomon suspected that the Queen of Sheba was Lilith because she had hairy legs, but they could not prevent him from seducing her. Adam insisted Lilith lay recumbent for sexual intercourse, she rebelled and in a rage uttered the magic name of God, rose into the air and left him.[259] Lilith was possibly a Venusian; three 'Angels' (Spacemen?) brought her back to Adam on Earth. Her children were beautiful, lived vast ages and flew to heaven. (Venus?) The Arabs believe in Djinns, the Chinese in Genii; magicians are said to conjure Elementals by words of power and to enslave them to perform tasks or produce things from the invisible realms like those apportations materialised at seances. Students of the Black Arts pronounced spells to raise devils and Christian Bishops like Tibetan lamas perform special rites to exorcise evil spirits. Throughout the ages all over the world a vast literature has accumulated to suggest that belief in denizens of the inner realms haunting mankind is surely the most ancient universal religion on Earth.

The last century of spiritualism, the revelations to psychiatrists, the paranormal studies of psycho-scientists, suggest the reality of transcendent states of existence. Materialist science dismissed the occult as superstition but recent researches into sub-atomic particles seem to offer surprising proof of the ancient beliefs. Researchers into cosmic rays and nuclear physicists in their cyclotron accelerators now speculate that their findings, exemplified by the elusive and potent neutrino, apparently confirm the existence of a parallel universe of matter vibrating at higher frequency than our own co-existing within the same space, thus confirming the astral planes of the occultists inhabited by Angels, Devas, Nature Spirits, Demons, Fairies, sometimes seen by Sensitives and even photographed. That wonderful occult record 'Oahspe' describes etheric hosts in etherean ships haunting our own Earth. The Borderland Scientists claim that many of the Spacemen visiting us today materialise from Etherean Venus, confirming ancient traditions of Etherean Teachers known surely to the Initiates of Babylon. It is fascinating to realise that our official science is now venturing into atomic occultism; perhaps in a century of progress our physicists may attain the Secret Wisdom of the Chaldeans and conjure down once again those Demons from Inner Space?

In 538 BC Babylon surrendered without a battle to Cyrus of Persia; twenty years later the inhabitants revolted and the great Darius razed the famous fortifications to the ground. An American Association, the 'Sons of Jared', claims that Darius and his son, Xerxes, were Watcher-Kings,[260] who like many notorious personages dominating history are believed to be of divine origin, Extra-terrestrials incarnating on Earth to enslave the human race. A fascinating theory not without reason! Darius began the great war against Greece in which the Persians suffered memorable defeat in 490 BC at Marathon where the Athenians swore the Gods descended and brought them victory. In 480 BC UFOS hovered over Salamis[261] when the Greeks smashed the invasion fleet of Xerxes, one of the most important battles in all history.

After the Persian conquests the old Gods of Babylon were eclipsed by Ahura-Mazda, the Iranian God of Zarathustra or Zoroaster. Initiates believe that through legendary ages many Avatars called Zarathustra incarnated to teach mankind; the last Prophet, known to the Greeks as Zoroaster, was born 660 BC in Azerbaijan near the Caspian Sea. Pliny claimed that Zoroaster laughed on the day of his birth, which was attended by prodigies in earth and sky. Plutarch spoke of his intercourse with the Gods like Lycurgus and Numa Pompilius; Dio Chrysostom, a contemporary of Plutarch, declared that Zoroaster was more conversant with the chariots of Zeus than Homer and Hesiod, suggesting that all his life he was inspired by Spacemen. As a child Zoroaster showed precocious wisdom, confounding the Magi; he studied religion, farming and healing, worked among the poor, then retired to a cave on Mount Sabalan to gain wisdom. One day at sunset the mountain became bathed in fire; suddenly the young hermit heard the Revelation of God; filled with cosmic understanding he descended to teach the Persians about Ahura-Mazda and his eternal struggle with Angra Manyu, Good against Evil. Zoroaster on the mountain finding enlightenment parallels Hammurabi, Minos and Moses, who also beheld God on mountain-tops; the fire on Mount Sabalan evokes the fire and smoke shrouding Mount Sinai, when Moses received the Ten Commandments from Jehovah; surely the fire was the radiance of a Spaceship; these prophets were instructed by Spacemen.[262]

In his home Zoroaster had celestial visions and held conversations with Archangels, whom we may regard as Teachers from Space. It is significant that he chose as the divine emblem of Ahura-Mazda the winged disk of Asshur, the God of Assyria, which is stylised prominently in the famous Behistun cliff-sculptures of Darius. The teachings of Zoroaster were written down in the Zend-Avesta and spread to neighbouring countries even to India. The worship of fire is probably a form of ancient sun worship, said to be the religion of the Space People. Ahura-Mazda (Ormuzd), Lord of Heaven, led Seven Amshaspends, Heavenly Hosts, in cosmic conflict against Angra Manyu (Ahriman) and his Demons of Darkness. This eternal war between the Gods of Light and the Lords of

Evil, parallels the struggle between Horus and Set, and may be an allegory of that actual War in the Heavens waged by Spacemen, so vividly described in the Hindu, Chinese and Greek Classics. Zoroaster is said to have ascended to 'heaven' to receive 'God's' instructions; we think of Enoch, Elijah, Romulus, even Adamski, and we wonder? During a Holy War Zoroaster was kneeling by the Sacred Fire when a Turanian soldier stabbed him in the back. Three hundred years later Alexander the Great dissolved the Zoroastrian priesthood, destroyed the temples and burned the Avesta desiring to establish the religion of Greece; centuries later the Persians and the Parsees restored the teachings of Zoroaster but much of the Avesta was lost. A modified form of Zoroastrianism worshipped Mithras, Leader of the Seven Amshaspends, identified with the Assyrian Sun God, Shamash; in the West he was seen as Atys, Bacchus or Apollo. 'Mithras' in Persian meant the 'Sun' and the 'Friend', symbolising the God of Love, the pagan Christ. Worship of Mithras was spread by the Roman legions across the Mediterranean world and rivalled Christianity which it threatened to eclipse.[263]

As Jehovah appeared to the Kings of Israel, so Ahura-Mazda materialised before the Achaemenid Kings of Persia; references in Livy[264] and Plutarch[265] suggest that about 500 BC Spacemen landed in the Middle East, while the cultivation of wheat in ancient times suggests aerial communication between Babylonia and America.

In 610 BC a middle-aged camel-driver in the hills near Mecca was brooding over the wickedness of the Arabs, when the 'Angel' Gabriel appeared and showed Mahomet a golden tablet,[266] which he bade him read. This revelation from 'Heaven' inspired Islam; later Gabriel escorted the Prophet on a trip to the Seven Heavens like Enoch—and (Dare we say, Adamski?) Hammurabi, Minos, Moses, Zoroaster, Mahomet, all communing with Celestials on mountains! Still we wonder?

CHAPTER FIFTEEN

Spacemen in Biblical Babylon

Our study of Babylon and the brilliant culture of the Middle East through two thousand years before Christ revealed in those colourful Epics, in the cuneiform tablets from the great Library of Assurbanipal at Nineveh and the wonderful discoveries of the archaeologists now enable us to view the Old Testament in reasonable perspective without that illogical awe which saw the Scriptures as divinely true. Until a hundred years ago all that was known of Ancient Egypt, Babylon and Persia were vague legends related by Greek and Roman writers, tales by travellers like Herodotus and baffling allusions in the Bible; of the histories by Manetho, Berossus and Sanchoniathon only few fragments remained. For twenty centuries hieroglyphics and cuneiform script held their secrets, great cities lay buried in sand; St Paul, the Christian Fathers and generations of scholars knew little of the civilisations of Antiquity, the past was a nameless blank; paganism was dismissed as devilish idolatry, science was cursed as witchcraft; the Earth was the centre of the Universe, the sole concern of God.

The civilisation of Babylon, the revelations of the Dead Sea Scrolls and the awareness of Extra-terrestrial visitations in the past, call for a complete re-appraisal of the events narrated in the Scriptures with a possible transformation in religious interpretation of the whole Bible story, which would revolutionise our fundamental conception of Judaism and Christianity, but our generation is not yet prepared for this new knowledge and remains immersed in the dusty doctrines of the past. Though many pregnant questions could be asked, our present references to the Old Testament must be restricted solely to incidents suggesting Extra-terrestrial manifestations in Babylonia.

Much of Genesis now appears to have been influenced by the old Sumerian Epics; it is most difficult to determine which passages are original, especially as the Semitic traditions, said to have been compiled by Moses for the inspiration of the Children of Israel in the Wilderness, were later revised by Ezra during the Captivity and subsequently by Jewish Rabbis before finally being agreed; scholars state that internal evidence in the Biblical text reveals at least four distinct sources. Recent illumination from the Dead Sea Scrolls shows many minor yet meaningful discrepancies in the Scriptures; more may soon be found.

The Garden of Eden has been situated by various authorities in many parts of the Earth and even on Mars,[267] conventional belief vaguely accepts it as somewhere in old Babylonia. The 'Lord' Who expelled Adam and Eve was not the Creator of the entire universe, in Whom we move and have our being, but the tribal God, Jehovah, possibly Commander of a Venusian space-fleet, for He was accompanied by Cherubim, which are generally depicted as creatures with a lion's body, human face and conspicuous wings, the Egyptian and Babylonian symbol for Spacemen. Adam and Eve may represent the early Atlanteans; expulsion from Eden may be a garbled memory of War with Overlords from Space followed by cosmic catastrophe, which changed the climate and made life harsh.

Enoch 'walked with God' and was translated to the skies on a whirlwind (Spaceship?); his son, Methuselah, begat Lamech, who according to the Genesis Apocryphon in the recently discovered Dead Sea Scrolls suspected before the birth of Noah that his wife had consorted with one of the Angels, who had descended from heaven and married the Daughters of Men. Her emphatic denial did not convince him.[268]

> 'Behold, I thought then within my heart that conception was (due) to the Watchers and the Holy Ones . . . and to the Giants . . . and my heart was troubled within me because of this child. . . . Bathenosh, my wife, spoke to me saying. . . . I swear to you by the Holy Great One, the King of (the heavens) that this seed was planted by you . . . and by no stranger or Watcher or Son of Heaven.'[269]

This Dead Sea Scroll clearly mentions Watchers and Holy Ones descending from the heavens; surely meaning Spacemen from the skies!

The Biblical story of the Flood may be a version of the older Gilgamesh Epic; both Ut Napishtim and Noah were warned by a God, possibly a Spaceman, who foresaw the catastrophe threatening Earth.

The early chapters of Genesis apparently describe events in Babylonia during the third and fourth millennia BC. The Sons of God (Spacemen) mated with the Daughters of Men, who bore them children, believed to be Giants, whose blasphemy brought them destruction in the Flood. Warned by the 'Lord' Noah saved his family and various animals enabling mankind to build civilisation again. Generations later in the Land of Shinar around Babylon in modern Iraq, men rebelled against the Gods (Spacemen) and built the Tower of Babel to storm Heaven itself; the 'Lord' came down, destroyed the Tower and scattered the survivors all over the Earth, so far that their descendants developed different languages. This confused story is probably some race-memory of the War between Spacemen and Giants mentioned in the legends of most ancient peoples throughout the world. Later the Tower of Babel became a popular name for the great temple of Marduk, whose summit contained a room with a large, elegant bed and a golden table, a sanctuary which none could enter, except the Babylonian women chosen by the 'God'.[270] Was this bride reserved for a Spaceman?

Abraham was born in Ur[271] about 2000 BC during the Middle Bronze Age, two or three centuries after Queen Shubud, whose magnificent tomb excavated by Sir Leonard Woolley revealed superb jewellery, exquisite gold ornaments and furnishings of an artistic excellence suggesting a sophistication which surprises us. Ur, principal port of Sumer, was a metropolis of the Middle East, trading with Egypt and India, the Mediterranean and the Black Sea, exchanging varied merchandise and all the fertile philosophies of the age. Sumerian religion with its colourful literature suggesting intercourse with Celestials from the skies, ruled men's daily lives, already the Magi were studying the stars. The Talmud states that on the night of Abraham's birth King Nimrod's magicians saw a brilliant star rise before them in the East, to their astonishment it swallowed or consumed four stars from the four quarters of heaven suggestive to us as a Mothership embarking four scoutships. Reared in such cosmopolitan society, Abraham surely acquired considerable culture and familiarity with all the religion-political thought and traditions of those fascinating times. The brief Biblical account of Abraham's migration to Egypt, then to Palestine amassing great prestige and wealth, even waging war against the King of Babylon, shows his mental stature comparable with our world-figures today.

The learned Ibn Aharon[272] with fantastic erudition throwing wondrous illumination on extra-terrestrialism in the ancient Semitic world deduces from the Zohar, the Sefer Sefirah and Sefer Yetsirah that Abraham was guided by an arrogant Spaceman called Y'hova, who wielded dictatorial and destructive powers. Y'hova was wrongly interpreted by the West as being the One God, the King of Kings, when in fact the early Israelites realised that he was only one of many Elohim or Spacemen; this was well-known by the Chaldeans who monitored the flights of the 'Power-and-Glory', the Spaceships from their lofty ziggurats.

The 'Lord' of Genesis[273] Who spoke to Abraham at his tent door accompanied by two Angels, Who guided him to prosperity and victory, cured Sarah, his wife, of her barrenness and promised to make his descendants into a great nation was surely a similar, even identical winged figure or Spaceman known to the Babylonians as Shamash who about the same time gave the tablets of Law to King Hammurabi. The Talmud described how Abraham was captured by Nimrod, who sentenced him to be burned at the stake; the wood would not burn, the Priests swore an Angel (Spaceman?) was flying around putting the fire out. In revenge Abraham called down an immense sun-darkening cloud of gnats, which devoured Nimrod's soldiers to the very bones. Shades of Hiroshima! The 'Mahabharata' and the *Shoo-King* suggest that Space Beings were active in India and China during the second and third millennia; if so, is it not likely that these Men from the Skies would land in the Middle East and influence great public figures possessing occult sensitivity like Abraham? Was the 'Lord' of Abraham the same 'Divine Man' who according to the Japanese *Sei-to-ki* descended under a sandal-tree in Korea about 2300 BC? Could He have been related to the 'Lord' who went hunting deer with Emperor Ono-hatsuse-Waka-Taka in old Yamato in AD 460, so genially described in the *Nihongi*?

In the seventh century BC Palestine, an unhappy buffer-state between Egypt and Babylon, was torn between these great Powers, subjugated by one side then the other in their imperial rivalry. After the defeat of Pharaoh Necho at Carchemish in 605 BC the Egyptians withdrew leaving Judaea to Babylonians. The pro-Egypt faction among the Jews rebelled in 597 BC; Nebuchadnezzar himself led his armies to storm Jerusalem; he sacked the palace and the temple and deported Jehoiachim and a number of important Jews to Babylon. This 'Exile' appears to have been somewhat exaggerated; the number of captive Jews was small, comparable to the foreign workers Hitler forced to Nazi Germany, although their treatment was much better. Even Jeremiah admitted that life under Nebuchadnezzar was hardly oppressive; the Jews enjoyed a higher standard of living than in Jerusalem; many prospered and became citizens of Babylon.

Among the 'Exiles' in a colony at Tel Abib near Nippur on the Chebar, an important canal of the Euphrates irrigation-system, lived a young Jewish Priest, Ezekiel, married, highly sensitive, whose impassioned and poetic mind revolted at the idolatries around him. With burning zeal he sought to convert the Jews to the religious ideals of the Patriarchs and prophesied destruction of Jerusalem unless the people returned to God. Such intuitive personality, strangely akin to our George Adamski, would certainly attract contact by the Space People watching the destinies of Earth.

In 593 BC Ezekiel was sitting by the River Chebar, when 'the heavens opened' and he beheld a strange and wonderful manifestation of the 'Lord',[274] completely outside his experience and comprehension, which he described in fanciful language, the only appropriate terms he knew, as irrelevant as Shakespeare having to explain a sputnik.[275]

'And I looked, and behold, a whirlwind came out of the north, a great cloud, and a fire infolding itself, and a brightness was about it, and out of the midst thereof as the colour of amber, out of the midst of the fire. Also out of the midst came the likeness of four living creatures. And this was their appearance, they had the likeness of a man . . . their appearance was like burning coals of fire, and like the appearance of lamps; it went up and down among the living creatures and the fire was bright and out of the fire went forth lightning. . . . Now as I beheld the living creatures, behold one wheel upon the earth by the living creatures . . . The appearance of the wheels and their work was like unto the colour of a beryl, and they four had one likeness; and their appearance and their work was, as it were, a wheel in the middle of a wheel. . . . As for the rings, they were so high, that they were dreadful, and their rings were full of eyes, round about them four . . . Whithersoever the spirit was to go, they went; thither was their spirit to go; and the wheels. And the likeness of the firmament upon the heads of the living creature was as the colour of the terrible crystal stretched forth over their heads above. . . . And when they went, I heard the noise of their wings like the noise of great waters, as the voice of the Almighty, the voice of speech, as the noise of an host; when they stood, and had let down their wings. . . .' (Ezekiel 1).

Ezekiel, like his Translators from the Aramaic, lacked technical knowledge yet despite this limitation he has given a marvellous description of a Spaceship and its occupants, at once recognized by all Students of UFOS, and unsurpassed until Adamski's famous meeting with Orthon in the Flying Saucer from Venus.[276] Generations of Bible scholars have felt baffled by this 'Vision' and view it as symbolic fantasy, even questioning Ezekiel's sanity, just as some scientists today dismiss Adamski's detailed description of the Spaceships.

Interpreting Ezekiel's words into modern terms it appears that the Saucer came from the North; as stressed by the Chinese, Egyptians and observers today UFOS apparently approach Earth through the vents in the Van Allen radiation belts in the sector of the North Pole. The crew of four wore space-suits and helmets like Oannes, that celestial Visitor to Babylon described by Berossus.

A year later the 'Lord' appeared to Ezekiel again.

> 'Then, I beheld! and lo', a likeness as the appearance of fire; from the appearance of his loins even downwards fire; and from his loins even upwards as the colour of amber. And he put forth the form of an hand, and took me a lock of mine head; and the spirit lifted me up between the earth and the heavens, and brought me in the visions of God to Jerusalem, to the door of the inner gate that looketh toward the north' (Ezekiel 8, 2-3).

In just such words might an articulate peasant in the remote jungles of Vietnam describe an airlift in an American Boeing to civilisation in Saigon.

In Chapter 10 Ezekiel embellishes his earlier description of the Saucer and its crew, whom he calls Cherubim, the same winged humans depicted in bas-reliefs by the Assyrians, and describes his conversation with the 'Lord' concerning the future, reminiscent of Adamski's discussion with the Venusian Master during his trip in a Spaceship.[277] The Saucer apparently landed Ezekiel in Jerusalem for a few days while he explored the depravity of the city, then returned him home to the Chebar. With blazing eloquence Ezekiel exhorted his countrymen to worship the 'Lord' and delivered vivid prophecies of future world wars after which the redeemed Jews would bask in the Glory of God.

A little known but remarkable account in Chapter 27 quotes the 'Lord's' description of the ports and commerce of the Mediterranean and the Middle East, from Tarshish to Arabia, Tyre to Persia, as though the vast scene were viewed from a Spaceship.

In 538 BC another young Jewish idealist, Daniel, was sitting on the bank of the Tigris just as fifty-four years earlier the prophet Ezekiel had sat beside the River Chebar, when he too beheld a wondrous apparition.

> 'And in the fourth and twentieth day of the first month, as I was by the side of the great river, which is Hiddekel. Then I lifted up mine eyes and behold, a certain man clothed in linen, whose loins were girded with fine gold of Uphaz. His body also was like the beryl and his face as the appearance of lightning, and his eyes as lamps of fire, and his arms and his feet like in colour to polished brass, and the voice of his words like the voice of a multitude' (Daniel 10, 4-6).

Almost the same words as Ezekiel's, even anticipating Adamski's description of Orthon from Venus.

The Celestial comforted Daniel with a brief prophecy of the turbulent future of the Middle East during the next four centuries and closed with allusion to eventual Apocalypse and Resurrection, reminiscent of the warnings of Ezekiel and the forebodings of Adamski today.

Daniel was just the man to attract the Space People, he closely resembled in temperament our own 'New Age' Philosophers who claim to contact the Spacemen. He was reared among the entourage of the exiled King Jehoiakin, thus having access to all the wisdom of the Jews and the Babylonians; he practised vegetarianism, drank water instead of wine, he had understanding of visions and dreams; Nebuchadnezzar after examination declared him to be 'ten times better than all the magicians and astrologers that were in his realms', a startling tribute in this Land of the Magi.

Uneasy lies the head that wears a Crown! Nebuchadnezzar was sorely troubled by dreams, hardly surprising for a Monarch who was destined to eat grass like a beast in the fields. The famous Chaldeans were baffled but Daniel in masterly revelation clearly impressed the King, who promptly made the young Jew ruler over the whole province of Babylon, a striking parallel with the promotion of Joseph that other well-known interpreter of kingly dreams, and tactlessly perhaps appointed Daniel Governor of the Wise Men; Daniel's friends, Shadrach, Meshach and Abednego were raised to high office in the Babylonian Civil Service. Nebuchadnezzar, possibly inspired somewhat craftily by the aforesaid Wise Men eager to belittle the Jews supplanting them, made a great image of gold and ordered all his subjects high and lowly to fall down and worship it or be flung into a fiery furnace. Shadrach, Meshach and Abednego nobly refused to bow down to the idol, Nebuchadnezzar in fury ordered the three to be bound and flung into the furnace superheated sevenfold. Watchers were astounded to behold the three martyrs walking unharmed amidst the fierce heat accompanied by a fourth 'Man' like the 'Son of God!' We are reminded of Abraham saved from burning at the stake by an 'Angel' or 'Spaceman'. Nebuchadnezzar was so awed by the demonstrable power of the Jewish 'God' he promptly promoted Shadrach, Meshach and Abednego 'in the province of Babylon'. Daniel is silent on his own attitude towards the golden image; however he retained his post as Chief Astrologer during the reign of Belshazzar, Regent for King Nabonidas.

Belshazzar gave a great feast with an Oriental extravagance degenerating to drunken orgy as the King and his Court mocked the God of the Jews drinking wine from the sacred golden vessels plundered from the Temple. Suddenly the ribaldry hushed.

> 'In the same hour came forth fingers of a man's hand and wrote over against the plaister of the wall of the king's palace; and the King saw the part of the hand that wrote' (Daniel 5, 5).

Belshazzar terrified summoned all his astrologers and soothsayers to interpret the cryptic writing on the wall. All the Wise Men stood baffled, then the Queen called for Daniel. The young Prophet surveyed the debauchery around him, studied the fateful words and read 'MENE. MENE. TEKEL. UPHARSIN.'

> 'MENE. God hath numbered thy kingdom and finished it. TEKEL. Thou art weighed in the balance and art found wanting. PERES. Thy kingdom is divided and given to the Medes and Persians. In that night was Belshazzar, the King of the Chaldeans slain. And Darius, the Median took the kingdom' (Daniel 5, 26-28, 30-31).

This dramatic tale of a phantom hand writing flaming words of warning on the palace wall heralding the death of Belshazzar and the downfall of mighty Babylon, has thrilled sixty generations as a miraculous Revelation of the Power of the 'Lord'. In our age of electronics we televise scenes from the Moon to our own fireside. Any Spaceship over Babylon could have beamed those fatal words on Belshazzar's palace wall; our cynical TV critics would no doubt agree that the production could have been much improved.

The Bible errs in stating that Darius conquered Babylon, historically it was Cyrus, whom Darius followed twenty years later. Cyrus occupied the city without bloodshed, he was noted for his clemency to all subdued peoples and authorised the captive Jews to return to Jerusalem to rebuild the Jerusalem Temple. A cuneiform cylinder records that he was welcomed as liberator from the tyranny of Nabonidus and Belshazzar, it suggests the startling yet plausible revelation that Jehovah and Mardouk (Merodach) were one and the same 'God', possibly a Being from Space, Who made contact with Cyrus himself, one of the most enlightened rulers of the ancient world, whose very birth like that of Moses was attended with mystery.

The Book of Daniel states that Darius preferred Daniel above the presidents and princes, evidence of the prestige of the young Jew; not unnaturally his jealous rivals plotted against him and persuaded the King to pass a decree that any man making a petition to God instead of to the King should be cast into a den of lions. As expected, Daniel ignored the command and was cast into the lions' den. The King was sorely anguished but the Laws of the Medes and the Persians could not be changed; next morning he went in haste to the den of lions and to his unfeigned delight found Daniel unharmed.

> 'Then said Daniel unto the King. O, King, live for ever! My God hath sent his Angel and hath shut the lions' mouths, that they have not hurt me' (Daniel 6, 21-22).

Could some Spaceman have charmed the hungry lions not to devour Daniel? The famous winged humans represented by Assurnazipal III and Shalmanezer II, the winged sun-disks in the carvings of Darius at Behistun, all suggest that the Babylonians accepted intervention by Men from the skies.

Learned commentators are puzzled by the Book of Daniel, their almost unanimous conclusion is that this apocalyptic work was actually composed about 166 BC to comfort the Jews during their terrible sufferings in the Persecution by Antiochus Epiphanes just prior to the Maccabean Revolt. Surely those early compilers of the Bible must have accepted the story of Daniel as true?

In 670 BC[278] the army of Sennacherib was destroyed at Pelusium possibly by nuclear-bomb; the Japanese claimed that in 660 BC[279] the 'Gods' assisted their Emperor Jimmu to victory; the Romans swore that in 498 BC[280] Castor and Pollux appeared at the Battle of Lake

Regillus; the Athenians believed that in 490 BC[281] Immortals materialised to aid them at Marathon; if so, Spacemen during the same period could have landed to inspire Ezekiel and Daniel in Babylon.

Is the Book of Daniel 'science fiction' or Hebrew anticipation of Adamski's *Flying Saucers have Landed*?

The Persians, who later assumed the mantle of imperial Babylon, for hundreds of years told wonderful tales of heroes and beautiful maidens soaring through the skies on magic flying carpets, which may have been race-memories of the Spaceships.

The fascinating history of Babylon from those ancient days of Oannes with its stormy Gods and dynamic Kings, its Magi and Prophets, unfolds a colourful panorama of a brilliant, restless civilisation surveilled by Spacemen.

CHAPTER SIXTEEN

Gods or Spacemen?

The fascinating history of the Ancient East blends with our modern insight of the inhabited universe and our development of space-travel into a wondrous, startling revelation giving new meaning to the destiny of Man. As we marvel at the UFOS now haunting our skies and question those 'contacts' with Beings from other worlds, we feel that all this happened before; the myths and literature of the old East illumine the Gods, Celestials from the stars, landing in Antiquity and teaching civilisation to Earth as we ourselves plan to do on Mars. Past, present and future appear to merge into an exhilarating, inspiring panorama dispelling the troubles from our tortured world, shining new purpose to life.[282]

From the mythologies and chronicles of India, Tibet, China, Japan, Egypt and Babylon, viewed in the light of our new knowledge, emerges a clear, consistent story covering the entire Ancient East. All traditions tell of Supermen from the skies,[283] Divine Dynasties ruling our Earth in a Golden Age, War in the heavens waged with fantastic weapons, world cataclysms, barbarism, then the rebuilding of civilisation under the guidance of Spacemen worshipped as Gods. Myth becomes science, the old fables subject to empirical proof; just as a chemist can predict the properties of an element he has yet to isolate, so we may synthesise the ancient histories of countries we have still to study, we can fabricate their mythologies by scientific method confident the legends must corroborate our plan.

As our research delves deeper into the few records extant to us, we resurrect in each country a glittering throng of Kings and Queens, heroes and scholars, patriarchs and priests, men and women of warm humanity just like ourselves, flitting down the dusty corridors of time pausing to play their destined part on this earthly stage under the eyes of Immortals from Space. We marvel at fabulous India where Gods and mortals wench and war in exotic rivalry; occult Tibet tantalises us with mystery and magic; old China enchants with wars in the skies in fantasies surpassing our science-fiction. On the cherry-blossom islands of Japan the temperamental Goddesses and eccentric Emperors merge somehow with Gilbert and Sullivan's *Mikado,* we confuse the Spacemen with that other wanderer, minstrel Nanki-Poo, and wonder if the Martian monarchs have as their object all sublime to make the punishment fit the crime. As we anticipate the familiar pattern of Gods or Spacemen is found in Egypt and Babylon; the Land of the Nile loses a little of its magic, even grandiose Babylon seems an imitation of bejewelled India; the Old Testament itself reads uninspired compared with the brilliant 'Ramayana' and the sublimity of the Upanishads. These glowing vistas of Antiquity when Gods mingled with men on Earth eclipse the vague pictures of Space Visitants today.

Excluding from our present study the Ancient West whose Classics sing of Sky Gods in Greece, Scandinavia, Britain and the Americas,[284] and support our thesis of the Extra-terrestrials, we can test the sequence of Divine Kings, war and catastrophe, in lands lacking literature from the past. Our conclusion that Celestials intervened on the continent of Asia and must have influenced primitive races all over the East seems proved beyond doubt; we can predict their legends before we read them, names may differ, the substance is the same.

Aborigines in Australia tell of a 'dream-time', a wondrous idyllic age in the past, their rock-paintings bear resemblance to the Tassili frescoes in the Sahara and petroglyphs in the Andes. The Polynesians of Malekula[285] remember 'winged women' who came down from the skies to give them aid, then flew back; it is intriguing to learn that the Polynesian word for 'Sun' is 'Ra' evoking all the wonder of Ancient Egypt. Easter Island's[286] giant statues and unsolved script still pose mysteries, and plausible explanations by learned scholars fail to convince. Natives of the Caroline Isles in their Haida Texts describe Wondrous Beings in flying-machines shaped like discs, who descended to Earth and taught their ancestors centuries ago; on many islands all over the Pacific tales are told of Kon-Tiki, a white-skinned culture-hero associated with the sun or moon. The Hawaiians use the word 'Akuwalela' for 'flying-cherubs', some race-memory of the solar-boats mentioned in the records of Ancient Egypt. African bush-men babble naïvely of Gods from the skies; Livingstone found the Tower of Babel story near Lake Ngami, a similar tradition exists in Mongolia. The Eskimos say their forefathers were transported by great white birds from lands devasted by flood and tell of Beings with shining faces sent from the stars; the Shamans of Siberia teach of Men preceding our present race who possessed boundless knowledge and threatened rebellion against the Great Chief Spirit, overtones of Atlantis and the Stanzas of Dzyan; the circum-polar races make a cult of the bear associating it with the North Star, which to the Ancients and to observers today coincides with the flight-path of Spaceships; perhaps the bear represented the primitive memory of Extra-terrestrials wearing spacesuits? Folk-lore of Vietnam states their first Kings came from heaven; Adepts believe the sands of the Gobi Desert shroud a fantastic civilisation buried long ago. Abandoned in the jungle of Cambodia the massive ruins of Anghor Wat[287] comprise temples and towers more than a hundred feet high rivalling the grandeur of Babylon; like the great Buddhist temple of Borobodura in Java the impressive sculptures on the walls include Gods with wings, there are intriguing representations of the 'man-fish', Oannes, the Teacher of the Babylonians, a Being from Space. The oldest part of Anghor Wat may date from dim Antiquity, many figures evoke Egyptian monuments and Assyrian tablets, some images resemble Poseidon and Vulcan, Gods of the Cabiri, worshipped in the Mediterranean ages ago. The foundation of the temple has been attributed to the 'Prince of Roma', possibly 'Rama' of the 'Ramayana' but Cambodian tradition makes the Founder of Anghor Wat come from 'Roma' at the western end of the world posing a fascinating mystery. The Khmers, apparently an Indo-European race linguistically related to Polynesia, achieved a remarkable and opulent civilisation; their priests were reputed to have accumulated large libraries, whose literature must have rivalled the Sanskrit epics of India.[288]

Today we tend to belittle the past and boast our age as the highest peak in human culture, despite its sadly apparent short-comings; the common man in the West certainly lives more princely than many a King centuries ago and enjoys marvels of genius which would have amazed the old magicians, yet the literature of Eastern peoples shows that the Ancients sometimes surpassed us in the very things of which we are proud. The Indian lyricise of spaceships faster than light and missiles more violent than H-bombs; their Sanskrit texts describe aircraft apparently with radar and cameras; the wonderful 'Mahabharata' rivals the 'Iliad', the 'Odyssey', the 'Aeneid', the plays of Shakespeare and most of our modern fiction all combined. The Tibetans in their occult manner could call down hailstorms on their adversaries and bewilder even themselves by materialising thought-forms; the Chinese rhapsodise of Flying Dragons, laser-beams, anti-gravity pills and human hibernation with an Oriental charm which confounds our Space Scientists. Egypt glories in her Pyramids and Sphinx; Babylon boasted of her Hanging Gardens and the famous Laws of Hammurabi. The religions and philosophies of the East distilled a sublimity of thought scarce attained in the West; the wonderful Indian system of Yoga, the Gnani Yoga of Wisdom, Raja Yoga of Mind, Hatha Yoga of Body, Bhakti Yoga of Love, Karma Yoga of Work, developed a discipline millennia ago blending mysticism with daily life, showing Man's relation to the Universe incarnating ever upwards to perfection to Union with God; this supreme and beneficent teaching now exercising widening influence in our Western world must surely have sprung from civilisations long vanished or have been taught to Earth by Spacemen. The fascinating Piri-Reis map shows Pre-Columbian America and the Antarctic coastline, cartography of vast antiquity. Even the familiar tales of our Bible reveal new wonders. Ezekiel's vision now appears to have been a Spaceship. Jonah's sojourn in the belly of a whale becomes a trip in a submarine, probably a spaceship plunging into the sea. The past teems with wonders, even to our modern eyes jaded with miracles.

Scientists of genius have transformed our Earth showering blessings unknown before, yet how shall it profit a Man to gain the world and lose his soul? These sorry times suggest our civilisation has lost that divine spark of wonder which alone can inspire humanity on our cosmic pilgrimage.

Opposition to Spacemen, apart from the natural egocentricity of Man and his fear of the unknown, stems from the astronomers, men of sincerity, whose assessment of the heavens has obliged them to condition people that Earth is the sole abode of life. Lately persuaded by advances in biology, most astronomers have recanted long-held beliefs and proclaim, alas, to deaf ears, that life must abound throughout the universe, except on the other planets in our solar-system. If neighbouring worlds remain uninhabited, Spacemen must originate from planets around the stars; since the stars are light-years away such travel must take decades even centuries; Spacemen therefore could not come to us, so the stories of Celestials visiting Earth in the past or the present simply cannot be true. Such lucid logic conceals the joke of the century!

Astronomers mesmerised by their own instruments swear the spectroscope shows no oxygen or water on Mars, though some rebels assert the spectroscope does show oxygen and water almost abundant as Earth's; many observers glued to their telescopes see the famous Martian canals, an equal number through the same telescopes do not; notwithstanding such fundamental disagreements, which would paralyse most professions, on any question of human life astronomers generally agree that Mars must be barren. Photographs telemetered in 1965 by the Mariner IV Mars Probe from a distance of 6,000 miles showed Mars as apparently deserted; the world heaved sighs of relief, the belligerent Powers need no longer worry about a Martian Invasion stabbing them in the back while they were so busy planning to war on each other; the public paid lavish tribute to the prescience of the astronomers. No life on Mars meant no Flying Saucers, no Spacemen, a triumph for official Science.

Alas for such elation! Meteorologists now casually reveal that thousands of photographs taken of our Earth by the satellite Nimbus I,[289] a mere 400 miles away, show not the slightest sign of life here. The astronomers who deny living creatures to Mars and more distant planets should now proclaim to the world that their wonderful instruments also prove that life does not exist on Earth. Suppression of facts is unscientific; if our own planet is uninhabited people have a right to know. Logic can deduce yet another reason why Spacemen never visit Earth. Has science not proved conclusively that none of us is here to meet them if they come?

Selenites on the Moon may have launched an Earth-probe to land in the Sahara, pictures telemetered back to Space Centre show the surface would support a Spaceship; data from instruments confirm the claims of lunar astronomers that Earth is too hot to allow life.

Proof that Earth was once ruled by Beings from other planets would be the fundamental discovery of our twentieth century; evidence from ancient literature may be confirmed beyond doubt by the archaeologists whose labours have so brilliantly resurrected much of lost Antiquity; any day we hope a spade might unearth some new scroll or sculpture proving the ancient Gods were Spacemen. Our Western culture was originally founded on the teachings of Greece and Israel, the Greek Philosophers and Christian Fathers may have been learned and pious men conversant with the wisdom of their own times, they knew nothing of the great civilisations of the old East and in their wildest flights of fancy could not have imagined our world today.

Many of our fundamental conceptions are based on false premises. We should sweep away the dust and dogma of centuries and study phenomena as they really happened. Today we realise our Earth is not the centre of Creation but a grain of dust in a space-time universe, including universes of various dimensions co-existing within our own, all paralleled by a possible universe of anti-matter.

Man stands on the threshold of a new, thrilling Cosmic Age challenging the stars; the present unrest on Earth shows that in his soul he yearns for Truth. All our conventional beliefs must be re-examined, the truth renewed, the false rejected. Man evolves by suffering in his pilgrimage from darkness to light. No man is wise but all men may be lovers of wisdom.

The word 'God' has at least two distinct meanings; The

Absolute, imagining the Universe, in Whom we live and have our being, and the local 'Gods' or Spacemen, who originate from some advanced planet and from time to time manifest among men.

What has been, shall be again! Earth now awaits our Brothers from the Stars, those Spacemen in the Ancient East.

BIBLIOGRAPHY

The Author wishes to express his gratitude and sincere acknowledgements to the Authors and Publishers of the literary works enumerated below and to all Authorities inadvertently omitted.

1 Apollodorus. *Loeb Classics.* Heinemann.

2 Hesiod, *Theogony Loeb Classics.* Heinemann.

3 Ovid, *Metamorphoses.* (Trans. Mary Innes). Penguin Classics.

4 Drake, W. R. *Gods or Spacemen?* Ray Palmer, Amherst, Wisconsin, 1965.

5 Sullivan, Walter. *We are not alone.* Hodder & Stoughton, London, 1965.

6 Plato. *Phaedrus.* (Lindsay, Dr A. D. Five Dialogues). Dent-Everyman.

7 Livy. *History of Rome. Book XXIV. 24 BC.* Dent-Everyman.

8 Leslie, Desmond and Adamski, George. *Flying Saucers have Landed.* T. Werner Laurie, London, 1953.

9 Kraspedon, Dino. *My Contact with Flying Saucers.* Neville Spearman Ltd., London, 1959.

10 Brunton, Paul. *The Wisdom of the Overself.* Arrow Books, London.

11 Hoyle, Fred. *Frontiers of Astronomy.* Heinemann, 1959.

12 Ingalese, Richard. *The History and Power of Mind.* L. Fowler & Co. Ltd., London.

13 Yogi Ramacharaka. *Gnani Yoga.* L. Fowler & Co. Ltd., London.

14 Ouspensky, J. P. *A New Model of the Universe.* Routledge & Kegan Paul, London.

15 Yogi Ramacharaka. *Fourteen Lessons in Yogi Philosophy.* L. Fowler & Co. Ltd., London.

16 Yogi Ramacharaka. *Gnani Yoga.* L. Fowler & Co. Ltd., London.

17 *La Vie existe-t-elle sur Terre? Planète* No. 12 s/o 1963. 42 rue de Berri, Paris, 8.

18 Vermeer, G. *The Dead Sea Scrolls in English.* Penguin, London, 1962.

19 Roberts, J. M. *Antiquity Unveiled.* Oriental Publishing Co., Philadelphia, 1912.
20 Voltaire. *Letter to M. Servier, 1770.*
21 Drake, W. R. *Gods or Spacemen?* Amherst Press, Wisconsin.
22 Frisch, Otto R. *Atomic Physics Today.* Oliver & Boyd, London, 1962.
23 Trench, Brinsley le Poer. *The Flying Saucer Story.* Neville Spearman Ltd., London, 1966.
24 Pauwels, L. and Bergier, J. *The Dawn of Magic.* Anthony Gibbs & Phillips, London, 1963.
25 Piccardi, Giorgio. *Alla ricerca di un metodo.* Pianeta, No. 1, M/A 1964, Firenze.
26 Bernhard-Bennet-Rice. *New Handbook of the Heavens.* Mentor, New American Library, New York.
27 Vallée, Jacques. *Anatomy of a Phenomenon.* Neville Spearman Ltd., London, 1966.
28 Martin, Charles Noel. *Si, la Vita esiste altrove.* Pianeta, No. 2, M/A 1964, Firenze.
29 Williamson, George Hunt. *Other Tongues, Other Flesh.* Ray Palmer, Amherst Press, Wisconsin, 1953.
30 National Aeronautics and Space Administration. *The Search for Extraterrestrial Life.* NASA, Washington, 1964.
31 Bracewell, Robert N. 'On Nous Cherche dans le Cosmos'. *Planète,* No. 19, N/D 1964. 42 Rue de Berri, Paris, 8.
32 Shklovsky, Joseph. 'La Vie et la Raison dans l'Univers'. *Planète,* No. 17, J/A 1964.
33 Avignon, Andre. 'L'étrange histoire des Satellites de Mars.' Fevrier, 1965. 'Phénomènes Spatiaux', GEPA. 69 Rue de la Tombe Issoire, Paris, 14.
34 Layne, Meade. *The Flying Saucer Mystery.* Borderland Science Research Association, Vista, California.
35 'Oahspe'. Venture Bookshop, P.O. Box 671, Evanston, USA.
36 Bergier, Jacques. 'Pour comprendre l'Anti-matière.' *Planète,* No. 15, M/A, 1964.
37 Davy, John. 'Lopsided Universe puzzles Physicists.' *The Observer,* London, July 3rd 1966.
38 Pauwels, L. and Bergier, J. *The Dawn of Magic.* Anthony Gibbs & Phillips, 1963.
39 Bernard, Dr Raymond. *The Hollow Earth.* Fieldcrest Publishing Co., New York, 10.
40 Fouéré, René. 'Seraient-ils des Revenants du Futur?' *Phénomènes Spatiaux,* June 1966.

41 Churchward, James. *The Sacred Symbols of Mu.* Neville Spearman Ltd., London, 1960.

42 Blavatsy, Mme H. P. *Isis Unveiled.* Vol. 1. Theosophical University Press, Pasadena, California, 1960.

43 Genesis, Chapter 1. v. 26.

44 Blavatsky, Mme H. P. *The Secret Doctrine. Vol. I.* Theosophical Publication Co., London, 1888.

45 Cerve, Wishar S. *Lemuria.* AMORC San-Jose, California.

46 *Brothers* Vol. 2, 1-4. 1944. Cosmic Brotherhood Association, Yokohama.

47 Pinotti, Roberto 'Siamo Extraterrestri'. *Clypeus, Anno III*, No. 1. Casella Postale 604, Torino.

48 Blavatsky, Mme H. P. *The Secret Doctrine. Vol. 2.*

49 Scott-Elliot, W. *The Story of the Lost Atlantis and the Lost Lemuria.* The Theosophical Publication Co., London, 1962.

50 Churchward, James. *The Lost Continent of Mu.* Neville Spearman Ltd., London, 1959.

51 Blavatsky, Mme H. P. *Isis Unveiled. Vol. 1.*

52 Evans-Wentz, W. Y. and Lama Kazi Dawa Sandup. *Tibetan Yoga and the Secret Doctrine.* Oxford University Press.

53 Brunton, Paul. *A Search in Secret India.* Arrow Books Ltd., London, 1965.

54 Saurat, Denis. *Atlantis and the Giants.* Faber & Faber Ltd., London.

55 MacDonnell, Arthur A. *A History of Sanskrit Literature.* Heinemann, London, 1900.

56 Paretti, Luigi. *The Ancient World.* Allen & Unwin, 1965.

57 MacDonnell, Arthur A. *A History of Sanskrit Literature.* Heinemann, London, 1900.

58 Ibid.

59 'Vascelli Interplanetari Nel Passato.' *Pianèta,* No. 1, M/A 1964. Firenze.

60 Wilson, H. H. *Rig Veda Sanhita. Vol. II.* W. H. Allen, London, 1854.

61 MacDonnell, Arthur A. *A History of Sanskrit Literature.* Heinemann, London, 1900.

62 Wilkins, W. I. *Hindu Mythology.* Thacker & Co., London, 1882.

63 MacDonnell, Arthur A. *A History of Sanskrit Literature.* Heinemann, London, 1900.

64 Mapes, Walter de. *De Nugis Curialium.* AD 1182. Camden Society. MDCCCL.

65 Bethurum, Truman. *Aboard a Flying Saucer.* De Vorss, Los Angeles, 1953.
66 Dutt, Romesh. *The Ramayana and the Mahabharata.* Dent, London, 1961.
67 Gordon, Cyrus H. *Before the Bible.* Collins, London, 1962.
68 Samaranganasutradhara by King Bhojadena. 11th century. *Gaewad's Oriental Studies.* 1924.
69 Dikshitar, Ramachandra. *War in Ancient India.* MacMillan, London, 1945.
70 Churchward, James. *The Children of Mu.* Neville Spearman Ltd., London, 1959.
71 Roy, Protop Chandra. *Bhisma Parva (Drona Parva).* Bharata Press, Bombay, 1888.
72 Obsequens, Julius Samuel Luchmans. *Libro de Prodigiis. Lugduni Batavorum.* 1720.
73 King, George. *The Nine Freedoms.* The Aetherius Society, Los Angeles, 1963.
74 Genesis, Chapter 19, verse 24.
75 Isaiah, Chapter 37, verse 36.
76 Giles, G. A. *Nennius and Gildas.* (Trans. Rev. W. Gunn). J. Bohn, London, 1861.
77 MacDonnell, Arthur A. *A History of Sanskrit Literature.* Heinemann, London, 1900.
78 Edwardes, Michael. *A History of India.* Thames & Hudson, London, 1961.
79 Dikshitar, Ramachandra. *War in Ancient India.* MacMillan, London, 1945.
80 'Vascelli Interplanetari Nel Passato'. *Pianèta,* No. 1, M/A 1964. Firenze.
81 Lacote, Felix. *Budhaswamin Brihat Katha Shlokasanigraha.* In French. Paris Imprimerie National, 1904.
82 Dickhoff, Dr Robert Ernst. *Agharta.* Fieldcrest Publishing Co., New York, 10.
83 Brinsley, le Poer Trench. *The Sky People.* Neville Spearman Ltd., 1960.
84 Cowell, E. B. and Thomas, F. H. *Harscha Charita of Bana.* Oriental Translation Fund, London, 1897.
85 Platts, I. *Boital Pachis.* W. Allen, London, 1871.
86 'Vascelli Interplanetari Nel Passato'. *Pianèta,* No. 1, M/A 1964. Firenze.
87 Williams, Alfred. *Tales from the Panchatantra.* Ed. Hertel. Cambridge, Mass. 1908.
88 Phylos the Tibetan. *A Dweller on Two Planets.* Borden Publishing Co., Los Angeles, 1932.

89 Adamski, George. *Inside the Spaceships.* Neville Spearman Ltd., London, 1966.

90 Eusebius, Pamphilius. *Life of Constantine.* Ed. Valezius. Cambridge, 1692.

91 Edwards, Frank. *Stranger than Science.* Pan Books Ltd., London.

92 Blavatsky, Mme H. P. *Isis Unveiled,* Vol. 1.

93 Agrest, M. 'Des Cosmonautes dans l'Antiquité'. *Planète,* No. 7, N/D 1962.

94 Lissner, Ivar. *The Living Past,* Penguin, 1957.

95 Blavatsky, Mme H. P. *The Secret Doctrine. Vol. 2.*

96 Rampa, Dr T. Lobsang. *The Cave of the Ancients.* Transworld (Corgi), London.

97 *Encyclopaedia Britannica.*

98 Maraini, Fosco. *Secret Tibet.* Hutchinson, London, 1952.

99 Harrar, Heinrich. *Seven Years in Tibet.* Pan Books Ltd., 1956.

100 Rampa, Dr T. Lobsang. *The Third Eye.* Transworld (Corgi), London.

101 Dalai Lama of Tibet. *My Land and People.* Weidenfeld & Nicholson, London, 1962.

102 Maraini, Fosco. *Secret Tibet.* Hutchinson, London, 1952.

103 David-Neel, Mme Alexandra. *With Mystics and Magicians in Tibet.* Penguin, 1936.

104 Evans-Wentz. W. Y. and Lama Kazi Dawa Sandup. *Tibetan Yoga and The Secret Doctrines.* Oxford University Press, 1958.

105 Evans-Wentz, W. Y. *Milarepa.* Oxford University Press.

106 Schiefner and Ralston. *Tibetan Tales derived from Indian Sources.* Paul, London, 1906.

107 Bernard, Theos. *Land of a thousand Buddhas.* Rider & Co., London, 1957.

108 Evans-Wentz, W. Y. and Bardo Thödol, *Tibetan Book of the Dead.* Oxford University Press.

109 Connor, Capt. W. F. *Folk Tales from Tibet.* Hurst & Blackett, London, 1906.

110 Schiefner and Ralston. *Tibetan Tales from Indian Sources.* Paul, 1906.

111 David-Neel. Mme A. and the Lama Yongden. *The Superhuman Exploits of Gesar of Ling.* Rider, London.

112 Roerich, N. *Altai Himalaya.* Frederick A. Stokes, New York.

113 Rampa, Dr T. Lobsang. 'Saucers Over Tibet'. *Flying Saucer Review.* M/A 1957.

114 Rampa, Dr T. Lobsang. 'Flying into Space'. *Flying Saucer Review*. M/J 1957. 21 Cecil Court, Charing Cross Road, London, WC2.

115 Churchward, James. *The Children of Mu*. Neville Spearman Ltd., London, 1959.

116 Kramer, S. N. *Mythologies of the Ancient World*. Anchor, New York, 1961.

117 Blavatsky, Mme H. P. *The Secret Doctrine*. Vol. 2.

118 Kramer, S. N. *Mythologies of the Ancient World*.

119 Cottrell, Leonard. *The Tiger of Ch'in*. Evans, London, 1962.

120 Werner, E. T. C. *Myths and Legends of China*. Harrap, London, 1956.

121 Paretti, Luigi. *The Ancient World*. Allen & Unwin, 1965.

122 Cottrell, Leonard. *Tiger of Ch'in*. Evans Bros., London, 1962.

123 Blavatsky, Mme H. P. *Isis Unveiled*.

124 Jacquetta Hawkes and Sir Leonard Woolley. *Prehistory and The Beginnings of Civilisation*. Allen & Unwin, 1962.

125 Matthew of Paris. *Historia Anglorum*.

126 Kramer, Samuel Noah. *Mythologies of the Ancient World*. Anchor, New York.

127 Werner, E. T. C. *Myths and Legends of China*. Harrap, London, 1956.

128 Graves, R. and Patai, R. *Myths of Ancient Greece*. Cassell, London, 1938.

129 Werner, E. T. C. *Myths and Legends of China*. Harrap, London.

130 Ibid.

131 Ibid.

132 Mackenzie, Donald A. *Myths of China and Japan*. Gresham Publishing Co.

133 Lorenzen, Coral E. *The Great Flying Saucer Hoax*. William Frederick Press, New York, 1962.

134 Matsumura, Y. J. 'Flying Saucers in Ancient Orient'. 1962. *Brothers*, Vol. I, No. 2. CBA Yokohama.

135 Wilcox, Elizabeth G. *Mu*. Den sjunkna Kontinenten. Parthenon. Hälsingborg, Sweden, 1964.

136 Sadler, A. T. *A Short History of Japan*. Angus & Robertson, London, 1963.

137 Creighton, Gordon. 'A Russian Wall Painting'. *Other Spacemen. Flying Saucer Review*. J/A 1965.

138 Matsumura, Y. J. 'Those Straw Rope Pattern Flying Suits'. *Brothers*, Vol. 2, Nos. 1-4, 1962. CBA Yokohama.

139 Kramer, Samuel Noah. *Mythologies of the Ancient World.* Anchor, New York.
140 Insole, Allan V. *Immortal Britain.* Rider & Co., London.
141 Sadler, A. L. *A Short History of Japan.* Angus & Robertson, London, 1963.
142 Bush, Lewis. *Land of the Dragon-fly.* R. Hale, London, 1959.
143 Aston, W. G. *Nihongi or Chronicles of Japan.* G. Allen & Unwin, London.
144 Bush, Lewis. *Land of the Dragon-fly.* R. Hale, London, 1959.
145 Cicero. *On the Nature of the Gods.*
146 Matsumura, Y. J. 'Flying Saucers Over Ancient Nippon'. *Brothers,* Vol. 3, No. 1, 1962, CBA. Yokohama.
147 Trench, Brinsley le Poer. *The Flying Saucer Story.* Neville Spearman Ltd., London, 1966.
148 Bede. *Ecclesiastical History.* Dent-Everyman, London.
149 Fort, Charles. *The Books of Charles Fort.* Henry Holt & Co., New York, 1941.
150 Mackenzie, Donald A. *Myths of China and Japan.* Gresham, London.
151 Maraini, Fosco. *Meeting with Japan.* Hutchinson, London, 1959.
152 Servier, Jean, 'Je ne crois pas au progrès'. *Planète,* No. 18. s/o 1964. Paris, 8.
153 Merezhovsky, Dmitri. *The Secret of the West.* Jonathan Cape, 1933.
154 Donelly, Ignatius. *Atlantis the Antediluvian World* (E. Sykes). Sidgwick & Jackson, 1950.
155 Petrie, Sir Flinders. *A History of Egypt.* Methuen, London, 1899.
156 Murray, Margaret A. *The Splendour that was Egypt.* Sidgwick & Jackson Ltd., London, 1959.
157 Davy, John. 'Man-like Fossils'. *The Observer,* London, 5th January 1967.
158 Herodotus. (Trans. E. Powell.) Oxford University Press, 1949.
159 Cory, I. P. *The Ancient Fragments.* W. Pickering, London, 1828.
160 Brunton, Paul. *A Search in Secret Egypt.* Arrow Books, London, 1962.
161 Cory, I. P. *The Ancient Fragments.* W. Pickering, London, 1828.
162 Ibid.
163 Ibid.

164 Murray, Margaret A. *The Splendour that was Egypt.* Sidgwick & Jackson Ltd., London, 1959.
165 Frankfort, Henri. *Before Philosophy.* Penguin, London, 1963.
166 White, John Manchip. *Everyday Life in Ancient Egypt.* B. Batsford, London, 1963.
167 Budge, Sir Wallis E. A. *The Book of the Dead. The Papyrus of Ani.* British Museum, 1895.
168 Settimo, Gianni. 'E nacquero gli Dei'. *Clypeus Anno I,* No. 2-5. Casella Postale 604, Torino.
169 Churchward, James. *The Sacred Symbols of Mu.* Neville Spearman Ltd., London.
170 Pinotti, Roberto. 'Space Visitors in Ancient Egypt'. *Flying Saucer Review.* M/J 1964. London.
171 Massey. Gerald. *Egyptian Book of the Dead and the Mysteries Amenti.* Health Research, Makeluma Hill, California.
172 Spence, Lewis. *Myths and Legends of Egypt.* George Harrap, 1915.
173 Spence, Lewis. *The Outlines of Mythology.* Premier. Fawcett Publications, New York.
174 Cory, I. P. *The Ancient Fragments.* W. Pickering, London, 1828.
175 Plato. *Phaedrus.* (Five Dialogues of Plato.) A. D. Lindsay. Dent-Everyman.
176 White, John Manchip. *Everyday Life in Ancient Egypt.* B. T. Batsford, London, 1962.
177 Budge, Sir E. A. Wallis. *The Book of the Dead. The Papyrus of Ani.* British Museum, 1895.
178 Ceram, C. W. *Gods, Graves and Scholars.* Gollancz and Sidgwick & Jackson, 1952.
179 Budge, Sir E. A. Wallis. *The Book of the Dead. The Papyrus of Ani.* British Museum, 1895.
180 Annales Laurissenses. *Migne's Patrologiae.* Tom. CIV. Saeculum IX. Anno. 840.
181 Annales Eginhardis. *Migne's Patrologiae.* Tom. CIV. Saeculum IX. Anno 840.
182 Boncompagni. Solas. 'Il Libro dei Morti'. *Clypeus, Anno II,* No. 1. Torino.
183 Ribera, Antonio. *El Gran Enigma de los Platillos Volantes.* Editions Pomaine, Barcelona, 1966.
184 Williamson, George Hunt. *The Secret Places of the Lion.* Neville Spearman Ltd., London, 1958.
185 Larson, Kenwood. 'The Great Pyramid'. A UFO Beacon. *Flying Saucers.* October 1966. Ray Palmer, Amherst.

186 Blavatsky, Mme H. P. *Isis Unveiled.* Vol 1. Theosophical University Press, Pasadena, California.

187 Gardner, Martin. *Fads and Fallacies.* Dover Pub. New York, 1957.

188 Hawkes, Jacquetta and Woolley, Sir Leonard. *Prehistory and the Beginnings of Civilisation.* Allen & Unwin, London, 1963.

189 Collinge, Edward G. *Life's Hidden Secrets.* Rider, 1952.

190 Blavatsky, Mme H. P. *Isis Unveiled.* Vol. 1. Theosophical University Press, Pasadena, California.

191 Trench, Brinsley le Poer. *Men Among Mankind.* Neville Spearman Ltd., London, 1962.

192 Beaumont, Comyns. *The Riddle of Prehistoric Britain.* Rider & Co., London.

193 Leslie, Desmond and Adamski, George. *Flying Saucers have Landed.* Hutchinson, Panther, 1957.

194 Williamson, George Hunt. *Road in the Sky.* Neville Spearman Ltd., London, 1959.

195 Mertz, Barbara. *Temples, Tombs and Hieroglyphics.* Gollancz, 1964.

196 Brunton, Paul. *A Search in Secret Egypt.* Arrow Books Ltd., London, 1962.

197 Collinge, Edward. *Life's Hidden Secrets.* Rider & Co.

198 Blavatsky, Mme H. P. *The Secret Doctrine.* Vol. 2.

199 Lamb, Harold. *Alexander of Macedon.* Robert Hale, 1946.

200 Blakeney, E. H. *A Small Classical Dictionary.* Dent-Everyman, 1928.

201 Hamilton, Edith. *Mythology* Mentor. New American Library, New York.

202 Velikovsky, Immanuel. *Oedipus and Akhnaton.* Sidgwick & Jackson, London, 1960.

203 Bratton, F. Gladstone. *The Heretic Pharaoh.* Robert Hale, London, 1962.

204 Velikovsky, Immanuel. *Ages in Chaos.* Sidgwick & Jackson, 1953.

205 Wells, Herbert George. *Outline of History.* Cassell, London, 1963.

206 Velikovsky, Immanuel. *Worlds in Collision.* Gollancz, 1950.

207 Keller, Werner. *The Bible as History in Pictures.* Hodder & Stoughton, London, 1964.

208 Gordon, Cyrus H. *Before the Bible.* Collins, London, 1962.

209 Murray, Margaret A. *The Splendour that was Egypt.* Four Square, New English Library, London.

210 Williamson, George Hunt. *The Secret Places of the Lion.* Neville Spearman Ltd., London, 1958.

211 Polano, H. *The Talmud.* Frederick Warne & Co., London, 1933.

212 Homer. *Odyssey.* (Trans. Alexander Pope.) Oxford University Press, 1931.

213 Trench, Brinsley le Poer. *The Sky People.* Neville Spearman Ltd., London, 1960.

214 Pauwels, L. and Bergier, J. *The Dawn of Magic.* Anthony Gibbs & Phillips, London, 1963.

215 Brasington, Virginia F. *Flying Saucers in the Bible.* Saucerian Books, Clarksburg VA, USA.

216 Thomas, Paul. *Flying Saucers through the Ages.* Neville Spearman Ltd., London, 1965.

217 *The Clarendon Bible.* Oxford University Press.

218 Wilkins, Harold T. *Flying Saucers Uncensored.* Arco Publications, London, 1956.

219 Flavius Philosostratus. *Life of Appolonius of Tyana.* Loeb Classics. Heinemann.

220 Drake, W. R. *Gods or Spacemen?* Ray Palmer, Amherst Press, Amherst.

221 Agrest, M. 'Des Cosmonautes dans l'Antiquité'. *Planète,* No. 7, N/D 1962. Paris, 8.

222 Lhote, Dr Henri. *The Search for the Tassili Frescoes.* Hutchinson, London, 1959.

223 Cory, I.P. *Ancient Fragments.* W. Pickering, London, 1828.

224 Saggs, H. W. F. *The Greatness that was Bablyon.* Sidgwick & Jackson, 1962.

225 Fernoglio, Alberto. 'Cronistoria su Oggetti Volanti del Passato.' *Clypeus. Anno III.* No. 2.

226 Blavatsky, Mme H. P. *The Secret Doctrine,* Vol. 2.

227 Bibby, G. *Four Thousand Years Ago.* Collins, London, 1962.

228 Churchward, James. *The Children of Mu.* Neville Spearman Ltd., London, 1959.

229 Cottrell, Leonard. *The Land of Shinar.* Souvenir Press, London, 1965.

230 Graves, Robert and Patai, R. *Hebrew Myths. The Book of Genesis.* Cassell, London, 1964.

231 Annales Eginhardi. *Migne's Patrologiae.* Tom CIV. Saeculum IX. Annus 840.

232 Cory, I. P. *Ancient Fragments.* W. Pickering, London, 1828.

233 Saggs, H. W. F. *Everyday Life in Babylonia and Assyria.* B. T. Batsford, London.

234 Herodotus. (Trans. E. Powell.) Book One, p. 183-5. Oxford University Press, 1949.

235 Saggs, H. F. W. *The Greatness that was Babylon.* Sidgwick & Jackson, London, 1946.

236 Herodotus. (Trans. E. Powell.) Book One, p. 183-5. Oxford University Press, 1949.

237 Diodorus Siculus. *Biblioteca Historica.* Oxford University Press, Oxford, 1956.

238 Spence, Lewis. *Myths and Legends of Babylon and Assyria.* Harrap, London, 1916.

239 Byron, Lord George. *The Destruction of Sennacherib.*

240 Laessoe, Jorgen. *People of Ancient Assyria.* Routledge & Kegan Paul, London, 1963.

241 *Cambridge Ancient History.* Vol. 3. 1925. Cambridge University Press.

242 Roux, G. *Ancient Iraq.* Allen & Unwin, London, 1964.

243 Culican, W. *The Medes and Persians.* Thames & Hudson, London.

244 Paretti, L. *The Ancient World.* Allen & Unwin, London, 1965.

245 Saggs, H. W. *The Greatness that was Babylon.* Sidgwick & Jackson, London, 1962.

246 Flavius Philostratus. *The Life of Apollonius of Tyana.* Loeb Classics. Heinemann.

247 Lamb, Harold. *Alexander of Macedon.* R. Hale, London, 1946.

248 Ceram, C. W. *Gods, Graves and Scholars.* Gollancz and Sidgwick & Jackson, 1952.

249 Hooke, S. H. *Middle Eastern Mythology.* Penguin, 1962.

250 Spence, Lewis. *The Outlines of Mythology.* Premier Books, Fawcett Pub. Co., New York.

251 Frankfort, Henri. *Before Philosophy.* Penguin, 1963.

252 Fenoglio, Alberto. 'Templi, Astrologici dei Caldei'. *Clypeus, Anno III,* No. 1. Torino.

253 Gordon, Cyrus H. *Before the Bible.* Collins, London, 1962.

254 Saggs, H. W. *The Greatness that was Babylon.* Sidgwick & Jackson, London, 1962.

255 Hooke, S. H. *Middle Eastern Mythology.* Penguin, London, 1963.

256 Feroglio, Alberto. 'Templi, Astrologici dei Caldi'. *Clypeus, Anno III,* No. 1. Torino.

257 Migne. *Patrologiae. Agobard.* Tom. CIV. Anno 840. *De Grandine et Tonitrius.* Saeculum IX.

258 Montfaucon de Villars. *Le Comte de Gabalis.* A. G. Nizet. Paris, 1963.

259 Graves, Robert and Paeti, R. *Hebrew Myths. The Book of Genesis*. Cassell, London, 1964.
260 *The Jaredite Advocate*. March 1965. Box 29026, Los Angeles, California.
261 Plutarch. *Themistocles XV*.
262 Gaer, J. *How the Great Religions Began*. Signet. New American Library, New York.
263 Vermaseren, M. J. *Mithras, the Secret God*. Chatto & Windus.
264 Livy. *History of Rome*. Book Twenty-one. Chapter 62. Dent-Everyman.
265 Plutarch. *Theseus*.
266 Gaer, J. *How the Great Religions Began*. Signet. New American Library, New York.
267 Trench, Brinsley le Poer. *The Sky People*. Neville Spearmann Ltd., London, 1960.
268 *Book of Enoch*. (Trans. Canon H. Charles.) SPLK, 1962.
269 Vermes, G. *The Dead Sea Scrolls in English*. Penguin, London, 1962.
270 *Herodotus*. (Trans. E. Powell.) Book One, p. 180-3.
271 Lissner, Ivar. *The Living Past*. Penguin, London, 1957.
272 Ibn Aharon. 'Extraterrestrialisme als historische studie'. *Dutch Disc Digest*. Lente 1961. I. Keukenmester. P.O. Box 537, Hague.
273 Genesis. Chapter 28, v. 2.
274 Jessup, M. K. *U.F.O. and the Bible*. The Citadel Press, New York, 1956.
275 Thomas, Paul. *Flying Saucers through the Ages*. Neville Spearman Ltd., London, 1965.
276 Leslie, Desmond and Adamski, George. *Flying Saucers have Landed*. Werner Laurie Ltd., London, 1953.
277 Adamski, George. *Inside the Spaceships*. Neville Spearman Ltd., London, 1966.
278 Isaiah, Chapter 37, v. 35-6.
279 Sadler, A. L. *A Short History of Japan*. Angus & Robertson, London, 1963.
280 Cicero. *On the Nature of the Gods*.
281 Plutarch. *Theseus*.
282 Drake, W. R. *Gods or Spacemen?* Ray Palmer, Amherst, Wisconsin, USA
283 Perego. Dr Alberto Interplanetarischer Verkehr in Erdgeschehen. *UFO Nachrichten*. No 8. August 1963. Wiesbaden.

284 Homet, F. *Sons of the Sun*. Neville Spearman Ltd., London, 1963.

285 Layard, J. *Stone Men of Malekula*. Chatto & Windus, London, 1946.

286 Heyderdahl, Thor. *Aku-Aku*. Allen & Unwin, London, 1959.

287 Blavatsky, Mme H. P. *Isis Unveiled*. Vol. 1. Theosophical University Press, Pasadena, California.

288 Lissner, Ivar. *The Living Past*. Penguin, London, 1957.

289 'Y-a-t-il de la Vie sur Terre?' *Planète*, No. 29, J/A 1966. 42 Rue de Berri, Paris, 8.

INDEX